Music Across the Senses

Music Across the Senses

Listening, Learning, and Making Meaning

Jody L. Kerchner

OXFORD
UNIVERSITY PRESS

Oxford University Press is a department of the University of Oxford.
It furthers the University's objective of excellence in research, scholarship,
and education by publishing worldwide.

Oxford   New York
Auckland   Cape Town   Dar es Salaam   Hong Kong   Karachi
Kuala Lumpur   Madrid   Melbourne   Mexico City   Nairobi
New Delhi   Shanghai   Taipei   Toronto

With offices in
Argentina   Austria   Brazil   Chile   Czech Republic   France   Greece
Guatemala   Hungary   Italy   Japan   Poland   Portugal   Singapore
South Korea   Switzerland   Thailand   Turkey   Ukraine   Vietnam

Oxford is a registered trademark of Oxford University Press
in the UK and certain other countries.

Published in the United States of America by
Oxford University Press
198 Madison Avenue, New York, NY 10016

Library of Congress Cataloging-in-Publication Data
Kerchner, Jody L., 1964–
Music across the senses : listening, learning, and making meaning / Jody L. Kerchner.
pages cm
Includes bibliographical references and index.
ISBN 978-0-19-996761-2 (alk. paper)—ISBN 978-0-19-996763-6 (alk. paper)
1. Music—Instruction and study. 2. Music appreciation—Instruction and study. I. Title.
MT1.K38 2013
780.71—dc23
2013008132

9 8 7 6 5 4 3 2 1
Printed in the United States of America
on acid-free paper

TABLE OF CONTENTS

LIST OF FIGURES

LIST OF RECORDINGS

Bach: Brandenburg Concerto #2 in F Major, mvt. 1 [Ransom Wilson and Gerard Schwarz, Los Angeles Chamber Orchestra, *Bach: Brandenburg Concertos, Suites in B Minor*]

Beethoven: Symphony #7 in A Major, mvt. 2 [Josef Krips, The London Symphony Orchestra, *Beethoven: The Complete Symphony Collection*]

Berlin: "Steppin' Out With My Baby" (*Easter Parade*) [The Texans, Blue Star, BS-1528, http://www.ceder.net/recorddb/viewsingle.php?Recordid=13047]

Bizet: "Overture" (*Carmen*) [Herbert von Karajan, Berliner Philharmoniker, *Bizet: Carmen (Highlights)*]

"Chigoku-Chiho No Komoriuta" [*The Music Connection*, Silver Burdett Ginn, 1995, Grade 8, CD #6, Track 5]

Copland: *Fanfare for The Common Man* [Leonard Bernstein, New York Philharmonic, *Copland: Appalachian Spring, Rodeo, Billy The Kid, Fanfare for The Common Man*]

Duruflé: "Sanctus" (*Requiem*) [Robert Shaw, Atlanta Symphony Orchestra & Chorus, *Fauré Requiem, Op. 48/Duruflé: Requiem, Op. 9*]

Gliére: "Russian Sailor's Dance" (*The Red Poppy*) [Eugene Ormandy, Philadelphia Orchestra, *Russian Orchestral Works*]

Handel: Act 2, Duet and Chorus, "Hail, hail, Judea" (*Judas Maccabeus*) [Nicolas McGehan, Lisa Saffer, Patricia Spence, Philharmonia Baroque Orchestra & U.C. Berkeley Chamber Chorus, *Handel: Judas Maccabaeus*]

Handel: "Hornpipe" (*Water Music Suite No. 2*) [John Eliot Gardiner, English Baroque Soloists, *Handel: Water Music*]

Liszt: Étude No. 3 in D-flat Major, "Un Sospiro" (*Trois études de concert*)[Lang Lang, *Liszt - My Piano Hero (Deluxe Edition)*]

Mozart: "Lacrymosa" (Requiem) [Carlo Maria Giulini, Philharmonia Orchestra & Chorus, *Mozart Requiem*]

Orff: "O fortuna" (*Carmina Burana*) [Seiji Ozawa, Boston Symphony Orchestra, New England Conservatory Orchestra & Chorus, *Orff—Carmina Burana*]

Rutter: "Magnificat" (*Magnificat*) [John Rutter, The Cambridge Singers, Choristers of St. Paul's Cathedral, and the City of London Sinfonia, *Magnificat, The Falcon, Two Festival Anthems by John Rutter*]

"Saqsahumanpi/Valicha" (Andean folk song) [Larry Crook, bombo (drum), Dan Dickey, (guitar), Tom Turino, kena (indigenous Andean flute)]; Accompanying CD to Thomas Turino (2010). *Music as Social Life.* University of Chicago Press.

Schubert: Piano Quintet in A Major, mvt.4, "The Trout" [Edgar Meyer, Emanuel Ax, Pamela Frank, Rebecca Young & Yo-Yo Ma, *Schubert: Trout Quintet, Arpeggione Sonata, Die Forelle D. 550*]

Strauss: "Sunrise" (*Also Sprach Zarathustra*) [Sir Georg Solti, Berliner Philharmonic, *Richard Strauss: Also Sprach Zarathustra, Till Eulenspiegels lustige Streiche, Salome: Tanz der sieben Schleier*]

Vivaldi: "Autumn" (*The Four Seasons*) [Various Artists, *The Best of Vivaldi - Classical Kids*]

Zeppelin: "Kashmir" [Led Zeppelin, *Mothership (Remastered)*]

LIST OF VIDEOS ON
COMPANION WEBSITE

▶Available online at www.oup.com/us/musicacrossthesenses
Access with username Music5 and password Book1745

ACKNOWLEDGMENTS

I have been blessed to spend over two and a half decades teaching music to children, youth, and young adults in public schools and higher education. To have had the opportunity to pursue that which I love and about which I am passionate has been an extraordinary adventure. What began as a question I had as a first-year music teacher in Swarthmore, Pennsylvania, has fed my curiosity about music listening for many years, and I still have so much to learn.

I am indebted to the many PK–12 music students who "helped me with my homework" for this book and the teachers who generously gave of their classroom and rehearsal time so I could research the topic of music listening. The inspirational music educators who assisted me were Melissa Ising Anderson, Jeff Meyers, Mark Parish, Carol Mason, Will Kish, Bronwen Davies Fox, Len Gnizak, Christine Pier, Ann Garvelink, Peggy Bennett, Joanne Erwin, and Betsy Gmitro.

I am also grateful to the school principals and superintendents, and students' parents for granting me access to their schools, teachers, and students. The participating schools and community groups for this project were: Oberlin High School, Oberlin Langston Middle School, Oberlin Prospect Elementary School, North Ridgeville Middle School, Elyria Northwood Middle School, Norwalk High School, Norwalk Pleasant Elementary School, Amherst Junior High School, Winnetka Crow Island Elementary School, Northern Ohio Youth Orchestra, Oberlin Choristers' Youth Chorale, and the Oberlin Conservatory Community Music School's MusicPlay.

Writing a manuscript can be a lonely process, yet I was fortunate to have astute readers, who are also stellar musicians and educators, to provide feedback on the chapters. Betsy Gmitro, Mary Mumbrue, and Bronwen Davies Fox provided feedback that helped shape my writing and clarify my ideas. Thank you for sharing your wisdom, expertise, and encouragement.

I am humbled that Norman Hirschy at Oxford University Press took a leap of faith by recommending this book for publication—one quite different from OUP's regular catalog listings. His guidance and enthusiasm for this project gave me the confidence to write the book I *wanted* to write. My gratitude is also extended to Kate Nunn at Newgen for her impeccable editing skill.

To Oberlin Music Education alumni Jessica Downs, Caitlin Roseum, and Lafayette Carthon, I am grateful to you for permitting me to include video excerpts of your student teaching and/or lesson materials in this book and on the Companion Website. Caitlin Roseum was also my research assistant during the spring of 2010, performing literature reviews and serving as videographer. Oberlin College student Zachary Jamieson shared his technological expertise during final video recording and postproduction of the video excerpts that appear on the book's Companion Website. Many thanks!

I would also like to thank the administration and Office of Sponsored Programs at Oberlin College for awarding me "Faculty Research Status" that included a sabbatical leave from my teaching and administrative duties during the 2011-12 academic year. It was a luxury to have time to focus on researching and writing. Without my Music Education faculty colleagues assuming some of my regular departmental responsibilities, however, my leave from campus would not have been feasible. I am especially grateful to Joanne Erwin and Peggy Bennett for their extra efforts within the Music Education Division.

Finally, I am grateful to my fan club: my parents—Shirley and Donald Kerchner—and my husband Mark Parish. Without your constant cheerleading and encouragement I would not have had the audacity to write this book. I extend my heartfelt thanks to Mark for keeping me in touch with and helping me celebrate my teaching roots in public school music education.

Music Across the Senses

CHAPTER 1

Principles and Foundations
of Music Listening

Music listening is a multisensory experience. We hear music, see or imagine musicians playing instruments or singing, tap feet and fingers to musical beats and rhythms, hum or sing a familiar portion of a song on a CD, and feel "moved" by music that evokes memories, associations, and emotions. Children, as natural consumers and creators of musical sounds, innately find access points—sensory portals—to enter, engage in, decipher, decode, create meaning of, and respond to music. They find "ear anchors," those musical moments that are familiar to their personal soundscapes, that have been acquired from prior musical experiences, and with which they compare new auditory experiences. Children, regardless of age, respond externally to musical sound—running, jumping, tapping, singing, dancing, talking, and smiling, for example. If they choose or are prompted, children find multisensory means—verbally, visually, kinesthetically, and musically—to describe to others what they are hearing and responding to as they engage in music listening experiences. It is often left to others—peers, parents, or teachers—to discern how these multisensory responses might relate to the music to which the children are listening.

Observing and listening to school-age music students, teachers can learn about their students' musical interests, perceptual and conceptual abilities, and readiness to move deeper into the myriad musical details of a particular musical listening experience. Students describe music they hear by using their own vocabulary; others struggle to find words that adequately represent their listening experiences. Some children confidently use words to describe music, but the language they use does not seem to depict it accurately—at least to trained adult musical ears. Some students doodle as they listen to music, but watching them create drawings as they listen to music seems to be a musical dance with pencil set to paper. Yet other students intuitively and insightfully move their bodies with the music. The students "know" and "feel" something about the music, but what is the nature of their understanding? How can music teachers gain access into the minds of music listeners?

How can students learn to access familiar and unfamiliar music using verbal and nonverbal media?

ABOUT THIS BOOK

Christopher Small (1998, 9) defined "musicking" as "the act of tak[ing] part, in any capacity, in a musical performance, whether by performing, by listening, by rehearsing or practicing, by providing material for performance (what is called composing), or by dancing." Music listening involves creative and re-creative interactions with musical sound and is foundational to every other musical behavior (i.e., performing, composing, improvising, critiquing). Reimer (1989, 70–71) stated that "since the major interaction most people have with music is as listeners, the task of helping them become creative in this most fundamental of musical behaviors is perhaps the most important in all of music education." About music listening, Elliott (1995, 274) stated that "listening ought to be taught and learned in direct relation to the musical practices and works students are learning in and through their own music making" or that they are listening to as audience members. He also mentioned that the study of music listening involves learning to critically reflect on music and its cultural and historical contexts. Therefore, music listening should be a vital component of PK–12 general music and performance ensemble curricular experiences if we are to nurture lifelong music listeners and appreciators.

Aligned with the *National Standards for Arts Education* (Consortium of National Arts Education 1994), Music Content Standard #6—"listening and describing music"—not only urges teachers to include music listening in music classes and rehearsals but also prompts teachers to provide students with experiences that enlist their creative thinking skills (Dunn 1997); imagination, perceptual, and discrimination abilities; and affective responses. Further, teachers are encouraged to help students develop and refine their verbal (and I suggest nonverbal) skills, so they can describe what they hear as they listen to music. Music-listening skill development and descriptive ability refinement (in verbal and nonverbal forms) that facilitate holistic and creative listening are essential to students' becoming independent musicians and musical connoisseurs.

Consequently, I have set forth music listening principles and pedagogical tools in this book based on my research into school-age children's verbal and nonverbal responses. This content includes: (a) music-listening pedagogical ideas that are based on children's stories and my interpretation of nonverbal representations of their listening experiences; (b) research findings related to children's (elementary and secondary school ages) cognitive processes and multisensory responses to music; (c) mapping and movement sequence examples in this book and on its Companion Website for teachers and students to use in classes or adapt to their own curriculum; and (d) means for assessing students' music listening development.

Reflecting on my career teaching K–12 music, I realized that my "passion points" and "wonderments" were related to music listening—the nature of children's music listening experiences. I had integrated music listening lessons into each of my classes. I taught how I was taught to teach music listening lessons: choose an interesting piece of music, tell the students what to listen for in the music, and discuss that musical "something" with the students after they had listened to the music. The sequence of instruction was predominantly teacher directed.

But what did I learn about what the students *experienced* by listening to music? How did the music listening experiences in those classes inform the students' music preferences and propensity to listen to and engage in music, then and in their future? Early on in my teaching I realized that, just because I "dropped the needle" onto the LP record and modeled focused listening, that did not mean the children brought the same mindset, experience, or interest to the music listening experience that I did as a trained adult musician.

As I expanded my teaching wonderments, I uncovered additional questions to ponder, some of which included: How could I get the children actively engaged in the music listening experiences? What are the students hearing as they listen to music? How do I know they are listening for the musical concept that I had presented to them? What do the students hear in addition to whatever I have asked them to listen for? How could I find out? Could the students tell me anything about their experience? How? What could I do to help students find meaning in their music listening experiences?

This book is based on extant developmental music research, constructivist philosophical and pedagogical perspectives, my own research and teaching, and the implementation of music listening pedagogical strategies that are research based and have been "test-driven" in music classrooms and rehearsal settings. The ideas and materials included in this book stem from my teaching and the research data collected from PK–12 students in classroom general music and choral and instrumental ensemble settings. The data included students' videotaped multisensory expressions as they listened to music individually and in communities of learners. Based on these data, I present multisensory tools and strategies designed to bring aural awareness to school-age music listeners—to bring students closer to hearing and understanding how the musical elements intertwine and relate to one another. The tools and strategies include verbal talk-alouds, mapping, and movement.

A *talk-aloud* is an experience during which students provide a running commentary of all that they think of, hear, or feel as they listen to a musical example. Also known as a *concurrent verbal report,* a talk aloud is similar to a commentator's giving a play-by-play call of a sporting event. *Mapping* invites students to capture musical events, moods, thoughts, and feelings on paper in the form of drawings, pictures, graphs, markings, and even words as they listen to a musical example. Finally, students create *movements/gestures* that represent what they hear in the music and what they are thinking and feeling. Theoretically, these multisensory descriptions represent insights into students' musical minds. In this book, students tell stories about their music listening experiences—their focus of attention, thoughts, and feelings. Other students share their drawings and movements inspired by the music. Pseudonyms have been used throughout the book to maintain student anonymity

The process of creating and using the multisensory tools will be discussed in each chapter, highlighted by PK–12 student research participants' verbal, visual, and kinesthetic responses. In addition to individual music listening experiences, I propose collaborative activities in which students listen to music and create responses within classroom and rehearsal communities of learners.

This book is designed to be a dynamic conversation among PK–12 students who have participated in my research project, students in general music classes and ensembles, you as reader-teacher-musician-researcher-life student, and me as author-teacher-musician-researcher-life student. What are your wonderments about music listening? What have you observed as your students listen and respond to music? What multisensory strategies do you use in your classroom and rehearsals that you find particularly effective?

I invite you to consider the music listening principles and tools presented in the following chapters and adapt them to fit your own music teaching and learning communities. Go to the book's Companion Website and observe how music teachers and students demonstrate the procedures and issues presented in each chapter. Use the maps and movement models presented in the text. Learn to "perform" them. Or, choose your own musical selections and design your own adaptations of the verbal talk-aloud, mapping, and movement sequence tasks.

▶   Go to the Companion Website and click on Video 1.1 for an introduction to the website.

A STORY UNFOLDS

To prepare our minds for thinking about PK–12 students' music listening experiences and skill development, I present a story. As you read it, think about how it might metaphorically convey principles to guide our concept of music listening pedagogy. What about this story intimates how children discover "what is," creating meaning from what they encounter in their musical listening environments and relaying those discoveries and meanings to others?

It is a warm, sunny summer day. A little girl, dressed in her favorite pink culottes and white tee-shirt, carries a net with a long aluminum handle as she sets out to capture some of the many butterflies that flutter in a meadow near her home. For several days, the young girl has watched the butterflies color the green grasses.

One day, the carefree child runs through the meadow and along a rippling creek. She closes her eyes and pauses to hear the sounds of the water rolling along its path. She smells the freshly cut grass while feeling the gently wafting breeze cool her small cheeks. With one eye open, she is delighted by seeing a few guppies swimming in an eddy.

Just ahead of her swarm small butterflies, dodging between the swaying grasses. As she approaches them, she places the net over her shoulder. She swings the net and finds she has caught something. Quickly, she places the content of the net into a glass jar and tightens the lid. She runs home to show her parents what she has found.

As the little girl enters her house, she tells her parents about the meadow, creek, smell of the grass, and the breeze, and especially the butterflies. After punching holes in the jar's lid, the child's parents question her about the content of the jar. She notes that the butterflies appear to be different—their wings, color, shape, and number of legs. The parents tell her that, while she had caught two small, white butterflies, she had also captured other bugs in the meadow—a fly, a grasshopper, and an unidentified insect. There was much more in that meadow than the little girl had originally thought. Satisfied with her expedition, the little girl takes the jar back into the meadow and releases its content.

The innocence of the child's journey and her discoveries in the meadow and in her home remind us that children learn by doing, exploring, searching, and investigating. They are creators of meaning in their own environments. In the story, the child explored the meadow and pursued the butterflies because she found them interesting and exciting. She simply wanted to play with them. No adult told her to find butterflies or capture any other type of insect. Students, who are encouraged to find something to explore based on their own interests, do so with great enthusiasm and vested interest. Students' investigative experiences lead them on an intriguing journey full of possible solutions and satisfaction by self-initiated questioning and discovery.

The child had not gone directly to the location where she initially saw the butterflies. Along the way, she wandered and experienced tactile, olfactory, visual, auditory, and kinesthetic sensations offered by the meadow, grass, creek, sunshine, and breeze. While an adult might consider her nonlinear path to the butterfly patch full of diversions, everything the child encountered along her trail was part of the composite butterfly-catching experience. That summer day was full of sensory experiences, only part of which was the act of catching butterflies. In the child's mind, the fertile process of exploring the meadow was likely as fulfilling as the prizes captured in her net—the butterflies and other bugs.

Finally, the little girl's parents asked probing questions. Instead of immediately telling their daughter that the jar contained creatures in addition to butterflies, they asked her to describe what she saw in the jar. As a family, they helped the girl compare, contrast, and classify the butterfly, fly, grasshopper, and other insect. The parents expanded her concept of "butterflies" by labeling them and the other creatures in the jar. The parents and little girl played roles that resemble those often assumed by teachers and students in music classes and rehearsal settings. In order to facilitate students' inquiry, discovery, and meaning-making, teachers ask questions that involve students in describing, naming, analyzing, synthesizing, making connections, and evaluating.

In the next sections of this chapter and in subsequent chapters, we will closely examine the musical behavior at the crux of this book—music listening. But before we consider the many facets of music listening from philosophical, physiological, cognitive (perceptual, affective, intuitive), and creative perspectives, I invite you to jot down *your* definition of the music listening experience—what type of music listening experiences you value, what types of music your students experience, what you value in terms of students' music-listening skill development, what resources and strategies you incorporate in your teaching–learning settings, and what short-term and long-term music listening goals you have for your students in your general music classrooms and rehearsals. What are your rationales for including (or excluding) music listening in your classrooms and rehearsals?

After reading the discussion about music listening, edit your definitions and rationales as you deem necessary. What might you add in order to expand your original ideas? What might you alter or delete? Were there any "sticking points" about music listening that confirmed or challenged your pedagogical values and beliefs? What questions arose when you read this chapter? Parker Palmer (1998, 2) wrote that, as teachers, "We must enter, not evade, the tangles of teaching so we can understand them better and negotiate them with more grace, not only to guard our own spirits but also to serve our students well." Let us dive into the deep waters of the music listening experience and the meanings children create from them.

FOUNDATIONAL CONSIDERATIONS
Music Listening

Of the soundscapes that infuse our daily life routines, we bring only portions into our immediate consciousness for consumption and consideration. Other sound patterns occur to us as mere sensory phenomena. Yet other sound streams pass us by without our awareness, memory, or acknowledgment. Such is the difference between "listening" and "hearing." The act of music *listening* involves the processes of receiving auditory stimuli (musical sounds), focusing on one or several musical elements, creating relationships among these elements, and then responding to those musical relationships. Conversely, *hearing* requires nothing more than the ears receiving auditory stimuli, which might simply pass beyond our ears and remain unnoticed. For example, I turn on the stereo while I cook or clean. I am aware there is music playing on the stereo, but I am not actively engaged in listening for meaning; the music stays in the background. But when I intentionally listen to music, my attention is usually focused while I (knowingly or unknowingly) attempt to uncover musical patterns and other elemental relationships. I might also "lose myself" in the music, marvel in my awareness of mood change, or wonder what about the music is acting as a "hook" and leading me on an emotional adventure.

Both Reimer (1989) and Mursell (1943) have written that when one actively listens *to* music, she or he becomes absorbed *by* the music. Her or his imaginative forces, prior experiences, culture, and preferences shape the music listening experience, while the music reciprocally shapes the person engaged in the music listening experience. A creative listener (Dunn 1997) compares the music in the moment to mental structures, scaffolding, representations, or schemes built on prior musical experiences. Cognitive dissonance during music listening—the disagreement between existing mental representations and unfamiliar sound phenomena—can be like perceptual and affective jolts to the listener. The ear and brain seek familiarity and connection by shifting the person's focus of attention. When the existing schemes are no longer sufficient in organizing and making sense of incoming stimuli, new cognitive paths are explored (building on paths taken during prior listenings). We construct and reconstruct meaning in the music we identify as "familiar," reformulate our concept of the music, or dismiss it as "unfamiliar." Imagine attending a concert programmed with music unfamiliar to you, possibly with sights and sounds outside of the Western musical canon. Some of us would choose to listen to and explore the musical sounds. Others of us might engage in an internal debate over whether or not the sounds we encountered were music. Yet others might find themselves losing interest in the concert, maybe even leaving the concert, because they could not (or chose not to) make sense of the music.

From a physiological standpoint, music listening occurs when someone performs or plays a recording of music, and the instruments or voices set sound waves into motion. Those waves displace air particles that our ears ultimately receive as auditory stimuli (perception) and which the middle- and inner-ear neurological apparatus sends forth to the brain as electrical impulses. Within the brain, the impulses seek neural connections. That is, the brain searches for mental structures (representations) that are similar to the in-coming stimuli. Cognitive processes such as focus, order, recall, comparison, anticipation, expectation, and juxtaposition of musical ideas are set into action. Meanwhile, the music is also affecting the body's physiology with changes in heart rate, respiration, blood pressure, skin conductivity and temperature, muscle tension, and chemical composition (Bartlett 1996).

The ability to perceive musical sounds is still only a part of a music listening experience. Affective response is another essential component. The term *affect* relative to music listening embraces complex human behaviors and traits, such as emotional involvement, aesthetic response, mood, interest, value, appreciation, preference, attitude, and taste. As our students listen to music, we cannot know for which of them the experience is pleasurable or tedious, since the process of music listening elicits infinite degrees of affective response dependent on individual listeners. Further, a student might respond favorably to the music one day and respond quite the opposite during subsequent listenings, since his or her musical moods and preferences, focus of attention, and desire to listen readily change.

When we listen, our brains and bodies do not engage in disparate, sequential processes—perception followed by affective response. Instead, there is simultaneous body-mind-affect functioning, which intimates musicking as holistic and organic to human beings. Perceptual and affective responses are inextricably linked, whether or not we are aware of the connection. Meyer (1956, 39) stated, "Thinking and feeling need not be viewed as polar opposites but as different manifestations of a single psychological process."

Adding to Meyer's notion of thinking and feeling as a single psychological process, thinking and feeling conjoin as a psychological process *situated and influenced by the listener's culture and society*. To that end, Bowman (2004, 29) stated, "[B]odily-constituted knowledge, of which music is a prime and precious instance, is not different in kind from intellectual kinds of knowing. Rather, the two are continuous, deeply involved in each other's construction, and each in turn ecologically situated in the social world." Blacking (1973) emphasized the cultural and biological components that influence the manner in which musical sounds are perceived and processed. He wrote, "Music is a synthesis of cognitive processes which are present in culture and in the human body: the forms it takes, and the effects it has on people, are generated by the social experiences of human bodies in different cultural environments" (1973, 89). Therefore, even if we listen to music by ourselves in the comfort of our homes, we are actually hearing it as a result of enculturation, and thus the music listening experience is one that is collective—ours, personally, and the groups with which we identify.

Let us also consider the role of intuition in the music listening process. Bruner (1960) described intuition as the intellectual and analytical solution to a problem or formulated conclusion about something without conscious analysis of it. It is a "felt," automatic knowing about something. "Intuitive listening" (Dunn 2006), then, might be considered a person's affective and perceptual tacit knowledge of music as it is heard, without the listener's going through the conscious process of analyzing the piece. It might be the deep-level thinking and feeling that transcend the conscious intellectual and feeling levels typically associated with externalized responses during music listening. Therefore, it is the affective, perceptual, and intuitive actions that constitute the definition of music cognition used in this book (Parsons 1976; Stokes 1990).

Multisensory Music Listening

Why the emphasis on *multisensory* music listening tools and strategies in this book? As teachers, we might observe students who prefer to experience, discover, and learn using a particular sensory modality—aural, visual, kinesthetic, tactile, and olfactory. Yet students absorb information through all of their senses to create, consciously or unconsciously, meaning in their environments. In Dura's (2002) philosophical study on music listening, she found that people listen to music with all of their senses, although some (like aural, visual, and kinesthetic) are primary among the other senses. People hear music and create aural and visual images relative to the music. But even the aural and visual metaphors, images, and associations are rooted in kinesthetic (bodily) understanding of the music.

Rita and Kenneth Dunn (1978, 1992a, 1992b; Dunn 2000) researched conditions most conducive to optimal learning. Through their work in schools, Dunn and Dunn found students to possess preferred learning styles—that is, the best combination of "domains" for interacting with instruction and materials, processing concepts, and creating an optimal, desired, learning outcome. Teachers embracing learning-style theory consider students' ideal environmental, emotional, sociological, physiological, and psychological conditions and then individualize instruction by accommodating the classroom's physical environment, schedule, assignments, and social interactions accordingly.

Howard Gardner, in his *Frames of Mind: The Theory of Multiple Intelligences* (1983), identified an initial list of seven distinct intelligences: linguistic, logical-mathematical, musical, bodily-kinesthetic, spatial, interpersonal, and intrapersonal. Since then, Gardner has considered the nature and feasibility of additional intellectual domains—naturalistic, spiritual, moral, and existential intelligences. Gardner defined an *intelligence* as "the capacity to solve problems or to fashion products that are valued in one or more cultural settings" (Gardner and Hatch 1989, 5). Further, he posited that, although an intelligence operates in an isolated area of the brain, all forms of intelligence function interdependently. Theoretically, a student comes to school having been born with an intellectual profile (Gardner 2006), indicating keen cognitive abilities in some intellectual domains and lower ability levels in other domains. Teachers are charged with providing learning opportunities that resonate with students' intellectual strengths while nurturing those intellectual domains that might provide learning challenges.

Recent research refutes models of modularity of brain functioning (i.e., single areas of the brain responsible for specific functions such as language, movement, music, etc.) and hemispheric brain functioning (i.e., right-brain versus left-brain functioning; see Demasio 1994). Neuroscientific studies suggest a much more complex integration of brain functioning than intimated by early models of brain function. By collecting data from *f*MRIs and PET scans during tasks such as listening to music, researchers have observed different portions of the brain engaging in simultaneous activity (i.e., blood flow), instead of activity being contained in only one portion of the brain (Langheim et al., 2002; Limb 2008; Zattore 2005). Moreover, the parts of the brain that are engaged vary according to changes that are perceived in musical elements, musical training, and tasks performed during music listening (Edwards and Hodges 2007).

Whatever your position in terms of multiple intelligence and learning-style theories, these views have powerful implications for thinking about teaching and learning. First and foremost is that as teachers we educate the *whole* child—body, mind, feeling, and spirit. Moreover, a single IQ test score cannot aptly define the richness of a student's cognitive abilities, interests, and personality. There is more to a student—more to discover and nurture—than the verbal and mathematical abilities that are typically deified in schooling and thus evaluated by standardized tests.

These theories also acknowledge that students bring myriad approaches, abilities, and preferences to their music listening experiences; therefore, teachers face the challenge of offering music listening opportunities that diverse learners can access. In this book, I offer multisensory tools that can be used to individualize music-listening skill development—tools that can provide students with different means for accessing and discerning what is "going on" in the music and possibly for expressing their responses to the music, regardless of its genre, style, or historical period. By experiencing music along various multisensory felt (i.e., cognitive) pathways (Blair 2008), students might build metaphoric (verbal, visual, kinesthetic) frames for knowing music and constructing personal meaning. Because the teaching and learning strategies presented in this book are multisensory, they can be used with students who are linguistically adept, but also with those for whom learning by listening to words, reading words, or expressing themselves with words is a challenge. And for those students who have a particular sensory learning-style preference, these strategies might potentially strengthen that means and other sensory modalities that are involved in musical perception and enjoyment.

What this book does *not* do is treat music-listening skill development as traditional aural skills training. While this type of training can inform people (mostly performers) of theoretical organization, sight-singing, and identification of musical elements aural skills exercises are rarely presented in the context of authentic musical excerpts.

What I have found most musically satisfying in my own teaching and learning is using excerpts from music about which one discovers something new with repeated listenings. This seems to be an organic process. Typically, people encounter music listening experiences as whole—complete—occurrences of musical sounds, rather than as a series of isolated pitches or rhythms. Of course, listeners' meanings are refined by learning about the music's sociocultural and historical contexts and the relationships of musical elements working in tandem.

Admittedly, people listening to music, in whatever space they choose, tend not to create drawn music maps, movement sequences, or running verbal commentaries. Nor do our students come to music classes and rehearsals as empty musical slates; they come with their personalized, informed musicianship from prior interactions with musical sounds. No one has to teach students to listen or respond to music. Thus, the multisensory strategies presented in this book act only as temporary tools that young listeners might employ to gain *enriched* awareness of what the music has to offer. Think of them as music listening "training wheels" that help students transition to the mountain bicycle. By using such tools and strategies, students may develop their listening ears and minds so they are consciously attuned to musical relationships and contextual information during future, independent music listening experiences. I regard music listening as an event that can engage and profoundly impact the body-mind-feeling-spirit; therefore, I value music listening pedagogy and learning experiences that are designed to nurture informed and independent music listeners. As teachers, it is our challenge to nurture students' innate musicianship so they are able to do better that which they already do naturally.

"Create-ive" Music Listening

When the term *musical creativity* appears in music-education research literature, it typically refers to someone engaged in music composition or improvisation tasks, and on occasion, to someone who demonstrates high-caliber technical and/ or expressive music performance skills. Musically creative students engaging in these behaviors—composing, improvising, and performing—demonstrate unique approaches to solving musical "problems" and producing clever, if not new, musical outcomes (i.e., compositions, improvisations, performance interpretations). These processes and products are observable, tangible, and measurable by evaluative criteria, however widely or narrowly music teachers and researchers might define those criteria.

What would happen if music listening were added to the list of musically creativity behaviors? Is music listening a musically creative experience? This is certainly an interesting, and complex, philosophical issue—one important to explore.

Peterson (2006) provided a compelling argument for music listening as a creative experience. She maintained that music listening, like composition, improvisation, and performance, is a creative act despite the fact that the products of music listening are not tangible. These musical behaviors, including music listening, involve novel ways of thinking, making connections, and refining perceptions. With each repeated listening, listeners might find new discoveries about the music and its inherent elemental relationships—another mark of creativity. Furthermore, these "aha" moments while listening to music are based on students' discovering, investigating, and problem solving in order to create their unique mental models of the music they encounter. Finally, Peterson posited that the quality of music listening experience depends on listeners' memory, the flexibility of their mental models, and their ability to create new music listening models upon each encounter with a piece of music.

Music listening requires active, focused, and responsive participation if one is to be engaged (perceptually and affectively) in the experience. As people listen to music, they consciously or unconsciously select musical features on which they focus, change their foci, get distracted, find "ear anchors," create stories, conjure up associations, and respond emotionally. They also remember some of what they hear in the music, and mentally juxtapose those musical ideas in order to compare, contrast, and find patterns. Finally, people reflect on their "real-time" listening in the moment to prior music listening experiences in order to determine "same" or "different."

Bamberger (1991) suggested that music listening is an active structuring of heard material. During repeated listenings, people regroup musical stimuli, create new sectional forms, appropriate their focus of attention to selected musical elements, and open their minds to musical aspects that they might not have heard in their prior music listenings. She also mentioned that the act of restructuring mental representations, resulting from music listening, is active, creative work, since new meaning is constructed. "Too often...the listener lets such [unfamiliar] works slip by, giving in solely to their familiar stylistic schemata. Failing then, to be roused from this 'state of passivity,' the listener will also fail to discover the 'ever new, internal logic,' the unique process which distinguishes the great work, that which makes it more than just another instance of a style" (Bamberger 1991, 309).

Ideally, people listen to music with open minds when they are presented with unfamiliar sound patterns and musical styles; however, it is unrealistic to think that musical preference and bias from prior music experiences do not affect how people listen to music. Listeners' motivations and desires to listen enable them to allow the music to unfold and construct meaning without passing initial, dismissive judgment of it as "different" and thereby unworthy of continued listening. People also construct personal and imaginative music listening experiences. Serafine (1988, 7) claimed that the cognitive processes employed here are unique to the musical domain, shared by listeners, composers, and performers, and that "cognition in music—in listening as well as in composing and performing—is an active, constructive process." Further, she suggested,

> The object [music]...is a fluid, changing thing, or else there are multiple objects, each constituted from some human-subjective point of view. At best, the central artwork/object is an idealized, hypothetical piece—the area of overlap among all the individual performances and conceptions of the work. This artwork is not a fixed, external object, but an abstract and fluid one that rests on human cognitive construction in all phases of its existence—composing, performing, and listening. (Serafine 1988, 67)

Because people are situated in diverse cultural milieus and possess varying degrees of cognitive (perceptual and affective) ability, listeners create uniquely personal music listening experiences. Needless to say, it is difficult to determine which music listening experiences are "creative" while others are not. During music listening, neither the internal cognitive processes nor the internal constructed products or changes to mental representations are observable or measurable. Therefore, music listening as a creative endeavor seems to be a creative activity different from composition, improvisation, and performance, even if there is overlap in the cognitive processes.

Consider this: *the cognitive processes employed during music listening do lead to creative products of music listening.* The processes, mentioned earlier in this chapter, include selecting, ordering, comparing, manipulating, reorganizing, and reflecting on music stimuli, thereby creating and revising mental models of a piece of music to which people have listened. Through the imaginative ways that listeners construct and assign meaning to musical patterns and relationships, they sophisticate their mental representations of the music during subsequent listenings. Thus, the creative products rendered during music listening are these redefined mental representations. They are dynamic, with listeners recasting them each time they listen to the same or different musical material.

Problematic, however, is that there is (to date) no empirical way of observing, describing, measuring, or evaluating the nature of listeners' mental representations or the quality of their music listening experience (i.e., perceptual acuity *and* affective response). Simply put, there is no direct access into listeners' minds during music listening so as to gain a holistic picture of the processes and products. Therefore, teachers and researchers are forced to rely on external modes—overt behaviors—that represent the "skeletal contents" of the mental processes used and the products generated during music listening experiences.

In this book, I invite you to explore students' observable responses—talk-alouds, maps, and movements—as behaviors that embody this musical thinking. We might, then, consider the act of drawing music listening maps—visual metaphors for what students are thinking, feeling, and hearing—as the embodiment of thinking creatively and musically in the moment. Or, the act of creating a gesture or sequence of movements—kinesthetic metaphors—to embody musically creative thinking. Or, talking aloud—verbal metaphors—to embody musically creative thinking.

I have asked students to represent their music listening experiences—perceptual and affective facets—via maps, movements, and words. As students create these types of external representations, we as teachers might gain useful insight into the processes by which students create their personal meanings of the music. That which is difficult to verbally describe might more fully be expressed metaphorically in nonverbal forms. Yet these metaphoric representations for thinking and feeling in musical sound can provide teachers with only a glimpse into students' music listening experience.

As teachers, we must remain mindful that students choose the features of the experience they want or might be able to share with us. The externalized representations also might interfere with the music listening process, as when students attend to and depict one musical event and many other musical events might pass by unnoticed and unreported. Further, these verbal and nonverbal representations will serve as levels of "translation," depicting a version transferred into metaphoric terms rather than capturing the essence of the students' music listening experience.

In terms of musical thinking, though, students' multisensory responses during music listening experiences represent observable, tangible products—externalized analogues of musical thinking in the moment. Like other musically creative tasks, they represent the result of problem solving: students are given a task of representing verbally, visually, and kinesthetically what they are thinking, feeling, and hearing as they listen to music, all of which are ways to personally express and represent musical sound and ideas.

In my research and teaching, I do not assess students' responses qualitatively as objects of art. Instead, I search the content and inherent musical meaning of the responses (often inferred). I treat students' responses as mirrors of their cognitive processes during their music listening experiences, while recognizing these externalized responses are incomplete accounts.

Repeated Listening

Music listeners create meaning of their present musical encounters in light of their past musical experiences. Throughout their attentive listening, people enlist cognitive processes to determine if their mental representations of the musical sounds are sufficient, or if they need to recast and rework their mental structures. But music moves quickly through time and space. I have heard children explain that they cannot remember or depict all they have heard, for they heard it only momentarily and then the music moved on. They did not have time to draw, or move, or talk aloud. Therefore, repeated listening becomes an essential strategy in helping students develop "deep" music listening skills (Shehan Campbell 2005).

Think of the initial presentation of an unfamiliar musical example as a mental skeleton; students might listen for and identify basic structural and expressive elements of that music. However, with each repeated listening, details of the musical excerpt are the flesh that is added to the musical skeleton. In my research (Kerchner 1996, 2005), I found that, regardless of age or music performance training, students exhibited a schematic framework in their verbal, visual, and kinesthetic responses, and that these frameworks were elaborated upon during each subsequent listening. Many students' responses developed from those capturing sparse descriptions of the music to subsequent responses that became more detailed (differentiated). Repeated listening, mental rehearsal, and musical familiarity contributed to the acquisition of detail that filled out the student listeners' mental representations.

Meyer (1956) wrote about the need for repeated listening:

> Because listening to music is a complex art involving sensitivity of apprehension, intellect, and memory, many of the implications of an event are missed on first hearing. It is only after we come to know and remember the basic, axiomatic events of a work—its motives, themes, and so on—that we begin to appreciate the richness of their implications. It is partly for these reasons that a good piece of music can be reheard and that, at least at first, enjoyment increases with familiarity. (46)

Therefore, repeated exposure to a piece of music facilitates familiarity, thus possibly prompting listeners to reformulate, reshape, and revise prior musical mental representations. Repeated listening also leads people to listen from different cognitive perspectives, finding musical sounds and elemental relationships they might not have heard before and, accordingly, allowing for new body-mind-feeling-spirit responses. Bamberger (1991, 264) describes this as "liberating their mental representation." Therefore, a primary function of music teachers is to lead students to listen to music with the intent of creating meaning—*listening-for-meaning*—through repeated listening and practice to become engaged, informed, and feelingful listeners.

PRINCIPLES OF MUSIC LISTENING

In the prior sections of this chapter, we explored music listening—the cognitive processes involved, its multisensory nature, and as an experience that is both creative and intuitive. Further, we considered rationales for including music listening as a cornerstone for general music classroom experiences and as a crucial component of performance rehearsal curricula. We also preliminarily explored multisensory tools that might act as "training wheels" for students' ears.

Having considered my own and others' research in these areas, I have created a list of music listening principles that serves as a rationale for including music listening in music curricula. We will explore these principles throughout this book. They might function as guidelines for how we teach music listening, helping us design classroom and rehearsal experiences that facilitate the development of students' music listening skills, and assisting us in assessing students' listening skills. Perhaps these principles could even serve as the connective tissue between the worlds of research and teaching praxis. What additional principles might you add to this list?

PRINCIPLES OF MUSIC LISTENING

1. Music listening is a skill worth developing. It is the foundation for musical behaviors, and attentive listening is key to human communication and interaction.
2. Each person has the capacity to develop music listening skills, regardless of her or his cognitive, physical, or musical abilities.
3. Each person creates unique music listening experiences that are influenced by past and present musical experiences.
4. Music listening can evoke internal and external responses to music's formal and aesthetic qualities.
5. Music listening requires creative and active participation.
6. Music listening pedagogical activities serve to focus students' attention on the music.
7. Masterful musical examples, regardless of style or genre, provide material for conceptual study in class and ensemble rehearsals.
8. Teaching strategies, not the music itself, suggest age suitability.
9. Repeatedly listening to musical examples, within a single class period and over the course of several classes, enables students to become intensely familiar with the musical "material" and to ascribe "deeper" levels of musical meaning.
10. Repeatedly listening to musical examples enables students to create, recreate, and sophisticate their constructed musical meaning.

11. Multisensory (kinesthetic, visual, aural, tactile) music listening tools can pro-
    vide multiple access points into the music for diverse students (i.e., cognitive/
    intellectual abilities, style preferences, linguistic skills).
12. Student responses can serve as springboards for subsequent musical discus-
    sions and explorations of other musical behaviors.

SETTING THE STAGE

In subsequent chapters, I present information specific to PK–12 students' verbal,
visual, and kinesthetic responses during music listening. Research artifacts (i.e.,
transcripts of students' verbal reports/talk-alouds, drawn maps, descriptions of
movements/gestures, and video recordings) will also be presented. The following
research procedure was implemented to procure individual student data:

RESEARCH PROJECT WEEKS 1 AND 2 (TWO 45-MINUTE INDIVIDUAL INTERVIEW SESSIONS):

1. Listen to musical excerpt only.
2. Listen to musical excerpt and provide concurrent verbal report (talk-aloud).
3. Listen to musical excerpt and draw a music listening map.
4. Listen to musical excerpt and add onto music listening map.
   4a. Verbally describe music listening map relative to the music excerpt.
5. Listen to musical excerpt and point to music listening map.
6. Listen to musical excerpt and create movement sequence.
7. View recording of movements and verbally describe them.
8. Verbal post-interview (Week 2 only).

The research task sequence modestly follows what is known as the
"whole-part-whole" or "synthesis-analysis-synthesis" sequence approach to music
curricular (and lesson) sequencing (GIML 2012). In this manner, students experience musical "information" from the largest possible whole (or chunk) that they can
manage, according to their levels of skill development, interest or motivation, and
focus of attention, and then they progress to smaller musical units for analysis. After
analyzing smaller pieces of the whole, students experience the small pieces placed
back into the complete musical unit. For example, second-grade students might
listen to a two-minute section of music, perhaps in AB form. During the analysis
portion of the lesson, they trace phrases with their arms and hands within each
formal section of the music. Enlisting repeated listening to the individual sections,
the students and teacher could determine how many phrases per section, which of

the phrases were the same or were different and how they differed. Finally, students listen to the same two-minute section as a whole unit, listening for the phrases and having pointer fingers to indicate the number of phrases.

The verbal, visual, and kinesthetic tasks demonstrated in this book were organized so that the student research participants would hear the musical excerpt "in tact" (synthesis) before they added another layer of complexity—the talking, mapping, or movement tasks (analysis). At the beginning of each listening interview session, the students listened to the musical excerpt without being asked to do any task, so they could gain a basic idea of the music excerpt. Then the students listened to the music excerpt while talking-aloud, mapping, or moving. Finally, the students reviewed their responses and verbally described them (maps and movements) or pointed to them (maps) while listening to the music—a synthesis-reflection piece of the procedure.

Each chapter of this book includes:

1. A rationale for the multisensory tool.
2. What I have learned from students who participated in my research projects (using particular multisensory pedagogical tools) about their music listening experience. PK–12 students "tell" their stories of engagement during music listening.
3. "How to" procedures and suggestions for incorporating the multisensory tools and strategies into the music classroom and rehearsal settings.
4. Sample music listening lessons that focus on teacher-generated and/or student-generated multisensory maps, movements, and verbal listening opportunities.

In the final chapter, I suggest strategies for tracking and assessing student music-listening skill development. At specific points in the text you will be directed to visit the book's Companion Website in order to see PK–12 students in action, providing responses as individuals, in collaborative groups, and in classrooms/rehearsals while listening to music.

RESOURCES

Bartlett, D. (1996). "Physiological Responses to Music and Sound Stimuli." In *Handbook of Music Psychology*, 2nd ed., edited by D. Hodges, chap. 9. San Antonio, TX: IMR Press.

Bamberger, J. (1991). *The Mind Behind the Musical Ear: How Children Develop Musical Intelligence.* Cambridge, MA: Harvard University Press.

Blacking, J. (1973). *How Musical Is Man?* Seattle: University of Washington Press.

Blair, D. (2008, August). "Do You Hear What I Hear? Musical Maps and Felt Pathways of Musical Understanding." *Visions of Research in Music Education* 11. Retrieved from http://www-usr.rider.edu~vrme/, September 29, 2011.

Bowman, W. (2004). "Cognition and the Body: Perspectives from Music Education." In *Knowing Bodies, Moving Minds: Toward Embodied Teaching and Learning*, edited by L. Bresler, 29-50. Dordrecht, Netherlands: Kluwer.

Bruner, J. (1960). *The Process of Education*. Cambridge, MA: Harvard University Press.

Consortium of National Arts Education. (1994). *National Standards for Arts Education: What Every Young American Should Know and Be Able to Do in the Arts*. Reston, VA: Music Educators National Conference.

Demásio, A. (1994). *Descartes' Error*. New York: G.P. Putnam.

Dunn, R. (2000). "Learning Styles: Theory, Research, and Practice." *National Forum of Applied Educational Research Journal* 13(1): 3–22.

Dunn, R. E. (1997). "Creative Thinking and Music Listening." *Research Studies in Music Education* 8: 42–55.

Dunn, R. E. (2006). "Teaching for Lifelong, Intuitive Listening." *Arts Education Policy Review* 107(3): 33–40.

Dunn, R., and K. Dunn (1978). *Teaching Students Through Their Individual Learning Styles*. Reston, VA: Reston.

Dunn, R., and K. Dunn (1992a). *Teaching Elementary Students Through Their Individual Learning Styles*. Boston: Allyn & Bacon.

Dunn, R., and K. Dunn (1992b). *Teaching Secondary Students Through Their Individual Learning Styles*. Boston: Allyn & Bacon.

Dura, M. (2002). *Music Education and the Music Listening Experience*. Lewiston, NY: Edwin Mellen Press, Ltd.

Edwards, R., and D. Hodges (2007). "Neuromusical Research: An Overview of the Literature". In *Neurosciences in Music Pedagogy*, edited by W. Grühn and R. Rauscher, chap. 1. New York: Nova Science.

Elliott, D. (1995). *Music Matters: A New Philosophy of Music Education*. New York: Oxford University Press.

Gardner, H. (1983). *Frames of Mind: The Theory of Multiple Intelligences*. New York: Basic Books.

Gardner, H. (2006). *Multiple Intelligences*: New Horizons. New York: Basic Books.

Gardner, H., and T. Hatch (1989). "Multiple Intelligences Go to School: Educational Implications of the Theory of Multiple Intelligences." *Educational Researcher* 18(8): 4–9.

Gordon Institute of Music Learning (GIML). (2012). Retrieved from http://www.giml.org/mlt_methodology.php on January 30, 2012.

Kerchner, J. L. (1996). "Perceptual and Affective Components of Music Listening Experience as Manifested in Children's Verbal, Visual, and Kinesthetic Representations." Unpublished doctoral dissertation, Northwestern University

Kerchner, J. L. (2001). "Children's Verbal, Visual, and Kinesthetic Responses: Insight into Their Music Listening Experience." *Bulletin of the Council for Research in Music Education* 146: 35–51.

Kerchner, J. L. (2005). "A World of Sound to Know and Feel: Exploring Children's Verbal, Visual, and Kinesthetic Responses to Music." In *Music in Schools for All Children: From Research to Effective Practice*, edited by M. Mans and B. W. Leung, 21–33. Granada, Spain: University of Granada.

Kerchner, J. L. (2009). "Drawing Middle-schoolers' Attention to Music." In *Musical Experience in Our Lives: Things We Learn and Meanings We Make*, edited by J. Kerchner and C. Abril, chap. 11. Lanham, MD: Rowman & Littlefield.

Langheim, F., J. Callicott, V. Mattay, J. Duyn, and D. Weinberger (2002). "Cortical Systems Associated with Covert Musical Rehearsal." *NeuroImage* 16: 901–8.

Limb, C. (2008). "Your Brain on Jazz: Neural Substrates of Spontaneous Improvisation." Library of Congress podcast, December 8, 2008, Retrieved from http://www.loc.gov/ podcasts/musicandthebrain/podcast_charleslimb.html.

Meyer, L. (1956). *Emotion and Meaning in Music*. Chicago: Chicago University Press.

Mursell, J. (1943). *Education for American Democracy*. New York: W. W. Norton.

Palmer, P. (1998). *The Courage to Teach: Exploring the Inner Landscape of a Teacher's Life*. San Francisco, CA: John Wiley & Sons, Inc.

Parsons, M. (1976). "A Suggestion Concerning the Development of Aesthetic Experience in Children." *Journal of Aesthetics and Art Criticism* 34(3): 305–14.

Peterson, E. (2006). "Creativity in Music Listening." *Arts Education Policy Review* 107(3): 15–21.

Reimer, B. (1989). *A Philosophy of Music Education*. Englewood Cliffs, NJ: Prentice-Hall.

Serafine, M. L. (1988). *Music as Cognition: The Development of Thought in Sound*. New York: Columbia University Press.

Shehan Campbell, P. (2005). "Deep Listening to the Musical World." *Music Educators Journal* 92(1): 30–36.

Small, C. (1998). Musicking: *The Meanings of Performing and Listening*. Middletown, CT: Wesleyan University Press.

Stokes, W. A. (1990). "Intelligence and Feeling: A Philosophical Examination of These Concepts as Interdependent Factors in Musical Experience and Music Education." Unpublished doctoral dissertation, Northwestern University.

Zattore, R. (2005). "Music, the Food of Neuroscience?" *Nature* 434: 312–15.

CHAPTER 2

Teachers Leading and Learning

The topic of this chapter might initially seem questionable in a book having as its focus the "who, what, when, why, and how" of multisensory music listening strategies. To look holistically at the pedagogy involved in teaching for students' heightened perceptual awareness, acuity, and affective response during music listening, however, that view must also include the examination of philosophical, curricular, and pedagogical perspectives, at one level, and teacher and student attitudes and habits of mind, at another level. These principles and perspectives intersect, and they can direct and redirect how students and teachers interact, as well as affect the willingness of both students and teachers to take risks together during the teaching–learning process.

In this chapter, we will examine those factors that influence, either directly or indirectly, student learning in music classrooms and rehearsal spaces, although the principles are equally applicable to general education classrooms, teachers, students, and curricular structures. We will explore, identify, and reflect on those teacher and student attitudes and behaviors that motivate and facilitate the joy of teaching and learning, as well as those factors that might hinder or prohibit the facilitation of hands-on, active, and creative music listening and learning experiences.

In the process, we will also consider verbal and nonverbal communication, presentational styles, teacher and student roles, feedback, questioning tactics, and teacher leadership styles. I encourage you to reflect on your teaching practice, and consider possible alternatives as a way of becoming an empowered music educator in your own teaching situation. Here, we will take inventory of what is is useful to teachers and students alike, as this kind of thinking challenges the bastion of beliefs, best practices, and preconceived notions about the nature of engagement in and with (i.e., "learning") music. Power comes when you take steps to ensure that you and your students are working toward being your "best possible selves" in a teaching–learning situation.

In our reflective practice, teachers regularly question, re-question, reconsider, revise, reframe, and revisit what they do in the classroom. They consider the effects (or lack of effect) that pedagogical, personal, and presentational habits of mind have on student learning. They create safe spaces in which students can eagerly participate in their classrooms or rehearsal communities of learners. Reflective practice can also affirm the efficacy of teaching and learning strategies that are aligned with our pedagogical values and can explain their effectiveness in accordance with what we intuit, observe, and assess concerning student learning.

TEACHERS EXAMINING THEIR PHILOSOPHIES

Examining your personal values is one way to reflect on what you teach in terms of music listening (and other musical) experiences and skills, including asking yourself why you teach them, in which classes you teach them, to whom you teach them, when you teach them, and how (pedagogically) you teach them. Some immediate responses to these questions might come to mind, based on your teaching experience and observations, curricular expectations, the research studies you have read, and your background in music education pedagogy. However, I ask you to think beyond the general notions of "why I teach music." While this is the philosophical question at the core of what we do as music educators, I encourage you to ask that question about your teaching of student music-listening skill development.

Why do you believe it is necessary (or not necessary) to develop students' music listening skills beyond those they already possess? To stimulate your thinking, consider the intellectual, emotional/affective, physical/behavioral, and social rationales you have for including the development of students' music listening skills in your music curriculum. Jot down your ideas and build on them as you read this chapter and subsequent chapters of this book.

Once you have considered these areas—your intellectual, emotional/affective, physical/behavioral, and social rationales behind your teaching—categorize those justifications into those that are strictly musical (e.g., studying music as an art form, learning about the relationships of various musical elements) and those that are extra-musical (e.g., ancillary benefits from developed music listening skills). Where are most of your rationales? Do you have more musical or more extra-musical rationales? Speculate as to why this is so, and consider how these rationales inform your philosophy and pedagogy of teaching for student music-listening skill development.

Shape your philosophical thinking into a statement about teaching for student music-listening skill development, as you answer the following questions:

1. Who does/does not need to develop music listening skills? (Students in performance ensembles? Students in general music classes? Students in other music classes? In which grade levels? Students possessing musical abilities? At what level of ability?)
2. In which type of music classes should the development of students' music listening skills occur? (Performance classes? General music classes? Music electives?)
3. What specific music listening skills do you want your students to develop and/or refine?

4. How are these skills developed throughout the students' PK–12 music experiences?
5. How often do you initiate music listening in your classroom?
6. How do you assess or evaluate the degree to which music listening skills are demonstrated and developed by individual students?
7. What are three pedagogical strategies you use in teaching music-listening skill development? Describe what those strategies look like in your classroom or rehearsal space.
8. What is/are your role(s) in your general music classes or ensemble rehearsals? What is/are the students' role(s) in those classes?
9. How do you communicate to the students, parents, and administration your students' progress in developing music listening skills?
10. How does your knowledge of recent research and the best-practices literature inform your understanding of music listening, learning, and student music development?
11. How does your teaching experience inform your music listening pedagogy?

Key to empowering yourself as an agent of change in your music-teaching setting is to consider whether or not your values—your philosophy for engaging students in experiences that will nurture their music-listening skill development and sophistication—align with what is actually experienced in the classroom or rehearsal setting. What follows are some principles to consider that might challenge or affirm your current rationales, while prompting you to move closer to making manifest those values in the music classroom or ensemble.

PLANNING FOR DISCOVERY LEARNING

This book is framed by *constructivist theory*. This theory acknowledges that students, regardless of age, are experienced learners who bring to the learning process a range of prior knowledge, skills, beliefs, and conceptual understandings that determine how they organize and interpret (assign meaning to) their environment. Jonassen (1991, 10) elaborates:

> Constructivism…claims that reality is constructed by the knower based upon mental activity. Humans are perceivers and interpreters who construct their own reality through engaging in those mental activities.…[T]hinking is grounded in perception of physical and social experiences, which can only be comprehended by the mind. What the mind produces are mental models that explain to the knower what he or she has perceived.…We all conceive of the external reality somewhat differently, based on our unique set of experiences with the world and our beliefs about them.

To this definition, I would add that we make meaning with our entire being—our body-mind-feeling-spirit selves. As unified entities, we interact with and create meaning in our environments, not only with our mental abilities but also with our feelingful selves. Therefore, in a constructivist classroom or ensemble rehearsal, students and teachers demonstrate discovery in creating (e.g., performing, listening, composing, improvising), interpreting, knowing, and feeling as individuals and as members of the learning community. Figure 2.1 lists the tenets of constructivism.

Constructivism, when applied to instruction in general education, and to music specifically, is not an innovative pedagogical perspective. Hints of constructivist ideology were evident as early as the sixth century B.C., with Lao Tzu, the Buddha, and Socrates, and later, in the writings of Kant and Schopenhauer. Similarly, constructivist thinking is at the core of educational theories and pedagogies espoused by Montessori (1946), Dewey (1997, 1964), Bruner (1966), Schön (1983), and Vygotsky (1978). The cognitive science revolution of the 1950s and 1960s mobilized an educational paradigm shift from behaviorism to constructivism. Prior to that time, psychologists and educators viewed students as the recipients of knowledge given by teachers, whereas constructivist "best practice" considers students as active creators of meaning and teachers as the facilitators of learning. Vygotsky (1978, 224) contended that students are not teachers' "instructional objects, but active agents." Constructivists acknowledge learning as a socially constructed, lifelong occurrence that is a direct result of the cultural, historical, socio-political context in which learners are situated. While the internalization of information and meaning occurs at the individual level, that internalization has its origin in society (Wertsch 1998).

For music teachers who embrace constructivism, a primary responsibility is to lead students to discover and create their own meaning for musical sounds, structures, and styles by facilitating group and individual problem-solving tasks or projects. Small (1977, 213) wrote that teachers engage students in learning "by acknowledging the inbuilt creative power of young minds, by harnessing and at the

---

Figure 2.1. TENETS OF CONSTRUCTIVISM

Tenets of constructivism include:

(1) students' active agency in learning through discovery,

(2) mental ordering (patterning) of information in creating personal meaning of an object or event,

(3) knowledge as variable, instead of being a single "truth,"

(4) development and involvement of students' self and personal identity in the learning process,

(5) social-symbolic relatedness of learning,

(6) creation of teacher-student learning partnerships,

(7) project-based learning/problem-solving tasks leading to discovery, and

(8) lifespan development.

---

same time releasing it to find its own solutions, or more fundamentally, to ask its own questions." At some time during music class, students should experience working independently *and* in small groups, as they pursue authentic musical tasks and "problems"—the kinds of tasks and problems that are experienced by people who engage in "real-life" musical experiences. Teachers who embrace constructivism determine the amount of scaffolding, providing students with detailed structure, directions, and task specification on one end of a continuum and offering them complete determination of a problem-solving task at the other end. Teachers who initially provide specific goals and tasks to achieve a goal may also wish to experiment with having students co-design the tasks or even lead the project. This decision is governed, of course, by the teacher's comfort level, prior student experiences in working independently and in groups, the level of trust between students and teacher, and the teacher's philosophical and pedagogical values.

From the constructivist perspective, members of problem-solving groups include students, teachers, and other musical experts in the broader learning community. In this manner, all members of the group share the roles of learner and informer. Teachers (senior learners) at times become students of their students (junior learners), while the students at times become teachers of their teachers—a learning partnership with fluid roles (Thurman and Welch 2000). To the projects or tasks the collaborators bring their own frameworks (mental structures built from prior experience) and perspectives; they negotiate and generate co-created meanings and solutions through a shared understanding of the problem and the discovery of possible solutions.

As music educators realize, there is rarely a musical absolute. Instead, there are multiple interpretations, phrasings, articulations, dynamic shifts, intonations, and vocal emphases that we consider in our performances, compositions, improvisations, and listening experiences. Music problem-solving tasks that engage students' perceptual and affective (i.e., cognitive) functioning and responses, their musical productions, and their reflective thinking skills prompt those students to seek multiple viable musical solutions, or truths. We learn from "experts," our own discoveries, and our social circles which musical practices are preferred, theoretically, historically, and aesthetically. We create understandings of musical sounds by thinking about and engaging with them. Thus, through the process of discovery learning, students can also explore and claim their personal musical preferences and identities as they engage in hands-on musical experiences.

What does constructivism look like in a music classroom or rehearsal space? What types of music listening projects might be possible? What types of individual and group projects involving music-listening skill development (exploration, creation, production, reflection) are facilitated in a music learning space? Advances in music software, personal computers, mp3 players, and iPads, and the expansion of the Internet have made music, especially authentic experiences, accessible to everyone. We can be "virtually" transported to performances worldwide and experience them within their own cultural contexts. Yet, project-based, discovery learning is by no means reliant on the use of technology, as the mapping, movement, and talk-aloud experiences in subsequent chapters demonstrate.

Before engaging your students in Internet searches, however, speak with your school principal and superintendent about how you would like to use technology in the classroom, give your rationale for choosing these learning experiences, and describe the learning outcomes you will be able to assess at the conclusion of the project. I found that steadfast school rules can be relaxed when teachers justify the use of technology as a tool that is aimed toward specific learning goals. Additionally, you can send e-mail messages to your students' parents, indicating that the students will be using online materials, describing the project's objectives and expected learning outcomes, and indicating the administration's support of this Internet use.

Here are only a few examples of problem-solving tasks and projects that you could try in your music classrooms and rehearsal spaces. These can be adapted for individual or small-group projects.

- Have students use Skype to connect with a musician or group of musicians in another country or elsewhere in the United States. By listening to and learning about others' musics via live performances or recordings, the students' aural soundscapes are expanded. Students could learn different rhythms and melodies (with or without lyrics), perform some pieces using them, and receive performance coaching in real time from native performers. Further, students can learn from world musicians how this different music is culturally and historically situated in those societies.
- Encourage students to use Skype to facilitate discussions between listeners (classroom students) and composers. Students can describe ahead of time, orally or in writing, what they are thinking, feeling, and hearing as they listen to a composer's music. These mini-descriptions, possibly critiques, then become fodder for dialog between the listeners and the composer. Age-appropriate aesthetic and philosophical discussions about a composer's decisions on how to affect audiences could be discussed. Further, these listening experiences and dialogs can become springboards for classroom and ensemble compositional tasks.
- Have the students compose something (e.g., a song, ballad, computer piece, "found sound" piece, commercial jingle, video game music), then find composers in the United States or abroad who are willing to critique the work. Or, have the students compose a piece "in the style of" a composition they have listened to and studied. Or, have the students get involved in a worldwide "jam session" (via Jam2jam) that involves listening to collaborators' improvised pieces, creating collaborative video and audio performances themselves, and recording the "final products" (Dillon, 2006). This improvisational opportunity can originate in listening lessons that include musics demonstrating improvisational techniques.
- Ask students to listen to recorded performances of world musics at websites such as http://worldmusic.nationalgeographic.com/. They can access these

sites on their laptops, iPads, or school computers. Additionally, iPad ensembles can be formed based on the world music sounds and songs that the students encounter, thereby using the sounds of authentic world instruments.

- Explore YouTube to examine video-music connections. YouTube, iTunes, and cell phone applications (apps) are ways to discover musical styles and genres from around the world, all easily accessible in classrooms or online media-converter sites such as zamzar.com or www.ilivid.com. These sites allow you to download the videos in a usable format, burn the video clips to a DVD, and subsequently use them in the classroom. Use a downloaded video or music piece to get students debating the role of video or images in the performance of a song. Probing questions to facilitate discussion might include: "How does video add to the performance of the music?" "How does it subtract?" "Does it engage the listener or distract the listener?" "How might the style or genre of this music help determine the images that are projected during the performance?"

- Explore sites such as Allmusic.com, a music database hosting short sound bites of musical of styles and genres; music is also listed by theme/mood and country. In the "motivation" category, for example, there are songs such as "Respect" by Aretha Franklin; musical styles include international, country, blues, jazz, reggae, R&B, rap, Latin, classical, pop, and rock. This type of site serves as only one of many stops for students exploring a potpourri of musical sounds.

- Explore soundjunction.org for a variety of music sounds or Freesound.org for a repository of sampled sounds—essentially, a sound bank for sounds not necessarily what some might consider "musical."

- Use the software package GarageBand for simple sound exploration (i.e., to gain familiarity with individual timbres and combinations of timbres, as well as tempo, note durations, sound effects, and recording sounds). This is excellent for recording voices into the software and manipulating their acoustic characteristics. It is easy to import music from iTunes or CDs to create musical collages or original compositions.

- Collect songs from student mp3 players, store the music on iTunes, and have the students create a musical mosaic à la *Musique concrete* and recent mashups as seen on television shows (e.g., *Glee*) and YouTube. Students can manipulate the features of the pieces by adding reverberation or repeating particular sounds, words, or consonants. Students can also place one piece of music on a track while simultaneously playing another piece on another track. These tasks can be done with recorded music, live music, synthesized sounds, or found-sounds in and around the school.

- Create a DJ (disk jockey) space: Students collect their favorite music in order to create a listening play list. The students play the role of DJ, introducing each piece with information about the performer and its descriptive musical features, while also providing the rationale for including that music on their play list (i.e., what in the music is appealing).

- Using GarageBand, have students record their personal musical journey. They can infuse sounds from their past and present musical soundscapes (i.e., pieces of songs, compositions, sounds from television, movies, nature, etc.) as the backdrop or for transitions in their stories of their musical pathways. This is an autobiographical way of learning about each student and helps validate each student's musical knowledge and experiences both outside of and during the music class.
- Create a music critic's corner: Following the model of a movie critic—Siskel, Ebert, Roeper, or a local newspaper music critic—have students select music of a particular style, period, or genre and critique the piece (i.e., describing what the music sounds like, highlight certain features) as well as the performer's execution of that piece. Students then discuss the primary points of each other's critiques, and ultimately, they rate the music as "thumbs up" or "thumbs down," or a mix of the two. A variation on this project is to have the students compare two different performances of the same piece, perhaps their own performances.
- Create music learning centers: Establish one, two, or several stations in your music classroom or rehearsal space (Burton 2012). Each station might focus on a different musical behavior: listening, composing, performing, improvising, reading notation, critiquing, arts connections, curricular connections to music, and cultural connections to music. Another option is to center on different behaviors involving music listening: critiquing, mapping, moving, being a DJ, creating world music listening collages, and exploring soundscapes. Using a sign-up sheet, students select their top two music learning centers; then, working independently or with partners, they rotate among the centers, completing a task or project affiliated with each center. You could offer perhaps one learning-center task or project per semester or grade reporting period. Students could also work on the learning centers during their study halls or other free time. Each center should have earphones, so the student activity at one center does not interfere with other centers or the regular, full-group class instruction.

You might have noticed that these music experiences do not follow traditional music class and rehearsal prototypes, as when students are the recipients of information about music or are learning how to perform a piece of music. You might have also noticed that even though the focus of these experiences is that of music listening, the activities exercise and refine a variety of musical skills and behaviors. While providing these student-centered experiences you might feel as if you are initially "courting chaos" in the class or rehearsal, juggling many musical experiences simultaneously. However, these independent and collaborative experiences inspire the students to take an active role in their music education and join the teaching–learning partnership. Setting the stage for such student-centered learning helps set the ethos and expectations for what the teaching and learning will look like in your classroom and rehearsal space.

LEADING EMPATHETICALLY

In an ideal world, all teachers would be pedagogical leaders who are caring, compassionate, charismatic, creative, and musically competent. They would also implement pedagogical strategies that help students meet their psychological, educational, musical, and social needs. Similarly in that ideal world, all students would be empathetic learners, coming to the teaching–learning partnership with open and curious minds, willing to try new educational experiences, enthusiastically engaging with their musical learning environments, and caring for and showing compassion toward their peers and teachers.

Empathetic leadership is a mind-set for building a music learning community. It is a teacher's determination to be emotionally, mentally, and physically in tune with his or her students. In line with the constructivist perspective, an empathetic leader is a music teacher who helps plot and facilitate the educational pathways for students, as well as being an authority and a senior learner who has both musical and pedagogical experience.

This position is diametrically opposed to the teacher-as-authoritarian model, in which the teacher is the sole expert and voice in the class or rehearsal. Perhaps it derives from the performance model—a stage, a podium, with actors performing for someone, with a conductor in charge of a chorus—that leads us, unfortunately, to think that teaching is also a performance. Instead, empathetic leaders are keenly aware of and responsive to the students' verbal and nonverbal behaviors, and they demonstrate musical and pedagogical skills in the moment, even making "in-flight" decisions about the direction of the lessons and rehearsals based on what they see, hear, and intuit.

The following list is a sampling of core values and beliefs that are embraced by empathetic leaders (Kerchner 2003, 121):

- Each person contributes to the music class or rehearsal dynamic.
- Each person has the right to an "equal voice" in class or rehearsal, in expressing questions, opinions, observations, or suggestions.
- Each person is capable of choosing, interpreting, imagining, deciding, evaluating, focusing, and performing in ways that contribute to the class's co-created understanding of musical experiences.
- Both teachers and students are learners and leaders.
- Music learning communities that are based on respect and empathy forge deeply rooted connections between people and the music.

Maxine Greene (1995) called for teachers to lead students to the "know-how" and provide the basic knowledge of an artistic domain (such as music), but then to provide opportunities for the students to discover musical meaning in their own, unique ways. As music teachers, we provide much more than information about music. We also use our musical and teaching experience to provide guidance, inspiration, and suggestions relative to the musical experiences that students have had and will continue to have inside and outside of our classrooms. True teaching and learning occur when students' imaginations are opened to the many possibilities for musical interpretation, sound structures, and expression of emotion and musical thought. Empowered teachers—empathetic leaders—enable students to seek that which is musically satisfying and meaningful on a personal level.

Empathetic leaders are responsible for modeling respectful, caring, and compassionate words and behaviors in the music classroom or rehearsal. Through these modeled behaviors, they demonstrate their expectations for student-teacher interactions in the music classroom. And because students feel emotionally and physically safe and cared for in this community of learners, they invest in their own learning experiences, develop trust and compassion, take risks in learning, and assume ownership of the role of "experienced insider" in the music learning process.

Verbal and Nonverbal Teacher Responses

Empathetic leaders are effective communicators. That means they craft their words to present, explain, clarify, prompt, question, suggest, comment, redirect, and encourage. Their words (as well as vocal tone, facial gestures, and body language) give students the information, and at times some mixed messages, about their musical progress, their roles in the classroom, their membership in the larger music learning community and classroom expectations.

In his book *The Four Agreements*, Don Miguel Ruiz (1997, 21) reminds us to "be impeccable with your words," while also stating that it is the most difficult of the agreements to implement. Ruiz explains:

> The word is not just a sound or a written symbol. The word is a force; it is the power you have to express and communicate, to think, and thereby to create the events in your life.... The word is the most powerful tool you have as a human.... [Y]our word can create the most beautiful dream, or your word can destroy everything around you. (26)

In our classrooms (as well as our personal lives), we can lift up, support, and honor those around us or we can demean, disparage, and discourage. The words we use with our students are so powerful that, in an instant, we can ignite motivation and trust or extinguish the will to participate, engage, and learn.

Using inclusive language such as "we," "let's," "our," "we'll," and "us" suggests that teacher and students are in and of the same music learning environment, that they are equal participants striving toward a common (as well as individual) goal. Saying things such as, "What we're going to do next is listen to a tune by Herbie Hancock" or "Let's raise our hands when we hear the first variation of the main melody" tells students that you are participating in the listening experience along with them. After all, you are not going to be doing something different (e.g., page through a book, write, appear uninterested) if the task involves active music listening. Further, such inclusive language indicates that you are not presenting the task *to* the students but, rather, facilitating learning *for* the community of students. The expectation, then, is that every member of the class will assume responsibility for participating in the task—we do this task together.

I have observed teachers tell their students not to talk while they listen to a musical example. Then, as the recorded music is played, the teacher asks questions or entertains students' comments. This has two negative outcomes: (1) it provides multiple aural stimuli that compete for students' attention, and (2) it contradicts the teacher's directive. Instead, simply remind the students that the class will discuss the music excerpt after they have listened to it, prompting them to jot down any questions or comments they might have as they listen. Teaching for music-listening skill development requires thoughtful spaces in which students can be fully attentive to the music.

As you might have noticed, students see through our words, straight through to our intent. No matter how encouraging a teacher's words may be, they mean little if the facial expressions and body gestures do not align with the words. A teacher's intent is lost if words of encouragement are stated in clipped, monotonic syllables and his or her face shows no excitement or compassion. Similarly, telling someone to "Stop!" is not meaningful if it is said with a smile or questioning eyebrows. Alternatively, as a classroom management tactic, teachers sometimes use the phrase "I need you to do this" or "I want you to do this." These phrases, however, are teacher-centered and sound manipulative and coercive. Why would students engage in a task because a teacher "needs" them to do it? Begging, pleading, sarcasm, and bullying might work temporarily, but these quick-fixes rarely build respect or inspire long-term student motivation to engage in the music learning community.

How, then, as empathetic leaders can we be effective communicators? In addition to using inclusive language, you listen to the inflection of your conversational voice, of your teaching voice, of your encouraging voice, of your questioning voice, and of your stern voice. You ask yourself if there is distinct difference in vocal tone for each of those situations. Does your inflection vary within the sentence? Remember, in any sentence there are syllables and words that are emphasized and those that are deemphasized as our voices change pitch. For example, a question typically ends with a rising vocal inflection. A directive, such as "Stop now" in response to unwanted student behavior, often involves the lower portion of one's vocal pitch, with equal emphasis on each word and on elongated vowels. Ensuring variety in your vocal inflections can reinforce the intent of your words while keeping the students' attention.

Next, look in a mirror and state something using your conversational, teaching, encouraging, questioning, and stern tones of voice. Is there anything about how your face looks when you say these sentences that either coincides or distracts from the intended meaning? What are your eyebrows doing? Your mouth? Your eyes? Practice in front of a mirror, saying the phrases you would use in a variety of contexts, and make your facial gestures match the intent and spirit of your words.

Effective teacher-communicators also have effective body alignment (posture) by maintaining open body postures (no crossing of arms or legs) that face the students; they use unobtrusive hand gestures to emphasize words or points of the lesson or rehearsal; they maintain eye contact with the group while acknowledging each individual student at least once during a class period; and they provide consistent messages in their verbal and nonverbal communications.

Respectful Listening

Your carefully worded questions can encourage your students to imagine, think in musical sound, dream, predict, compare, contrast, anticipate, speculate, critique, reflect, challenge beliefs, and question. However, student responses—verbal or nonverbal—fall on deaf ears if you are not attuned and responsive to the precious information that students offer. Even if you are aware of your students' responses, the challenge is to know what to do with them in the moment—how to engage, deflect and redirect, or ignore—without appearing dismissive or disrespectful. Respectful listening includes hearing, considering, reflecting, and responding— and appropriately taking action or deciding to take no action. Empathetic leaders question and listen with the intent to discover and understand their student informants.

Teachers and students enter the art of engaged listening by being attentive, sincere, and open to others' words, thoughts, and opinions that might be aligned with or contrary to those they hold. Empathetic leaders are listeners who are as willing to be convinced by others as they are to convince others. Of course, even when debating an issue, it is the topic being debated, perhaps passionately, that is discussed and considered; it is not the objective of either debater to be called personally into question or stripped of her or his integrity.

An attentive and sincere listening posture includes person-to-person eye contact ("soft" eyes instead of intense eyes; relaxed eye contact instead of staring or glaring), engaging facial gestures (expressions), and nonverbal interactions (a head nod, smile, frown, hand gesture). In terms of body proxemics, a teacher walks toward a person who is speaking, keeping an open body posture. In other words, you remove any real and/or socially constructed boundaries (a music stand, a podium, a desk, an instrument) that might separate you from the speaker. You observe the student's body language in order to gauge whether or not you are encroaching on the student's personal space while communicating.

Respectful listening also includes the insertion of an occasional phrase such as, "Oh," "Hmm," or "I see"; these reflect your involvement in the speaker's communication. And empathetic listening is devoid of interruption until the speaker's thought is verbalized completely. Then, it is useful to summarize the speaker's point by saying something like, "I think I heard you say" or, "I am going to summarize. Tell me what I am missing or misinterpreting," or "I'm unclear about the one point you made. Could you tell me more about that?" This ensures that you have grasped the speaker's intent.

Another level of empathetic listening involves extrapolating information from students' multisensory responses (verbal, visual, kinesthetic), then taking that information and using it as a platform from which to introduce new musical vocabulary terms, elements, or concepts. This helps students make musical and nonmusical connections, and challenges them to listen deeply and in ways they might not have yet experienced. This type of empathetic listening takes students from where they are in terms of their listening skill development and responses to music and directs the flow of the lesson from concrete to abstract learning. It is a joy when students surprise me with their perspectives on a music listening example, as they have stated in profound terms and images that I had not considered.

Questions that Stimulate Learning

Asking your students questions sends the message that you value their opinions, comments, responses, and questions. It is saying, "You have something to offer," or "I have something to learn from you." Questions are most frequently posed in order to:

- Initiate discussion
- Gather suggestions, opinions, observations, and evaluative comments
- Show a general interest in people
- Give individuals "voice" and equal opportunity to express themselves
- Generate a "holding pond" of ideas that result from group brainstorming and problem-solving sessions (Kerchner 2003, 125)

Open-ended, divergent questions elicit more descriptive responses than questions that students can respond to simply by saying yes or no. Such open-ended, multiple response questions include:

> "Why?"
> "What did you notice?"
> "How did it feel when you heard that?"
> "How would you describe the piece?"
> "What in the music made you think of...?"
> "What is the difference between...?"
> "Why do you suppose...?"
> "How does this compare with...?"

A teacher's verbal prompts invite the students to expound on or clarify their initial responses. These prompts might include statements such as, "Tell me more about..." and "Tell us how you arrived at that response." To encourage other students in the class to engage in a response that has been offered by a student, try a phrase such as, "Let's continue with that stream of thought" or "Who would like to contribute another idea on that topic?"

Empathetic leaders use empathetic questioning when they plan their classroom lessons or rehearsals. As a part of their lesson plans, student teachers with whom I have worked have scripted questions in the plan that serve to initiate discussion or to transition from one musical experience to another. Crafting these questions in the moment can be challenging, especially in terms of wording and sequencing the flow of the lesson. Therefore, when scripting such questions for a lesson plan, consider the following when determining which questions to ask, when, and for what reasons:

1. What information do I want the students to discover, experience, or understand?
2. What do I want my students to discover by asking this question?
3. What information do the students need to know in order to respond to my question?
4. Did I teach that in a prior class? Did the students experience that concept, skill, etc., in prior class experiences?
5. In what order will I ask the questions, according to the goals/objectives of the class?
6. Which questions elicit descriptive student responses? Which are yes or no questions? Which are open-ended questions? Which require a specific fact or answer? Which type of question do I seek at this point of the lesson?

The last question to add to this checklist is, "Which levels of the Bloom's taxonomy am I covering in my line of questioning?" Bloom's *Cognitive Taxonomy* (1956) refers to the mental skills needed to accomplish a task, from the very basic levels to the higher order levels of thinking. Anderson (as described in Pohl 2000) renamed and reordered the labels on Bloom's original taxonomy, changing the noun labels into verbs to describe specific behaviors enlisted at each level. Listing the simplest levels to the most complex levels of thinking/behavior (Anderson's labels are in parentheses) on the taxonomy, the order is:

Knowledge (remembering)
Comprehension (understanding)
Application (applying)
Analysis (analyzing)
Synthesis (evaluating)
Evaluation (creating)

Each higher-order level of thinking subsumes the thinking skills exercised in the previous levels. For example, in order to demonstrate mastery of a musical concept or task at the analysis level, students would enlist mental operations also found at the knowledge, comprehension, and application levels on the taxonomy.

In light of these labels, teachers might wish to reflect on the formulation of the questions and/or directive statements they will pose to their students. Which levels of thinking/behavior are being addressed? How frequently are these mental skills engaged because of the questions you will pose? Of course, not all levels of questioning will be included in a single lesson, since lesson ideas unfold and evolve from introductory to mastery levels over the course of several days or weeks. Similarly, the questions vary depending on the students' ages and ability levels.

To assist in this analysis, I provide a few cue verbs, based on Kassner (1998), that indicate specific levels of questioning grounded in Bloom's and Anderson's six levels of cognition.

- *Knowledge* (remembering): define, describe, identify, know, label, list, name, outline, match (e.g., "How would you define the word *forte*?")
- *Comprehension* (understanding): summarize, predict, interpret, explain, give an example of, compare, anticipate (e.g., "Explain how Beethoven changed the pattern in order to add interest to the music.")
- *Application* (applying): show, demonstrate, produce, use (e.g., "As a class, use the syllable *ta* to demonstrate the dynamic level you heard in the beginning of the musical example.")
- *Analysis* (analyzing): analyze, compare, contrast, break into smaller pieces or chunks (e.g., "How does the first phrase of the musical excerpt compare to the second phrase in terms of texture?")
- *Synthesis* (evaluating): create, compose, combine, rearrange, reorganize, plan, design (e.g., "Now that you have listed features of three vocal (singing) styles from around the world, provide a summary chart. What do they all have in common? What are stylistic traits specific to a particular culture?")
- *Evaluation* (creating): evaluate, critique, defend, judge, decide, justify, explain (e.g., "How would you (and the composer) possibly justify the inclusion of found-sounds and natural sounds in the recorded composition?" "Why does it work? Why does it not work? What might be an alternative solution?")

Anecdotally, students seem to benefit from experiences that provide them with a concrete knowledge base before they move to the higher-order levels of thinking. Students need to have mastered the knowledge, comprehension, and application levels of mental operation before moving on to tasks requiring abstract thinking or demonstration of complex cognitive behaviors. Moving between the levels on the taxonomy, however, is not typically linear. Depending on your students' demonstration of knowledge during multisensory tasks, you may decide to retreat to a prior level of interaction with the experienced musical sound before progressing onward to higher-order levels of thinking.

Feedback that is Encouraging

In response to students' questions, comments, and multisensory representations, teachers have the choice of providing verbal or nonverbal feedback that either "feeds" or "starves" the minds, bodies, and spirits of their students. Teachers' comments can be encouraging, nurturing, and constructive (feedback that feeds) or they can be degrading, demeaning, and destructive (feedback that starves). Empathetic leaders provide feedback that is honest, direct, sincere, and encouraging, all said with words that a students will want to hear rather than having them "tune out." Empathetic leaders not only provide constructive feedback to students but also clear paths for their continued improvement and greater sophistication of thought and musical behavior.

Observational feedback literally conveys what the teacher has noticed about the students' responses or task performances. For example,

> "Your music maps are so different from one another."
> "We're closer to identifying the name of the mystery instrument we heard in the musical example."
> "You did it."
> "Hmmm. I'm not sure about that description. Let's listen again and see if we can add more specific words this time."

Notice the differences in tone and effect in saying the same thing, but in a manner that "starves":

> "Well these are not the types of music listening maps I was expecting. I thought you might pick up on the things you've been learning since the last lesson."
> "We've listened to this music three times, and you still do not know the names of these instruments."
> "I don't know what you are saying."
> "You're wrong."

The teacher's word choices and manner of delivering feedback might have an immediate, if not long-lasting, effect on how students engage in the remaining portions of the music class or rehearsal. Certainly, negative or sarcastic comments discredit student skills and intelligence, and call into question the teacher's credibility as a compassionate person worthy of respect. While some teachers might defend using sarcasm as an attempt at humor, these careless words and quips can be dangerous and often are misconstrued by students, even if they laugh and seem unaffected. While we teachers think students understand when we are joking by using sarcasm, we must remember that our students are not adults who can typically differentiate between evaluative comments and sarcasm. What specific, productive information does sarcasm provide such that it cannot be conveyed without resorting to using it?

Teacher (and peer) feedback also includes acknowledgement ("Okay," "Yes."); nonverbal cues (a nod of the head, a smile, a thumbs up); probing questions to clarify, challenge, or initiate further discussion ("What did you mean by…"); repeating the student responses so that everyone is able to hear them; and evaluative comments ("No, that wasn't the trumpet playing the melody, but it is an instrument that requires air to play it. Does anyone else have ideas about which instrument played the melody? Right, the flute!").

What is intentionally missing from this list of feedback cues are words that provide no specific information to the student. These include "Good," "Good job," "No," and "Okay." They are quick and handy responses for teachers, but students end up receiving no more specific information about their task performance, project, or response than if there had been no feedback at all.

I encourage teachers to reconsider any observational feedback that begins with the words, "I like the way…." Again, instead of giving pure observational feedback or acknowledgment, this phrase indicates that you, as teacher, are judge. While students naturally try to please their teachers, they should not learn to rely on a teacher's opinion and judgment as the only source of assessment. Instead, teachers should encourage their students to develop their own evaluative criteria, based on high standards, and to use those criteria in evaluating their own and their peers' work. That students learn to trust their informed judgment, in addition to and independent from others, is part of developing their independent musicianship.

Observation of the Process

The verb *observe* finds its origins in the fifteenth and sixteenth centuries, and means "to attend to in practice, to keep, to follow" and to "watch, perceive, notice" trends for future study and remark." Empathetic leaders develop keen observation skills so that they can see, assess, reflect on, and respond to their own and their students' verbal and nonverbal reactions "in the moment" during the teaching–learning process. Observation is usually the first behavior in the web of teacher cyclical analytical processes—observation, assessment, reflection, and response. Informed "in-flight" decision making can take the form of (1) revisiting foundational musical material that students have yet to master, (2) redirecting a lesson according to student skill demonstration or the questions/comments they raise, or (3) aborting a lesson segment if it is time to move on to something new or if the pedagogical strategies seem not to be working.

Observation can also lead teachers to gauge the musical, physical, social, and pedagogical climate of the classroom or rehearsal, for subsequent review and reflection. Because of time constraints, teachers often rely on their memory in thinking about classes they have taught. Yet memory is selective and mainly calls up only that information that, for some reason, "sticks" in the mind. Furthermore, there are variables that taint memory, that even skew the perception of reality. There is perhaps no perfect way to replicate the complex teacher-student learning environment in order to later review and reflect on it. However, teacher videos are a useful, yet admittedly not comprehensive, aide in observing, reflecting, and improving the quality of instruction and learning. As the saying goes, "Seeing is believing." In developing their observational skills, and reflecting on their successes and failures, teachers can better direct their efforts toward nurturing their students to observe and provide feedback on their own, and their peers' music projects and performances, in ways that are specific, honest, and constructive.

No matter how objective teachers try to remain during the observation process, there will always be hints of biases, preconceptions and misperceptions, ego, and judgment that impede the clarity with which they observe their students and themselves. Yet one's perception of a situation is indeed one's reality. What one teacher observes while reviewing a video of his or her music classroom might not be another reviewer's perception while reviewing that same video.

The purpose of the observation process is simply to record data to be analyzed subsequently, in an effort to determine those areas that require change and improvement in the conditions necessary for effective teaching and learning. Reserving judgment until after the data are recorded is essential, yet difficult, since teachers are personally invested in the actions they review on video. Prejudgment serves only to cloud teachers' eyes, ears, and intuition, making it difficult to grasp holistically what they experience via video.

Empathetic leaders tend to review video recordings of classroom music lessons and rehearsals by focusing on several areas that include the:

- Physical classroom setting (location of chairs, instruments, learning centers, etc.)
- Teacher-student verbal interactions (inclusive language, feedback, questioning, tone of comments or questions, responsiveness to comments or questions)
- Teacher and student nonverbal behaviors (i.e., eye contact, tone of voice, body posture, facial and hand gestures, movement of students and teacher in the classroom, proximity of teacher to students, student-peer interactions, teacher-student interactions)
- Music pedagogy and musical experiences (i.e., flow of lesson/sequence, use of questions, feedback, percentage of musical experiences vs. talking, teacher- vs. student-centered classroom, teacher and/or student musical modeling techniques, extent to which students and teacher achieve lesson goals, objectives, and standards)

Because there are vast amounts of sensory information upon which teachers might focus during observations, there are at least four types of observation tools that can assist in the process. You might find that, after using these tools, your in-flight observations and decision making become more acute, for you have practiced bringing specific issues and details to your attention. These observational tools include: (1) thick description, (2) questioning guide, (3) timed (interval), and (4) checklist (Erwin, Edwards, Kerchner, and Knight 2003).

A *thick description* is a narrative or transcript of verbal interactions, teaching and learning details, and teacher impressions that give information regarding classroom atmosphere, pedagogical techniques, and evidence of student musical learning— instructional and learning processes and products and the environment in which they occur. While this tool is labor intensive, teachers might find the written "story" of their classroom lesson or, better still, a portion of a lesson, to be useful in recre- ating mentally, physically, and emotionally the essence of what occurred in class. After writing the narrative, the teacher can then analyze it for trends and themes that might emerge, that lead the teacher to consider his or her next steps in planning for and facilitating student music learning in future music classes.

A *questioning guide* is a set of predetermined questions that focus the teacher's attention during the video review. Responses to these open-ended questions require the teacher's descriptive analysis. Figure 2.2 is an example of a music classroom

---

Figure 2.2. QUESTIONING GUIDE FOR OBSERVATION

I. Classroom environment:

1. How might the classroom's physical set-up effect the student-teacher interaction?
2. How does the classroom depict a relaxed, comfortable, and purposeful learning environment?
3. How does the teacher vary the intensity level, or is there a "sameness" to the class?
4. How are routines and well-defined procedures made evident?

II. Teacher and student behavior:

1. How does the teacher maintain a learning environment conducive to learning? (i.e., lack of put- downs, sarcasm, and the like?
2. How does the teacher show support and encouragement?
3. How does the teacher react with sensitivity to the students' needs and feelings?
4. How do facial and body language reflect concentration, interest, and enthusiasm as opposed to boredom and frustration?
5. What evidence of mutual respect did you observe?

III. Pedagogy:

1. Describe teacher instructions. Do the students appear to know what is expected?
2. Describe the levels of the teacher's questions.
3. How does the teacher practice "preventive medicine" (i.e., classroom management)?
4. When and how does the teacher present instruction, provide corrective feedback, and reinforce instruction on the class content?

IV. Students' musical thinking/engagement/performance

1. How are students actively engaged in musical thinking and/or performing? Describe students' responses to teacher questions and instructions.
3. What behaviors do students exhibit that indicate achievement of teacher's and/or students' musical goals?
4. Given your observations, what MUSICALLY did the students learn in this lesson?

---

or rehearsal questioning guide. The guide is flexible: a teacher could, for example, focus on only one section of questions or address one or two questions per section.

The timed (interval) and checklist tools are closely related; both are quick and easy to use, and require tallying the frequency of a student's or teacher's behavior as it occurs during a class period or rehearsal. For a *timed (interval)* observation, the teacher predetermines the interval unit of observation (i.e., every minute, every five or ten minutes), and then notes the occurrence of a single or several behaviors of interest. For example, perhaps the teacher wants to observe the frequency of his asking questions within five-minute intervals; while watching the video, he records the number of questions he poses at the beginning of the timed period, at the five-minute mark, at the ten-minute mark, and so on, until the class concludes. Unfortunately, this timed (interval) tool does not capture what happens *during* the five-minute intervals, only at the five-minute marks. On the other hand, teachers can use the tool to track when in the class period a specific teacher or student behavior most frequently occurs.

Checklists usually list more than one teacher or student behavior to be noted during a video review. Unlike the timed observation (interval) tool, the checklist tallies the frequency of a behavior regardless of when it occurs during the class period (see figure 2.3). For example, in reviewing a video of her 40-minute class period, the teacher might notice that she provided 15 "Good" statements as a form of feedback, yet did not provide specific information about *what* was good about the student's musical or other behavior. Without being given specifics, the student might not recognize which behaviors (i.e., use of head voice, recognition of many musical events during a mapping experience, the expression used during the movement sequence) he should continue or eliminate. Therefore, the teacher might want to amend her style of providing specific feedback to the student.

Figure 2.3. OBSERVATION CHECKLIST

Focus: Teacher feedback

Type of feedback↓	Frequency→
Affirmation and acknowledgement of students	
Verbal probes and prompts	
Follow-up questions	
Specific praise	
Empty responses (i.e., good, ok, good job, etc.)	
Divergent questions (i.e., open-ended questions)	
Yes/No questions	
Criticism	
Silence	
Non-verbal	

Reflection and Changes

After empathetic leaders have observed and analyzed their teaching videos, they identify specific areas for change and prescribe specific solutions for making those changes. The importance of reflective thinking is not in the act itself but, rather, in the actions that stem from it, made manifest in future music class teaching and learning experiences. *Not* engaging in this reflective practice only reinforces existing pedagogical techniques, strategies, and mind-sets that may not be effective or best practices.

In order to engage in reflective thinking, a teacher must develop and refine the following professional habits of mind (Kerchner 2003, 125):

- Trusting in oneself and others
- Curiosity for learning about self and others in the teaching–learning partnership
- Openness of mind in order to challenge thinking patterns and teaching behaviors, and to modify existing teaching strategies of classroom environments
- Sharing thoughts and feels about teaching and challenges with mentors and colleagues
- Supporting other educators and students who are engaged in reflective thinking (the "evaluation" level of Bloom's higher-order thinking)
- Observing interactions between self and students
- Listening to mentor, colleagues, students, and self in order to understand and learn about the teaching–learning partnership.

Let us explore three types of reflective thinking guides: (1) free-form, (2) prompted, (3) critical incident, and (4) noteworthy moments. Obviously, these are only some of the possible tools you could use to stimulate your reflective thinking. Rarely are "good/bad" or "effective/noneffective" assessments enlightening; however, since they provide no observational evidence to substantiate the teacher's assessment or lead to prescriptive suggestions for future lessons.

Free-form reflections quite naturally address two basic questions, not necessarily as separate entities, while also providing prescriptive solutions for revising any facet of the teaching–learning partnership that needs attention:

1. What about the lesson was effective? Why was it effective?
2. What about the lesson needs revision? Why?

Free-form reflections are usually stream-of-consciousness reports, regardless of whether the teacher is writing the reflection in a journal, talking aloud to a confident (i.e., mentor or trusted colleague/administrator), or thinking without externalizing that reflection.

Prompted reflections are based on, but not limited to, a set of predetermined questions that stimulate analysis and assessment of specific pedagogical practice and student music learning. The questions call teachers to hone in on specific pedagogical strategies employed in the class or rehearsal, levels of student engagement, and the dynamic between students and teacher. Examples of questions that prompt reflection might include the following listed below.

1. How were you able to alter your plan to fit the educational needs of the children at the time of class? How did you change your plan? Were you able to "think on your feet?" Did you achieve the lesson goals (objectives)? How do you know that your lesson objectives were met?
2. Describe the students' musical engagement and learning. What needs to occur in future lessons to provide increased amounts of student engagement? What needs to occur in future lessons to create an environment of student success, achievement? What are the next steps in building on students' prior knowledge and experiences?
3. How responsive was the class to the lesson? How responsive were you to students' responses? Describe your personal interaction with the class during the rehearsal. What would you do differently/the same in the next class?
4. Did your questions promote foundational and higher-order thinking skills? Did the class ask you questions? Describe the comfort level as you attempted to respond to their questions. What would you do differently in the next class?
5. Describe the pacing of the lesson. When did you "hang on" too long to an idea or concept? How did you know when/feel it was time to move on? What motivated your decision?
6. How did you feel in the role of a conductor, musician, and educator? Did you command authority? Too much authority? Was there a mix of teacher- and student-directed teaching and learning? How do you know?
7. Describe any classroom-management issues that might have been a concern to you or the students. How did you handle the situation? What would you like to change should a similar incident occur?

The following is a portion of a student teacher's reflection on a lesson, based on question prompts. As you read the reflection, notice the ownership of pedagogical technique and empathetic leadership that the student teacher exhibits. How would you guide this teacher in continuing her reflective practice? What additional questions or prompts might you provide for this reflection? What constructive feedback would you provide?

Sample Teaching Reflection

I can barely believe that I taught the same lesson to the same grade level, for both classes were SO different. Given what I had observed during the past two weeks, I anticipated the first 7th-grade class to be more challenging than the second. I might have known that, with middle school general-music classes, anything is possible! Of course there were three major external factors contributing to students' responses and attention today: (1) there was an assembly early in the day, (2) it was a rainy afternoon, and (3) once again, I asked the students to be actively involved for the full 42 minutes of time.

I struggled today, particularly with the last 7th-grade class. In fact, I cut the class short, for I was becoming frustrated and exhausted. I had lost the attention of most students, and I allowed my frustration of the classroom to cloud my motivation to continue in class. I'm not saying that this was the best way of handling the situation. In fact, until another time, I will need to express my expectations of students' attention and interaction. I mentioned this last week; clearly they needed a more stern reminder this week. Simply stating that raising their hands was the appropriate signal to speak was not enough. I need to project authority, without seeming stifling.

I also continue to feel so "new" to this music class environment. I don't know how to handle the set-up of the class. I don't like the clusters of students and the distance from me that the class set-up creates, and yet this IS the classroom, and I am a guest within the music classroom setting. How can I change this? I WANT to work with the environs, and I want to work with the students, but I'm in conflict with the classroom set-up. Might I try having all students move their chairs in rows in front of the desks? What will the real music teacher think? Should I be concerned about her reaction? Will the movement of chairs and students cause more instability within the classroom environment? Might a semi-circle work? Sitting on the floor will not work (too cold and dirty on the tile floor).

I also noticed today that I was skeptical about enforcing student behavior. The class was not "out of control" today, but there were several students who really "tested the waters." I addressed some of the students by name and used verbal and nonverbal cues and reminders, but I didn't want to give too much attention to individual students. I certainly did not want to give them what they expected—yelling and an interruption of the class lesson. I needed to be stern with my facial gesture and in my direction. I also should have spoken with a student (Jeremiah) after class. The fact remains; this is not my class, but when I teach, it is my class. In the first class, simply waiting for students to refocus their attention worked. How different these two classes were!

Related to prompted reflections are *critical incident* reflections, based on Burnard's (2004) "critical incident charting" idea. In this type of reflection, teachers identify those specific moments in which things changed directions (positively or negatively), analyze possible reasons for their happening, and provide prescriptions for improving the situations in future classes. Think of a winding river; at each curve, the river changes momentarily or over the course of many miles. The same is true of the teaching–learning partnership in music classes or rehearsals. There are pivotal points in the lesson that change the content and dynamic of the class. The follow-ing questions might stimulate recognition of and reflection on those river-bend moments. Teachers might even wish to sketch a winding river and label each curve with specific class happenings. Consider these questions:

1. At what moment in the class did you feel most engaged with what was happening? Why?
2. At what moment in the class did you feel most disengaged with what was happening? Why?
3. What action that anyone (you or the students) took in class did you find most affirming or helpful? Why?
4. What action that anyone (you or the students) took in class did you find most puzzling or confusing? Why?
5. What was the most musical moment (students) in your class? Why?

The following is a critical-incident reflection submitted by a student teacher in a col-legiate secondary school music-methods course. She had taught a lesson segment in a sixth-grade general music class that served as the course's teaching laboratory. (Her lesson plan is found in chapter 4; it involved teaching adapted folk dance steps to accompany the *Valicha*.) What about this reflection captures your attention? What trends do you see? What additional details would you want to have about the situations she described in her reflection? How would you guide her teaching and her reflective thinking processes?

Sample Lesson Reflection

1. At what moment in the class did you feel most engaged with what was happening? Why?

I felt the most engaged during two moments in each of the classes: (1) while discussing tone color in the listening example, and (2) while teaching the dance moves to the class. While discussing tone color and instrument use with the students, I felt like I really had the chance to ask meaningful and insight-ful questions and more importantly, to relate the current lesson to things the students had learned about in prior lessons with the other [collegiate] stu-dents and the general music teacher. The discussion that blossomed out of my few simple questions was informative for me (because I was able to better understand what the students were focusing on and thinking about) and for the students (because they were able to tie my lesson to the Japan, Africa, and the five elements lessons and learned about a new set of instruments). During those moments, I felt invigorated and inspired by my own and my colleagues' teaching, and by the students' abilities and motivations to learn.

I also felt very engaged while teaching the dance to *Valicha*. Watching the videos, especially, I thought that the students appeared very engaged during the dancing. I thought this was more obvious during the second class, when all of the students had scarves and I was able to observe whether or not the ideas we talked about (melody/flute/voice = arms, rhythm/*charango* = feet) were present in the motions. They were! While not all of the students were performing the correct *charango* rhythm in the feet, they were at least keeping a steady beat and performing the moves with the entire class. I thought that the introduction and review of the dance steps was well-delivered and that the students and I were really communicating well.

2. At what moment in the class did you feel most disengaged with that was happening? Why?

I felt the most disengaged at two points in the first class—at the beginning of the lesson and when I performed the map on the screen. The beginning of the lesson felt disjointed—part of the experience of team teaching, I suppose—but it was tough to smoothly transition between the two lessons. The students were riled up from dancing with Charlotte (the other student teacher), and I'm not sure I took the appropriate steps to refocus them. Instead of giving them a clear direction and fluid opening, I fumbled with the computer (again, a fact of life with team teaching) and tried to keep the students' attention. In the future, I will aim to have a clearer opening for my lesson, a catch phrase or strong opening question to catch the students' attention as I did with my African drumming lesson. This opening was not as strong, and as a result, I think it set the stage for a very disjointed and distracted lesson. Fortunately, my language and directives became stronger as I went on, and we did get through a lot of the material.

Performing the map on the projector was also difficult and disengaging for me, because I felt that the classes needed the guidance of someone performing the map with them, but I wasn't able to observe the students as they were supposed to be listening and performing the map on their own. I was able to later see on the videos that the students performing on the individual maps was one of the most successful parts of the lesson, but at the time, I felt like anything could happen as I had my back turned or that the students could get off task. In the future (and if I had just a little more time) I might change the steps of the lesson just a little bit: perform the map once by myself as the students listen and watch, perform the map as the students perform with fingers in the air, ask for a student volunteer to perform the map on the projector as the class performs in the air so that I can observe and walk around, then hand out individual maps, ask for another student volunteer and repeat as the class performs on individual maps. This version of the activity would not only give me a chance to walk around and observe, but it would also reinforce to the students the idea that we are actively performing the map, not just looking at it and listening.

3. What action that anyone (you or the students) took in class did you find most affirming or helpful? Why?

The most affirming part of the lesson was to hear almost absolute quiet and see the concentration from the students in both classes when they were given their own maps to perform. I had been worried that the maps would be too hard for them to follow or that they would talk through the lesson. What I observed during class and what was confirmed in the videos was quite the opposite! The students were quiet and attentive, and seemed to be engaged and intrigued by the map. What's more, some of the students that we have typically had trouble motivating were actively participating and performing the map accurately! While I don't have any proof, I have observed that the kids in these classes that are also in band, choir and orchestra tend to be the ones volunteering and participating, and those who are not sit quietly or are inattentive. I wonder if that has anything to do with feeling "unmusical." In any case, I firmly believe that having the chance to "perform" in a nonperforming general music class was a positive experience for the students. For me, it was a chance to see my hard work in creating a map and a guided listening lesson come to fruition and succeed in including the entire class.

4. What action that anyone (you or the students) took in class did you find most puzzling or confusing? Why?

The most puzzling action of the lessons was my classroom management of the 6th period class. For whatever reason, the first class was very energetic (which is normally fine) but this week the energy was paired with being completely distracted! This made for a difficult time for both my colleague and me. It's hard to present material if your students aren't even aware of you! What was puzzling for me about this situation was how I chose (in the moment) to deal with the talking and goofing around. Some of it was handled well, such as taking the time to move a few of the students who were being distracted by those around them or standing closely to students who were talking, but for the most part, when I needed the class' attention, I just said "Eyes and ears here, please," and continued on – whether they were listening and attentive or not. I know that it is better not to do that, but I still did!

Frustrating indeed, since thinking back to how I felt teaching, I thought the entire lesson was a struggle to get them to just pay attention. What was the reason for their hyperactivity? How could I have handled that better? The interesting thing was that the class settled down almost instantly once they had their own maps in hand. I would hesitate handing them out prior to performing the map as a group, but perhaps that is what this class needed—an option to work individually while we tackled the listening as a group. If I were to repeat the lesson under similar conditions, I might try handing out the map first and seeing if that made a difference.

5.What was the most musical moment (students) in your class? Why?

I felt that the most musical moment for the students took place when the students performed their individual listening maps for *Valicha*. Watching the videos, I had the chance to see that the students were not only participating and paying attention as I mentioned earlier, but were performing and moving their fingers with the melody, some of them tapping their feet or fingers to the steady beat as they moved their fingers and pencils on the map. After performing the map as a group, the students really seemed to grasp the ideas of tone color, rhythm, and melody within the listening example and the map itself. To watch the students perform their maps with such gusto and grace was a very gratifying moment for me, because even though they weren't singing, dancing, or playing an instrument, these students were actively participating in music class, seemed to be enjoying themselves, and were doing so in a musical way—something that I imagine all music teachers strive for.

The final reflective thinking tool is the *noteworthy moments* reflection. Teachers choose four "noteworthy moments" (positive or negative, effective or ineffective), one "moment" for each of the following categories: (1) teacher pedagogy and pedagogical tools employed, (2) classroom climate, (3) students' active musical understanding/thinking/performing, and (4) teacher and student behaviors.

For each notable moment, the teacher rates the moment as (a) a counterproductive act, (b) a missed opportunity, (c) an effective action, or (d) a masterful action. As an entry in a journal, the teacher lists the noteworthy moment in each category and writes explanations for their ratings, supporting them with specific, observable evidence and specific prescriptions for improving upon the moments they selected. This could also work as a conversational reflection with a colleague or mentor or as a mental reflection that is not documented or shared.

The following is a student teacher's noteworthy moments reflection. Notice the information that could have also been shared in critical incident, free-form, or prompt reflections. What bits of information provided in the reflection are unique to this type of reflection? What does the addition of assessment comments provide the teacher doing the reflecting? The person reading the reflection? What personality types of teachers and student-learners might best utilize this reflective thinking tool? What other tools for reflective thinking have you employed?

Sample Teaching Reflection
Pedagogy: *Effective action*

I thought having the students view the call chart and then later the listening map that I created was an effective pedagogical strategy. I used repeated listening, so that the students were able to become more familiar with the music example. I think the sequencing of the lesson (call charts and listening maps) was very strong. I did not skip any of the major points of my lesson plan, and yet I felt flexible enough to address student responses. I particularly found the first class exciting when the students were able to speculate about the markings found on my listening map, and then compare their expectations with what actually happened. The entire sequence was slower in the second class; I was distracted. I needed to stop and express exactly that. I wonder if other students were distracted, too? How did that hinder their learning and engagement?

Although this is the second "effective action," and I know that I'm asked to identify only one per category, I thought that the introduction to the lesson (the review and the rhythmic comparison of "Mt. King" and "Mary Had a Little Lamb") was quite creative. It appeared from the students' reactions that they enjoyed it as well. Furthermore, beginning with "Mary Had a Little Lamb" gave them something concrete before moving to that rhythm in a new context of "Mt. King."

Climate: Counterproductive action

As I mentioned earlier in the reflection, many of the students were off, and I did not insist on it. Some students were writing, reading, talking, and while I used closer proxemics, this strategy was definitely not enough. In future lessons, I need to voice my concerns and expectations of their interaction and engagement. The second class's content was not conveyed as smoothly as in the first class, because their energy was not focused.

Musical learning/goals/objectives: Effective

The students participated in the activities and achieved the goals that I had set out for them. However, not ALL students participated. Not all of the students were on task. Nonetheless, my lesson was not lecture-style. I had planned and presented them with various ways of getting to know "Mt. King" and of the idea that the composer turned a repeated pattern into a larger piece of music. I think the review of *ostinato* and repeated rhythmic pattern at the beginning of the class set up later successes in the lesson. The level of understanding seemed to be appropriate for the seventh-grade classes. I was even happily surprised that some students came up with the words, *accelerando* and *crescendo*.

Student active engagement: Missed opportunity

While these students were engaged in body percussion and visually following listening maps, their body language (tapping hands, swinging necklaces, giggling, singing along) suggested that I should have made an "in-flight" decision to do something with movement—something that would have gotten them out of their seats. I did not respond to the bodily information that gave me. I had planned for the visual and aural learners, but what about the kinesthetic learners? Next time, anticipate this type of reaction.

TAKING ACTION

Palmer (1998, 11) wrote that "as good teachers weave the fabric that joins them with students and subjects, the heart is the loom on which the threads are tied, the tension is held, the shuttle flies, and the fabric is stretched tight." Palmer clearly understood that teaching is more than teachers demonstrating skillful technique and mastery of methodology. Empathetic leaders bring the very fabric of their being—heart, soul, and spirit—into the classroom or rehearsal. The topics of this chapter—philosophy, curriculum, empathetic leadership, questioning, listening, observing, providing feedback, and reflection—are some of the many skills effective teachers develop throughout their careers.

The information in this chapter might have "stretched the fabric" of your notions about teacher, student, teaching, and learning. Maybe these ideas reassured you by providing gentle reminders of the behaviors that facilitate making connections with students. Yet some principles might have even ignited your reflective curiosity to risk trying something out of the ordinary—whether in terms of your teaching practice, habits of mind, or leadership skills. How you interpret and implement these ideas will be unique to your personality, teaching style, teaching experience, and classroom environment.

At the heart of these philosophical and curricular perspectives, empathetic leadership qualities, and reflective practices is the journey to understand ourselves and the students with whom we interact. Without understanding who we are, especially as leaders in the classroom, it is difficult to understand our students as individuals and members of a community of learners. By continuously questioning "So what?" and "Why?" we begin to understand the evolution of our perspectives on teaching and learning, as well as our students' behaviors (i.e., learning, collaboration, engagement, attitude, willingness, and motivation).

Here is the punch line: Once you examine your philosophy about music teaching and learning, ask yourself how these values and beliefs are made manifest in your classroom or rehearsal. Do you *do* what you say you do? How do you know? If there is a lack of alignment, then what gradual steps could you take to get on the path where your ideology, musicianship, and classroom environment become synchronous? If there is alignment, how could what you know and do be even further refined?

In the next chapters, you will explore some of the multisensory teaching tools I have found effective in nurturing children's listening skill development. The pedagogical tools and strategies are couched in the principles and habits of mind and behavior that have been presented in this chapter. Decide where along the continuum you choose to be in terms of empathetic leadership—an authority on one end and an authoritarian on the opposite end. Also, recognize when you are more likely to act at one end of the spectrum or the other. As you read, envision your best self and the students' best selves collaboratively transforming your music classes into inspirational spaces of learning and interaction.

REFERENCES

Bloom, B. S. (1956). *Taxonomy of Educational Objectives, Handbook I: The Cognitive Domain.* New York: David McKay.

Bruner, J. (1966). *Toward a Theory of Instruction.* Cambridge, MA: Harvard University Press.

Burnard, P. (2004). "Using Critical Incident Charting for Reflecting on Musical Learning." *Mountain Lake Reader: Conversations on the Study and Practice of Music Teaching* 3: 7–24.

Burton, S. (2012). "Making Music Mine! A Centers-based Approach for Middle School General Music." In *Engaging Musical Practices: A Sourcebook for Middle School General Music,* edited by S. Burton, chap. 12. Lanham, MD: Rowman & Littlefield.

Dewey, J. (1997). *How We Think.* Mineola, NY: Dover.

Dewey, J. (1964). "School Conditions and the Training of Thought." In *John Dewey on Education: Selected Writings,* edited by R. Archambault, 229-241 . Chicago: University of Chicago Press

Dillon, S. (2006). "Jam2jam: Networked Jamming." *M/C Journal* 9(6). Retrieved March 15, 2012, http://journal.media-culture.org.au/0612/04-dillon.php.

Erwin, J., K. Edwards, J. Kerchner, and J. Knight (2003). *Prelude to Music Education.* Upper Saddle River, NJ: Prentice-Hall.

Greene, M. (1995). *Releasing the Imagination: Essays on Education, the Arts, and Social Change.* San Francisco, CA: Jossey-Bass Publishers.

Jonassen, D. (1991). "Objectivism vs. Constructivism: Do We Need a New Philosophical Paradigm?" *Educational Technology, Research, and Development* 39(3): 5–13.

Kassner, K. (1998). "Would Better Questions Enhance Music Learning?" *Music Educators Journal* 84(4): 29–36.

Kerchner, J. L. (2003). "Stepping off of the Podium: Leveling the Playing (and Singing) Field." In *Musicianship in the 21st Century: Issues, Trends, & Possibilities,* edited by S. Leong, 113–29. Sydney: Australian Music Centre.

Montessori, M. (1946). *Education for a New World.* Madras, India: Kalakshetra.

Palmer, P. (1998). *The Courage to Teach: Exploring the Inner Landscape of a Teacher's Life.* San Francisco: Jossey-Bass.

Pohl, M. (2000). *Learning to Think, Thinking to Learn: Models and Strategies to Develop a Classroom Culture of Thinking.* Cheltenham, Victoria: Hawker Brownlow.

Ruiz, D. M. (1997). *The Four Agreements.* San Rafael, CA: Amber-Allen.

Schön, D. (1983). *The Reflective Practitioner: How Professionals Think in Action.* London: Temple Smith.

Small, C. (1977). *Music, Society, Education.* New York: Schirmer.

Thurman, L., and G. Welch (2000). *Bodymind and Voice: Foundations of Voice Education.* Collegeville, MN: VoiceCare Network.

Vygotsky, L. S. (1978). *Mind in Society.* Cambridge, MA: Harvard University Press.

Wertsch, J. (1998). *Mind as Action.* New York: Oxford University Press.

CHAPTER 3

Listeners Moving

Music Listening as Embodied Experience

The world we live in is in constant motion. The cycle of day into night, the seasons of the year, and the planting, growing, and reaping of yearly harvests—all remind us that nothing remains in stasis, including our own body cycles. Our hearts beat in rhythm, our breathing takes on regulated inhalation and exhalation patterns, our eyes blink, we awaken and then sleep, and we walk in unique, measured gaits. Like our environmental surroundings, we are not the same in one moment as in the next.

Movement is a natural and necessary function in our lives. Through our bodies, we sense motion around us, that which is inherent in the process of change. And through our bodies, we feel, experience, and activate motion that causes change in our surroundings. Movement is situated, negotiated, and defined within our socio-cultural arenas. Communities of people embrace movement (e.g., dance) as ritual or functional means for communication and/or expressive purposes (artistic and emotional). Furthermore, our social worlds influence how comfortable we feel while moving our bodies, which movements have accepted meaning within our communities, and which are valued (or devalued) in the public eye.

Merleau-Ponty (1962) purported that we know the world through our bodies (i.e., the unified body-mind-feeling-spirit entity) as life in motion. Juntunen and Hyvönen (2004, 200) summarized Merleau-Ponty's perspective: "Understanding arises first at the bodily, pre-reflective level; any intellectual processing occurs afterwards." Therefore, it is through our bodies that we first experience the world, and what we learn is relative to our bodies interacting with the world around us. Young children do not rely on verbal understandings of their environment; they explore by touching, tasting, moving, and smelling. In a quest for independence, teenagers seek to follow their intuitions and desires—to do something active—in order to experience (and learn from) the results of their actions, instead of heeding adults' verbal rationales. Through our active corporeal experiences, we create cognitive, physical, emotional, and spiritual meanings of the motion and changes in our surroundings. It all starts with the body living in motion, changing, and pre-intellectually understanding the world—that which is called *embodied knowing*.

Music, of course, is an artistic form that consists of heard and felt movement of sounds in space and over time: moving toward a cadence, moving to the height of the melodic passage and phrase, changing, reposing, creating the cycle of tension and release, the feeling of instability and resolution, and sounding rhythms that drive us to the climax and repose of a musical section. Music performers actively engage (move) their bodies as they play instruments or sing: an arm moving the bow across strings, lips buzzing on a mouthpiece or reed, arms and upper bodies moving mallets across a xylophone, lungs breathing deeply, and body muscles supporting the onset of a sung phrase. Performing musicians experience the kinesthetic acts of making music that holistically represent thinking, feeling, intuiting, and moving externally and internally.

To make only the obvious links between our bodies, movement, and music, however, is to oversimplify a complex relationship. Movement associated with music performance is not the only way for us to know music in and through our bodies. Have you ever been "transported," while listening to music, to some mystical place that captivates your entire being? Have you been "moved" to tears by music that at once evokes personal meaning and connects you to the humanness of those listening alongside of you? Have you felt goose bumps while listening to music? Have you been called by music to tap fingers and feet, clap to the beat, move in your seat, or dance? Have you ever imagined a favorite song or piece of music and felt "moved" by it, even though you hear no sound? Have you ever danced to a song, when there is no music to be heard? Music listening is a behavior that allows listeners to be "moved" by and with the music in covert (implicit) and overt (explicit) ways, knowing and feeling music in and through their bodies.

The *Oxford English Dictionary* (2012) defines the verb *embody* as the process of "giving a concrete form to an idea, quality, or feeling" and "to include or contain (something) as a constituent part." As they listen, musically untrained and trained human bodies engage with musical sounds at the visceral, emotive, and cognitive levels as ways of embodying musical sound. In her review of philosophical literature on music listening, Dura (2002, 246) suggested that we hear music with our whole body, but also in reaction to it, and that the ears serve merely as focal organs for perceiving musical sound.

In addition to the theories regarding physio-emotional relationships to music, there are propositions about how another organ—the brain—receives, decodes, and stores musical sound. Bruner (1966) proposed the enactive mode of forming mental representations (action-based knowing) as one of three nonhierarchical modes in which the brain stores and deciphers information it receives (the other modes being iconic and symbolic). Gardner's (1983) theory of multiple intelligences included the bodily-kinesthetic intelligence, along with musical and other intelligences, and suggested there is an operational locus of control in which the brain deals with movement—a "modularity" theory of brain function and process-ing. However, Chen, Penhune, and Zattore (2008) refuted modularity theory based on their research findings that demonstrated *f*MRIs of people's brains during music listening. They found primary points of activation in auditory centers and other areas of the brain, including portions of the bodily-kinesthetic center of the brain. This seems especially true when the people had listened to rhythmic chunks of music.

Listeners experience music with the body and mind, and they implicitly and explicitly ascribe meaning to it. We might not possess sufficient words to describe what we know and feel as we listen to music, however, because our musical embodi-ment takes us to deeper levels of musical understanding than words allow us to describe.

As music educators, then, it is our responsibility to lead students into musi-cal awareness and consciousness of how relationships among the musical ele-ments and structures lead to bodily-mindful-feelingful experiences. Juntunen and Hyvönen (2004, 199) called for the end of "disembodied intellect." Instead, they called for music educators to acknowledge the embodiment of musical sound and give it credence as a way of knowing in the same manner as we validate and value intellectual reasoning. The authors suggested that students should not experience music only by talking about, analyzing, or describing it. Experientially, students must first feel and internalize musical sounds in their bodies. In fact, Juntunen and Hyvönen wrote that movement provides the foundation for all other intellectual understanding.

Dalcroze (1921/1980, 39) stated, "Musical consciousness is the result of physi-cal experience. Musical consciousness can be acquired by repeated experiences of ear, voice, and movement of the whole body." Further, in Dalcrozian methodology, "the goal is to show music's heard and felt qualities in body movement [and] to help students to become more aware of kinaesthetic sensations" of the music (Juntunen 2004, 203). Students engaging in gestures/movements during music listening can transform musical sounds into concrete, bodily manifestations of the inherent musical qualities. Further, movement provides students the opportunity to dem-onstrate not only what they hear perceptually in the music but also their affective responses to it (Ebie 2004).

Movement is often incorporated into elementary general-music classes. Sometimes these kinesthetic gestures reflect actual musical events or qualities of a song or listening example, or they can exist as movement experiences for the sake of having children move. Music methodologies, typically reserved for the very young-est students, exist that provide specific, sequential strategies for incorporating movement into music classes. Somehow, however, we seem to have forgotten that *all* students—not only those in preschool and elementary school—benefit from coordinated movement experiences. Kinesthetic metaphors—movement—can facilitate students' bodily feeling and knowing of musical sounds and their relation-ships, while also increasing their awareness of all the music has to offer, perceptually and affectively. Movement experiences during music listening might also appeal to those students who prefer to learn by doing and those whose vocabularies prohibit them from verbally expressing what they are thinking, feeling, and hearing as they listen to music.

MOVEMENT STRATEGIES FOR MUSIC LISTENING

For the purpose of this book, I define movement strategies as student-generated or teacher-generated movement sequences or gestures that relate directly to some aesthetic or formal quality of music that students experience as they listen. More specifically, *gesture* can be defined as "a movement of part of the body...to express an idea or meaning" (Leman and Godøy 2010).

Some music educators might have students tap a steady beat or stand when they hear the return of a formal section or motivic idea. These gestures certainly provide teachers immediate feedback as to which students recognize a particular musical element or formal musical structure (e.g., phrase, section, tonality). Other music educators might implement Dalcroze Eurhythmics, Laban or Feldenkrais movement exercises, or Orff body percussion into their classes. Yet other music teachers might incorporate curricular units of movement exercises based on the recordings and materials produced by Phyllis Weikart (1982) or folk dancing into the curriculum. These examples are viable means for incorporating movement during music listening, if the music educators lead the students to discover how the movements *relate to the music.*

Therefore, I propose an eclectic method embracing a variety of student movement experiences, many which land somewhere on the continuum between nonlocomotor clapping and locomotor sequences and folk dances. My basic premise for incorporating movement during music listening experiences is this: keep it creative, simple, musically relevant, and expressive in its "performance" with the music. After all, gestures and movement sequences should enhance students' focus of attention and musical awareness while being unobtrusive to their music listening experience.

Anecdotally, I have found Dalcroze movement experiences to be an effective pedagogy in developing musicianship skills, particularly music listening skills and internal musical thinking skills, for music students regardless of age. However, I will not delve into Dalcroze movement strategies in this chapter, since there are numerous teacher and student resources that provide a wealth of information on each method relative to developing students' musicianship skills (see Black and Moore 2003; Joseph, 1982; Lindeman 2011; Mead 1994).

There are two broad categories of movement sequences and gestures— teacher-generated and student-generated—that we will explore in this chapter. *Teacher-generated movement sequences* are custom-made, by the teacher, to fit the students' and teacher's musical teaching–learning needs in general-music classrooms and rehearsal settings. Teachers create a series of kinesthetic gestures that help focus students' attention on specific musical features or qualities. The younger the music student, the simpler the movements should be; full-body and symmetrical, gross-motor movements tend to work best. At the elementary-school level, I recommend focusing the students' attention on only one or two musical events, qualities, or concepts per listening. For example, suppose a teacher would like students to focus on melodic contour. The teacher might create a series of full-body and arm motions to indicate the rise and fall of the melody while also indicating aspects of performance style (i.e., *legato/staccato*; peppy or melancholy; scalar or jumping between pitches).

Student-generated movement sequences are those created "from scratch" by the students. They use their whole bodies or body parts and move with the intent of representing their personal music listening experiences—what the students are thinking, feeling, and hearing as they listen to music. This is an experience that promotes discovery learning: "In the discovery approach, the teacher guides the children so that they can find their own solutions to stated movement problems in response to a musical excerpt played" (O'Hagin 1998, 17). Students create their movement sequences in the moment, while they listen to the music for the first time, or as the product of repeated listenings during which they plan their series of movements.

Having students create their own movement sequences and performing them can assist teachers in understanding their individual students' perceptual and affective responses. From a constructivist perspective, student-generated movement sequences can also provide teachers insight into "where the students are" in terms of their natural focus of attention, cognitive abilities, and progress toward developing, refining, elaborating, and reflecting on new features that are discovered in the music during repeated listenings. Then, teachers can base subsequent curricular experiences on the information students initially provide through their movements by (1) introducing new musical vocabulary and (2) presenting different musics that demonstrate the same musical feature the students described kinesthetically in the original listening excerpt.

Examples of movement experiences that teachers might use in order to develop music listening skills, and which can be created by students or teachers, include: (1) movement sequences, (2) free-style movement, (3) body sculptures, and (4) movement montages. Teacher-generated movement sequences and student-generated free-style movements seem to be two popular kinesthetic tools currently used in music classrooms. But there are many other creative and engaging ways for students to feel the music with their minds and bodies. The four types I offer are not meant to be an exhaustive list; however, they might be additions to your newly or continuously developing pedagogical movement tool collection.

As I mentioned earlier in this chapter, *movement sequences* are series of gestures (kinesthetic representations) that are used to point to—highlight—musical events, formal structures, or aesthetic qualities (i.e., mood, style), typically as they occur chronologically in a music listening excerpt of one to two minutes in length. Movement sequences involve all students in the class doing the same movements or gestures simultaneously to represent musical events, elements, or formal structures.

Free-style movements are movements created by individual students with the intent of demonstrating what they are thinking, feeling, or hearing as they listen to a musical excerpt that is no longer than one minute. The process involves the students exploring and experimenting in the creation of movements that best fit some aspect of what they hear and feel during music listening. Typically, free-style movement is improvisatory and is performed as an in-the-moment response to musical sound. Additionally, it is an activity for students working independently within a full-class, free-style movement situation.

For the third category, think of a marble sculpture of a horse. It is stationary. It is three-dimensional (i.e., length, width, depth). The sculpture is not an actual horse but, rather, a resemblance that depicts key features, some which might even be exaggerated, of a horse. Unfortunately, a sculpture implies stasis and three dimensions, both antithetical to music consisting of movement and the inclusion of the fourth dimension—time/space. However, a sculpture can still convey motion. This is the idea behind creating small-group *body sculptures*.

Each student in the group, comprising approximately five students, depicts a different facet of a one-minute-long music excerpt by contributing a single gesture with the whole body or a single body part that is frozen in time and space. Once the students have experimented with possible solutions, they place their frozen gestures alongside the other students' gestures in their group to form the larger "whole" sculpture that represents the amalgam of key features of the musical excerpts.

Similarly, each student in the group might choose to create a gesture for a single facet of the music. For example, if students determine they wish to represent the music's topography of dynamic contrasts, each student might create a gesture indicating those dynamic changes as they occur in the music (i.e., abruptly, gradually, degrees of loud/quiet, silence, etc.). Imagine one student crouched to the ground, another in a seated position with hands pointed to the ground, and then a third on the ground pointing to another person who has arms extended above his head. This sculpture could be depicting *pianissimo* becoming *mezzo forte*, then *subito piano* becoming *fortissimo*. Obviously, this pedagogical strategy requires repeated listening to the musical excerpt.

Movement montages are similar to the small-group body sculptures. They both involve students creating movements, working in small groups, and individuals representing a musical element or formal structure that they perceive in a music listening excerpt. Movement montages, however, require students to perform their respective movements representing a musical element or formal structure at the time that it is heard in the excerpt. Furthermore, the movements are not frozen, as is the case with body sculptures but, rather, flow with the music through time and space. A group of students might create one or a series of gestures to depict that which they heard and felt during the music listening. The movements might be juxtaposed and sequential, flowing from one person's movement to the next person's movement—a group choreographed performance.

A variation on the musical montage is for the teacher to assign a "musical focus point" to each small group. For example, one group might focus on depicting the melodic movement as played by a flute. Another group might create a gesture for the timpani that sometimes accompanies the melody, but at other times accompanies the string section (another small group assignment). After the members of each group create their movements to depict the assigned musical focus point, the groups act as an ensemble, performing their movements at the time their focus points occur in the music example. This experience facilitates the focus on one musical feature, but also allows students to begin to understand (kinesthetically and visually) when other features occur. Video recording the group's ensemble performance and reviewing it is helpful in drawing student attention to some of the many musical events that occur simultaneously in the music example.

We as teachers must be sensitive to those students in our music classes and rehearsals who have some sort of motor delay or disability. Movements and gestures can easily be modified so that students can remain in a wheelchair, for example, but still participate in a least restricted environment. Instead of using full-body movements through time and space, students with special needs might use a single body part or only parts on one side of the body. Enlist the student's one-on-one aide or even a student in the class who is willing to assist the student in a wheelchair with an upper-body motion or a gentle physical manipulation of a limb. Always consult the student, the teaching aide, or the case team at the school for the motions that the student can complete safely and without pain, either independently or with the gentle assistance of someone else in the ensemble.

What types of movement opportunities have you found useful in your general music classroom? In your rehearsals? What did you observe in the students' moving, listening, and learning that provided evidence for your conclusions? Why were the movement experiences in your music classroom successful tools for developing music listening skills? Why did you decide to use movement as a strategy in your classroom or rehearsal? What would you need to do if you wanted to begin incorporating movement in your classroom or rehearsal? On the Companion Website, you will be able to view movement sequences and gestures created by individual students, groups of students, and teachers in research and music classroom settings. Perhaps these models will inspire your movement creativity.

MOVING FOR MEANING

As mentioned in chapter 1, the order in which I conducted my individual research interviews to gather data for this book was: "whole" listenings, talk-aloud, mapping, and movement. Notice the order of the tasks. Given the research and theoretical literature, putting the music listening movement task as the students' first task following the "whole" listening might have been more pedagogically sound than having the students begin by talking about their listening experiences. However, I wanted the students to do the tasks with which they had experience—talking and drawing—before the movement task in order to establish a sense of comfort within the research environment. Otherwise, some students would have had to create movements in front of a relative stranger. I anticipated the students becoming frustrated, thus inhibiting their willingness and ability to remain "open" during the remaining portions of the interview, if the first interview task had been the kinesthetic one.

Similarly, the second task was also familiar (drawing), even though creating a music listening map was a new activity. By the time we arrived at the movement task, then, the students had become more familiar with each other, as well as with me, so much of their inhibition or self-consciousness was thwarted. Consequently, I make the argument that, while the order of the interview tasks was not the most pedagogically sound, it was the most participant-friendly.

My case for the task order is somewhat supported by the interview participants, who frequently mentioned that the movement sequence was their least favorite of the music listening tasks and that it was also their most difficult and "embarrassing." In a music class or rehearsal space, teachers and students are gradually able to build a community of trusting learners that encourage each other to take risks, where they can experiment with moving within a safe space. However, I did not have the opportunity to build such long-term relationships with many of my student research participants.

In the section that follows, I present individual students' responses and my descriptions of their movements while listening to musical examples. These students were in grades two, five, eight, and eleven. Similar to my investigations of students mapping (chapter 4) and verbal responses (chapter 5), I played the roles of teacher and researcher, since many of these students (in grades two, five, and eleven) were already in my music classes taught in public school and community music venues. I present the results of my interviews with individual students during two research sessions and my teaching of whole-class movement experiences. In all cases, except for the class of middle-schoolers who listened to Strauss's "Sunrise" (from *Also Sprach Zarathustra*), the students listened to an excerpt of the Bach Brandenburg Concerto #2 in F Major, movement 1 (BWV 1047), approximately 2"20' in length.

After the initial listening, talk-aloud and mapping, the students provided kinesthetic descriptions while they listened to the music excerpt. The participants elected to either stand or sit in an area of the room that was open and free of classroom materials or equipment. The directions I gave the students included the following:

[D]escribe the music through your movement. I am asking you to create motions with your whole body or parts of your body as you listen to the music. Pretend that I am unable to hear the music or anything you might say. I will want to look at your movements to get an idea of what you are thinking, feeling, or hearing as you listen to the music. Remember, you are not expected to create a dance.

I video-recorded each student's movement task, after which she or he and I viewed the recorded gestures, and the student verbally described the relationship of their movements to the musical example.

The following are the individuals' voices telling their stories and my interpretations of their movement sequences. To observe the students' conscious or subconscious depiction of subtle musical detail through movement, I invite you to go to the Companion Website. I also encourage you, as a student of your students' verbal and nonverbal behaviors, to look for "the musical" in the students' movements— no matter how simple or complex their demonstrations. Consider, also, these focus questions while you observe students moving to music:

1. What do the students demonstrate in their gestures that represent what they perceive in the musical example?
2. Which movements seem indicative of students' affective responses to the music?
3. How might you confirm your speculations?
4. How do the movements seem to represent embodied musical knowing?
5. What information about the students' music listening experiences might have remained unearthed if they only had the opportunity to describe the music listening example verbally?
6. What about the students' body language suggests that they are comfortable or uncomfortable doing this task?
7. What would you do for individuals and for classes of students to help alleviate any apprehension?
8. What personal, musical, social, cognitive "variables" might be affecting the students' responses?

Finally, can you imagine how the students' movements might have been the same or different if the listening example were another piece of music, such as rock, jazz, gospel, or popular music? How might presenting students with music of a different style or genre affect your research findings or the students' willingness to participate?

Listening to and Observing Michele

▶ Observe Michele perform her movement sequence while listening to music. Go to the Companion Website and click on Video 3.1.

Michele, a second-grade female (age seven), was a student in my general music class for two years (Kerchner 1996, 2001, 2005). A quiet and somewhat reserved personality, Michele exhibited enthusiastic participation in the activities offered in the music classroom setting. At the time of the interviews, Michele had taken only two months of private piano instruction.

Her parents reported that Michele preferred to listen to popular, rap, musical theater, and country music. They also described what seemed to be limited music listening opportunities for Michele at home: she heard her brothers practicing their musical instruments and her father's "oldies" music on the radio. They also stated they occasionally attended outdoor jazz and pop concerts. There was no description, however, of Michele's purposely listening to music as an activity integrated into her home routine. Her parents remarked that Michele enjoyed dancing to music when she heard music that she liked; specifically, she enjoyed participating in musical productions. Her parents also mentioned that drawing, listening to music, and creating movements were all activities that Michele enjoyed.

Several of Michele's kinesthetic descriptions from the interview movement tasks recounted information that she had also presented in her verbal and mapping responses. Typical of her verbal and visual responses, Michele's motions reflected melodic contour. As she heard each segment of the descending melodic trumpet sequence in the Bach excerpt, she incrementally lowered her arms. She also moved her index finger up and down in a jagged fashion to follow the flute scalar contour. Michele's hand and arm motions gradually moved to a higher plane as the music progressed toward the statement of the primary thematic material in the key of the subdominant.

Similar to the first movement task, Michele moved her arm in a perpendicular manner during the scalar flute material. Not only did this gesture capture the musical contour, but it also depicted the melodic rhythm. In addition, Michele demonstrated her perception of a repeated-note trumpet rhythm. When Michele viewed her motion that coincided with the contour of sixteenth-note scalar string and continuo parts, she explained that the violin was "hopping," her description of scalar contour and short note values. As she heard the music, Michele either used her entire arm or her index finger to move up and down with each sixteenth-note.

As with her other verbal descriptions, Michele described the music in relation to her movements as "flowing," "wigglier," and "shakier." She used kinesthetic adjectives to describe the musical motion and instrumental articulations, even though she did not describe what she perceived in technical musical terms. When Michele struggled to find words to describe her movements or the music, she reverted to using her voice to produce descriptive sounds such as vocables (i.e., "doi-ing, doi-ing") or singing a melodic pattern—vocally and musically using metaphors to describe the musical sounds in the listening excerpt.

The jagged and smooth lines that Michele exhibited in her maps were transferred to her kinesthetic gestures. Considering the motions from the movement tasks, Michele used jagged motions during the *tutti* sections of the music and smooth gestures to depict solo instruments playing. Other gestures reflected her awareness of the violin when she pretended to play the instrument during the violin solo. Another example was Michele's sensitivity to instrumental embellishments. Michele shook her index finger during some trumpet and flute trills. She reported that the music "stayed in the same spot," while she extended her hand and fluttered it back and forth.

Confused by this statement, I asked her to explain. Michele said that the music sounded as though it "stayed in the same spot, but then went to a higher string," but continued to shake her hand. She pointed to the lines on her map in which the jagged points were in close proximity. She explained that the music "was going side to side. It sounded like staying in the same spot, but it sound like it was going side to side." Perhaps her statement relayed her perception of notes having short durations or that she was trying to describe the embellishments, such as trills, that she heard in the music. Either way, Michele stumped this researcher and teacher regarding the specific meaning of her descriptions.

Michele's linear thinking tendency was most apparent in her movement responses. She provided a sequential kinesthetic account of the music as it unfolded. Although she mentioned that mapping was her favorite of the interview tasks, Michele noted that the movement task was the easiest. Coincidentally, she provided the greatest number of responses and the most musical detail in the kinesthetic mode of response. In this situation, it seems that Michele's task preference did not influence the repleteness of her movement responses. Perhaps Michele considered the movement task the easiest mode in which to represent her music listening experience, since it was the least obtrusive in her descriptions. She could allow her body to respond to the musical nuances as they passed through time and space, without relying on words to describe them. Maybe her kinesthetic responses required less translation from the musical sound to external response than would the verbal and visual (mapping) responses. I observed a natural kinesthetic component to Michele's music listening experience that was not evident in the verbal and visual response modes.

I discovered that Michele provided the greatest number of varied topics (musical themes) in her kinesthetic descriptions of the music. Furthermore, this information was more detailed, more differentiated than the general, global descriptions of the music she provided in the verbal and visual response modes. Although contour captured her attention in her verbal, visual, and kinesthetic responses, Michele's motions also alluded to melodic rhythm, beat, embellishment, and notational duration, along with formal properties. Michele did not verbally describe these musical features in great detail, yet the coordination of her movement and the music intimated that she might have perceived these musical characteristics. Her movements also reflected more detail about musical events than appeared in her verbal and visual responses. Further, Michele mentioned that she depicted "happiness" in each of her verbal, visual, and kinesthetic responses.

Listening to and Observing Maribeth

▶ Observe Maribeth perform her movement sequences while listening to music. Go to the Companion Website and click on Videos 3.2 and 3.3.

Maribeth was a precocious fifth-grade female (age ten), whose behavior and speech were mature beyond her chronological age (Kerchner 1996, 2001, 2005).

An obvious extroverted personality, Maribeth was articulate and animated during the interview sessions. Her parents described her as a person who listened to music "very intently" at home. Further, they noted that Maribeth frequently sang at home and danced to her favorite songs. To complement these organic experiences, Maribeth's parents enrolled her in dance classes. At the time of the research study, she had also taken private piano lessons for three years and had participated in the fourth-grade school recorder ensemble that I had taught at the elementary school.

Aligned with her parents' descriptions of her music-dance-acting activities at home, I was not surprised that Maribeth "acted out" scenes from stories she had created for each repeated listening of the music excerpt during the verbal and visual interview tasks. Similar to the content of her talk-alouds and maps, Maribeth's movements told stories of a dance party, ballet, and being an orchestral conductor.

In the first interview kinesthetic task, Maribeth pretended to be dancing with a partner. Whenever she heard the primary theme of the Bach or any of its thematic segments sprinkled throughout the musical excerpt (the "stronger parts"), she used footwork that corresponded to the steady beat. As long as the music was "jumping" (during the *tutti* sections), she continued to dance. During the solo instrumental sections, however, Maribeth stopped or acted out another part of the story she had created.

Maribeth displayed what I interpreted as affective response to the music in her expressive facial gestures, particularly in the first kinesthetic task. The characters she depicted held particular moods, seemingly those that coincided with Maribeth's (and/or the character's mood that she was depicting) own affective response to the music. For example, she made a sad face as she listened to a descending trumpet melodic sequence, but her expression changed to a happy face at its conclusion. She made another sad face later during a transitional section of music, and she stated that she was sad because no one at the party had asked her to dance. Maribeth revealed that the music made her sad because "it gets softer and some of the new instruments came in that were maybe lower."

Coinciding with the rhythmic descriptions of the music that had captured her attention in prior listenings of the excerpt, Maribeth illustrated her notion of steady beat, downbeat, subdivided beat, melodic rhythm, and embellishments in her conducting gestures of the second interview session. Maribeth's second "scenario," different from the first interview session, consisted of her being the conductor of an orchestra, the scene she had described earlier in the second interview during her talk-aloud and on her map. She used an Orff xylophone mallet to conduct her imaginary orchestra in duple meter. Maribeth described:

> I was kind of in this other place. I was in the music room, but then I imagined I was in the symphony. And I was thinking that I could do the conducting, be the conductor, and then switch off from being the conductor and then horn player or trumpet, um, but it didn't really match, because if I just jumped into the place, you wouldn't exactly get it.

In her duple conducting pattern, Maribeth physically emphasized the beats whenever she heard the *tutti* sections and primary thematic material of the Bach excerpt. Her motions were larger, heavier, and on a deeper plane than her other conducting gestures. "Harder" beats, as she described, indicated the "stronger parts" of the music. Maribeth also recognized segments of the primary thematic material that were combined to form a transitional section of music. With each fragment of a melodic sequence, Maribeth's conducting gesture grew larger. Clearly, rhythmic events and the music's mood and style seemed to capture Maribeth's attention, given the kinesthetic representations of these features.

In addition to rhythmic descriptions, Maribeth recognized different instruments in the musical excerpt. She captured the sixteenth-note continuo accompaniment and the scalar contour of solo instruments, by shifting her visual focus and body stance to the areas of the orchestra in which those instruments might be located. In fact, Maribeth provided conducting cues to some of the instrumental sections at the time they were to enter the music.

The second interview kinesthetic task captured Maribeth's awareness and overt response to specific events in the musical excerpt. It was during this task that her perceptual and affective "voice" as a listener was revealed to me. Her conducting gestures indicated her perception of beat, subdivided beat, phrase, melodic rhythm, dynamics, embellishment, texture of the various instrumental parts, contour, motive, and theme, as well as a linear style of thinking. Maribeth conducted musical events happening in the moment. Even though there was a story at the foundation of her movement sequence, it played a secondary role to her fully playing the role of conductor. The conductor "story" did not obscure the subtle perceptual and affective responses Maribeth provided, while her first kinesthetic task responses focused wholly on the details surrounding her story of being at a dance party.

As we reviewed the video recording of her conducting, Maribeth narrated what was going on in the conductor's (Maribeth's) mind. She shifted pronouns in her verbal descriptions of the conductor—from the use of "she" to "I" (i.e., "Now what she's going to do right now is to think, *How do I make this sound distressing?* and *How would I make my orchestra know the music is distressing with my hands?*"). Maribeth was aware of and could easily express the conductor's thinking processes—her own thinking processes—as she created the scene via kinesthetic gestures.

Maribeth was also able to provide verbal rationales for her kinesthetic responses. She was aware not only of the thinking involved in her kinesthetic responses but also the level of concentration she maintained throughout the kinesthetic (and verbal and visual) interview tasks. Maribeth was deliberate in creating her movement sequences. Before she began the kinesthetic task in the first interview, she asked for "time to think." Reflecting metacognitive operations, she explained, "I was thinking about what I would do when like, I knew some of the parts were stronger than others, so I was thinking, *What would I do in those parts?* So, I was really thinking."

She also admitted that she did not always know which role to assume in her stories she created during the kinesthetic tasks. "I didn't know whether to be in the audience or up on stage. I didn't know whether to be the conductor, the director, the bad guy." She explained that there was a lot to think about and "very little time" in which to make decisions. The music evolved and she had to think quickly in order to capture the musical moment *and* make decisions about her story line and characters. My wonderment remains: was she aware of all the musical events to which she responded kinesthetically during the listening experience, or did her body (i.e., her conducting gestures) respond subconsciously or intuitively while she was consciously creating her story? The evidence appears to suggest a combination, for she was aware of the instruments and when her visual attention needed to change among her imaginary orchestra members.

Maribeth's verbal, visual, and kinesthetic responses in both interview sessions were full of programmatic information. I could not, however, completely rely on Maribeth's verbal descriptions of her kinesthetic responses, since she only recounted her stories rather than describing actual musical events or her affective responses to the music. Therefore, I had to infer the relationship between elements of her stories and the music by observing her perform the kinesthetic task while simultaneously analyzing corresponding musical events. Maribeth provided few verbal details regarding the connection of her story details and the music, even when I verbally probed for this type of information.

Her stories were connected to her prior personal experiences. When I asked her "what in the music" helped her decide which story to create, Maribeth explained that "Most of the things [in the stories] I've seen or done. Like I've been in a ballet. I've seen a ballet. I've seen a conductor on TV. Most of this had to do with dancing." Maribeth imagined herself as a part of her own story, since she created the stories during the interview tasks based on her life experiences. Her real-life musical encounters, experienced during her dance and instrumental lessons, were automatically associated with the music listening interview sessions.

During the post-interview, Maribeth did not hesitate to express her uneasiness with the kinesthetic tasks. Having found this to contradict her (and her parents') reported enjoyment of music and dance, I asked Maribeth to describe the difference between her dance classes and creating movements to describe a musical example. She said, "I love to dance, but not that way. So there were a lot of, I like dancing jazz and other types of music, so this wasn't my favorite thing." Was it the music that did not fit her scaffolding of "dancing" or moving? Was it the actual task of moving or the music that she did not enjoy? Perhaps Maribeth was uncomfortable moving during the interviews, because the kinesthetic task required her to perform a solo rather than a group movement choreography typically experienced in dance classes. During the interview kinesthetic classes, Maribeth was asked to create movements spontaneously as she listened to the music. In her dance classes, however, the teacher taught her and her peers specific movements to perform at specific moments in the music. Maribeth stated,

It [a dance lesson] is easier because everyone's dancing in the class....And when I'm a solo, when she [the teacher] says, "Maribeth, let me see that again," I know that everyone has to do it next. And because she taught it to me...I mean, I make up dances sometimes at home, but I mean, I pick out the music. You see, that's the difference.

Maribeth also described the effect of repeatedly listening to the Bach excerpt. Familiarity, owing to the repeated listenings and task repetitions, allowed Maribeth to concentrate more intently on the music instead of the task performance. She said that she did not "listen as well" during the first interview session as she did in the second interview session, because it was easier to listen and to concentrate in the second interview. She said she "knew what we were doing," and she already had the music in her head from the first interview session.

Repeated listening also had a negative effect on Maribeth's music listening experience. Her tolerance of the performance tasks dwindled by the end of the interview sessions. Further, she reported that it was "annoying" and "boring" to listen to the same musical excerpt so many times. With each repeated listening, however, Maribeth added new detail about the music or her stories she had enacted during the movement tasks. She created new stories but held onto the general internal representation of the musical example from previous listenings. Maribeth recognized that there were multiple ways to listen to a musical excerpt. Her imagination had been engaged, had "removed" her from the interview session, and had "relocated" her in the musical experience.

Observing a Sixth-Grade General Music Class

▶ Observe middle-schoolers perform a teacher-generated movement sequence while listening to Strauss's "Sunrise" (*Also Sprach Zarathustra*). Go to the Companion Website and click Video 3.4.

Since 1997, undergraduate and graduate students and I place teaching and learning principles and theories into practice by observing and team-teaching in local middle school general-music classes in a variety of school districts. It is an opportunity for us to collaboratively plan, teach, and assess teaching ideas and strategies presented in the methods class and place them into action with "real" teenaged general-music students.

One of the middle schools where we conducted our teaching and learning lab is in a suburban neighborhood with a population of approximately 28,000 residents and a school-district population of approximately 4,000 students. At that time of our teaching, general music was required for all sixth and seventh graders, while it was an elective for eighth graders. Typically, the class of students remained seated in chairs on choral risers throughout the class period. Prior to this particular lesson, the middle-schoolers, the undergraduates, and I had interacted once, weekly for six weeks. The students were on the "quarter" system, having four nine-week marking periods to the school calendar.

Using the music teacher's curriculum, an objective for the class period was interval and octave recognition and performance, specifically do-sol-do patterns using Kodály-Curwen hand signs, singing, and movement during a music listening experience. Another objective was simply for the students to participate in the singing, playing (Orff instruments), listening, and movement experiences—all which remained relatively new experiences for the students.

The first portion of the class consisted of the students singing do-sol and do-sol-do with hand signs, identifying the hand signs, and playing the patterns on Orff instruments (beginning the pattern on different pitches). We also played an "inner hearing" game, whereby we reviewed all diatonic hand signs and intervals. The students took turns creating three-pitch (two-interval) patterns: a student showed the hand sign, gave a starting pitch, and the rest of the class did the hand signs and sang the syllables for each pitch. The idea was for the creator of the pitch sequence to identify if what the class sang was actually what the leader's hand signs had represented.

Next, the task was to place the do-sol-do pattern into a music listening context using Strauss's "Sunrise" from *Also Sprach Zarathustra*. I expected some students to be familiar with this music, as it was used in the movie *2001: A Space Odyssey* and in numerous popular television commercials. Indeed, my assumption was accurate. As a focusing directive prior to listening to "Sunrise," I instructed the students to raise their hands when they heard the pattern do-sol-do in the music. Most of the students indicated their recognition of the do-sol-do pattern that repeated three times in the beginning of the segment. One student, Teddy, who had not seemed engaged during the first part of the class, suddenly added movement of his own to the music. He pretended to play the timpani when he heard it in the music, and then he pretended to be running in slow motion after the do-sol-do repetitions. Suddenly, he "came alive" with the music. Oddly, a few students raised their hands (and then quickly retracted them) during each of the last three chords of the music. True, the music had concluded on the high "do" that they had recognized earlier in the piece, but there was not the exact replication of the do-sol-do pattern.

When the music ended, I asked the students, "So how many time did the pattern occur?" A young man responded, "Three times." Then I continued with a focusing question for a repeated listening of "Sunrise." "This time when you hear the do-sol-do (I sang and showed the hand signs), think about which instrument is playing that pattern." The music concluded, and I repeated the question, "Which instrument played the pattern?" Another young man said, "French horn," to which I responded, "No, not the French horn, but you are definitely in the right instrument family." A young woman raised her hand and offered, "Trumpet?" I asked the class if anyone else thought it was the trumpet. Only a few students raised their hands.

Then I asked if there were any other ideas about which instrument played. The students mentioned "tuba" and "trombone." We discussed that it was one of the highest, not lowest, members of the brass family—the trumpet. A student reminded me that someone had already given that answer, but I told him that I had not said she was wrong and that no one else in the class had indicated that they thought she was correct.

The final segment of the class involved a movement segment I had created to highlight specific features of the music: (1) do-sol-do pattern, (2) specific instruments (timpani, trombone, trumpet, string bass/organ), (3) phrases, (4) melodic contour, and (5) intensity/dynamics. (See "Ideas for Movement Lessons," Lesson #1, that appears later in this chapter for the actual movement sequence description.) Because there was much repetition of thematic material (do-sol-do) and other repeated melodic and rhythmic material, "Sunrise" was a perfect piece for which a movement segment could be easily created and performed.

Before the students gathered in a circle on the floor in front of the choral risers, the students and I reminded each other of the behaviors that might be the "best choices" while we participated in the movement sequence (e.g., maintaining personal space, lots of listening, following directions, not being silly, knowing when to stop when the music stops). Once the students found their spaces within the class circle, I gave them a focus question: "What in the music made me [the teacher] decide to do these particular movements?" I noticed that one student was standing on the risers and not following directions. I stated that we needed Kevin's participation and then I indicated a "great spot" for him within the class circle; he joined us and participated. I started the music, and the students echoed my movements.

The students (and two undergraduate students) participated enthusiastically in the movement sequence. There were giggles during the timpani segments that followed each do-sol-do pattern; at that time, they were jogging in place. Throughout the sequence, I observed smiling faces and focused attention. At the conclusion of the sequence, a girl wearing a bright orange sweater, Susan, was moving from a higher to lower plane to indicate the dynamic change, and accidentally hit her bottom on the floor. This was accompanied by an "ouch!" and giggling.

We returned to a sitting position in our class circle. I restated the original question, "What in the music made me do the different motions? What about when we did this (body at floor, middle, stretch positions)?"

Teddy responded, "It went lower to higher."

"Why do you think I chose the lower to higher movements?" I asked.

Susan eventually answered, "Do-sol-do." Then I demonstrated another movement (arms moving in angular motions from high to low during trombone section). "How about this one?"

A girl answered, "Drum?" and I responded, "Not quite. That was played during this part" [I jogged in place]. I repeated the movement associated with the descending trombone line to which Teddy responded, "The sound was going down."

"Yes, the sound was going down. Did you catch which instrument?" Another girl said, "The brass instrument."

"You are in the right family; it was a low brass instrument." Another student guessed, "A baritone?" while another responded, "I forget the name of that instrument!"

It was time for a repeated listening to focus on the trombone part that was giving the students difficulty in identifying and naming it. "Let's check that part out again. How about this?" I demonstrate the fingers tapping on the floor that indicated the soft organ/string bass introduction and conclusion of "Sunrise." "I was like low and stuff."

"Yes, it was low. Was it loud or soft?"

The students answered, "Soft."

I reposed my question, "But what instrument was playing?"

After some students incorrectly guessed, I said, "That's a challenge instrument for us. So now we have two things to listen for next time—this (I demonstrated the trombone descending line movement) and this" (I performed the organ's low, fingertip movement on the floor).

While we repeated the entire movement sequence, I provided verbal cues just prior to the point when the organ and trombone movements were to be performed. I noticed Teddy incorporating his own movements again, particularly the slow-motion running placed in his arms and legs, with the other movements I had created in the sequence. When the music ended, the students eagerly raised their hands, for they wanted to tell me what they had discovered about the "mystery instruments." They figured out that when we crouched down and moved our fingertips gently on the floor, they heard the organ. Someone had said it was drum, an indication that he heard the low rumbling introductory sound.

The second mystery sound occurred when we moved our arms in descending steps. The students were excited that they had discovered (or finally guessed) that the gesture was performed when the trombone played. The lesson concluded with our discussion of program music and why the composer might choose this music to represent a sunrise.

Listening to and Observing Steven

Observe Steven perform his movement sequence while listening to music. Go to the Companion Website and click Video 3.5.

Steven, grade eleven, was a participant for three years in the high school community choir that I directed. He was a polite and reserved young man, and he was a leader within the tenor section with his secure, newly changed voice. In addition to singing with the community choir, he sang in his high school's choir and took piano lessons for several years. Yet, when I asked him to describe his music listening habits outside of school, he said that he only listened to music with his parents in the car. He stated that he never listened to music by himself or with friends in other venues. After rethinking my question, Steven stated that he actually did listen to music, because he heard it on television and in commercials and movies.

Similar to Michele and Maribeth, Steven experienced the talk-aloud and mapping tasks prior to the movement task in both individual interview sessions. As the Bach excerpt began with the *tutti* primary theme, Steven moved his entire arm up and down in wide, curvy, legato waves with his right arm and then created larger circles on a higher plane. During the solo sections sprinkled between the return of the *tutti* sections, he moved his right hand in small circles on a plane at waist level. Steven used his left hand to keep somewhat of a steady pulse while moving his right arm up and down during the *tutti* section that followed the introductory oboe solo. At the point of the first trumpet solo, Steven created medium-size circles with his hand, but ultimately returned to the wide, curvy, legato waves during the *tutti* sections. He continued to use circles and figure-eight movements until the conclusion of the excerpt, varying the size of the gestures with the dynamic levels and possibly the musical tension that built before the statement of the primary theme in the key of the dominant.

Steven viewed the video of his gestures, and he provided elucidating information about his music listening experience. He told me that the excerpt "starts out with a lot of dips and curves, kind of a circular motion in that opening statement…it goes up and down." During the first solo statement, I commented that his movements seemed to change.

"Yeah, it gets a bit lower and softer. Here it gets back to the big dips and curves, before it gets softer again." Clearly, Steven was describing the timbral and formal structural changes between the alternating solo and *tutti* statement in the concerto.

About the trumpet solo, Steven said, "It's fast and quick and jubilant. Not in volume, not in the performance. Not all the time, though." As the trumpet played a descending trumpet sequence, he mentioned that the music is "getting smoother, slower, and more connected here. But then it changes a bit; it gets slower." Perhaps this statement reflected the slower melodic rhythm that he perceived and the minor tonality that acts as transition into the dominant statement of the primary theme. I probed him on this, for I was unclear that my interpretation was accurate. I asked, "What was getting slower?"

Steven paused to ponder. "No, it's not slower, it's smaller and a little bit quicker."

I questioned, "Are the notes quicker or is the tempo speeding up?"

"I think the notes are moving faster, not the overall tempo. There are more notes in a little space."

Steven changed the subject by telling me that the next part would be "circular" and "leading somewhere.…It's picking up with more notes now." He appeared to be anticipating the musical events before they actually happened on video. These statements seemed to corroborate my hunch that Steven reflected the tension and musical transitions into the dominant statement of the primary theme at the conclusion of the excerpt. To summarize Steven's first movement interview task, he seemed to respond to and kinesthetically represent his perception of: primary thematic material, solo/*tutti* formal sections, melodic contour, repetition/contrast, dynamics, tension/resolution, foreground and background musical material, mood, subdivision of pulse, and steady pulse.

Similar to the first interview session, Steven's movements in the second interview session demonstrated global (general) descriptions of musical events also included in his talk-alouds and mappings. However, during the second interview tasks, his verbal, visual, and kinesthetic responses included an increased amount of detailed information about his perception of and response to the Bach excerpt.

Once again, Steven depicted the *tutti* statement of the primary theme with large, legato, wavy curves while using smaller wavy curves during the solo statements. Similarly, his left hand was engaged at the same point (*tutti* prior to the flute solo) along with his right hand. New to the kinesthetic tasks was Steven's hand patting downward in the melodic rhythm of the trumpet playing repeated, short notes. He also drew small circles before a trumpet trill. During the trill, however, his hand movements increased in speed, seeming to capture the scalar movement of the accompaniment. At the point where the trumpet produced longer note values, Steven moved his hand in slower curves and figure-eights. As he heard the descending trumpet melodic sequence, Steven created increasingly lower movements at the center of his body for each segment of the sequence. His wavy, legato curves became larger and on a higher plane as the music approached the statement of the primary theme in the key of the dominant.

As I listened to Steven describe his gestures while he viewed them on video, it occurred to me that he used the same word to relay his perception of musical events. For example, he used the words *small* and *smaller* to describe several musical contexts. At one point, he said the solo parts were "smaller, but it still goes up and down. It is not as pronounced as this part [he creates a large, legato, wavy curve]. That's the orchestral part." I presumed "smaller" meant the solo sections only, until he used the word to describe segments of the first ascending melodic sequence. I asked, "When you say 'smaller,' what are you describing now?" He responded, "A softer, calmer, more relaxed feel." Yet, at another point, Steven referred to the segments of a melodic and rhythmic sequence as "small bits."

Steven described the music in the background as a "bit chaotic underneath"— that is, the sixteenth-note accompaniment. He said the music was "more intense" during the final sequential transition into the key of the dominant. "It's a good change," he added.

In the post-interview, I asked Steven to compare his music listening experiences and responses in both interview sessions. He responded, "Sometimes I'd pick up something that I didn't the first time. I heard different instruments this time. Sometimes I could pick out the violin and the group of strings, where I couldn't do that the first time." He further explained that he changed his mind about the "whirl-wind" part that he heard in the first interview; he heard it as "chaotic" during the second interview. He also recounted that the music was "kind of cheerful, relaxing, and calm, even though it was repetitious."

From Steven's multisensory responses, it seems that he perceived and depicted musical elements, instruments, and formal sections of music (i.e., solo/*tutti* sections, repetition, sequences). He depicted no associations or stories as he listened to the music, only formal properties. The manner in which he presented information about the music was linear, for he provided a chronological synopsis of musical benchmarks in the music. Although Steven mentioned that talking about the music was his favorite and the easiest in which to provide description, he provided sparse, undifferentiated (i.e., general, lacking detail) information about what he heard, thought, or felt as he listened to the Bach excerpt.

Given Steven's shy, reserved demeanor, I wondered how those personal qualities might have affected the quantity and quality of his multisensory responses. Observing him listen to the music, I could almost see him thinking with the intent to describe. How might the movement task, or the other interview tasks, have hindered his thinking and listening? And, how much more did Steven perceive and feel than he felt comfortable reporting kinesthetically? To what extent did he soak up musical detail subconsciously? Steven's listening experience remained a mystery to me, for the listening energy he exuded did not seem to be reflected in the details of his kinesthetic responses. I sensed I did not know the depth of Steven's musical, perceptual, and emotional experiences during the music listening tasks, exhibited in his kinesthetic (and verbal) responses.

STUDENTS INFORMING TEACHERS: IMPLICATIONS FOR MUSIC LISTENING PEDAGOGY

From the interviews of individual students, the kinesthetic mode of response elicited detailed musical information that was often not contained in students' verbal responses. We heard Maribeth's and Michele's stories of their kinesthetic responses; however, these students might be kinesthetic outliers. They provided more perceptual and affective information in their responses than in the verbal and visual modes. They depicted continuous motion that enabled them to react, consciously or unconsciously, to the musical events as they unfolded. Steven, however, is an example of the many other students' kinesthetic responses that I encountered during the research interviews: providing general responses without detail, using a limited kinesthetic vocabulary, and providing delayed reactions to the music rather than in-the-moment movements and gestures.

Students, regardless of age, mentioned that the kinesthetic mode was the least preferred mode of response. Consequently, it also solicited the fewest detailed responses from the students. The students also stated that responding kinesthetically was challenging because there were two competing layers to the task—listening to the music and trying to create appropriate movements to describe the music. I find this explanation interesting, since the kinesthetic task was experienced after several listenings to the Bach excerpt, and since the students did not mention this difficulty relative to the mapping experiences that had occurred earlier in the interviews. Afer all, both tasks had required layers of translation from sound to symbol.

The examples of the students in classroom settings, however, depicted the students' general willingness to participate in movement experiences if trust and safety have been strongly established between teacher and students. To that mix, effective classroom movement experiences incorporate a learning sequence that facilitates success and enjoyment. Of course, there might be students reluctant or unwilling to participate. It has been my experience, however, that once those students see their peers and teacher doing the movement sequence, they eventually join the group. Patience and the avoidance of power struggles are key principles.

From my observations of students' movements and gestures, it appears that students initially attended to musical "ear anchors" that marked beginnings and ends of phrases, sections, tonality, and harmonic tension and resolution, along with other prominent musical elemental changes (i.e., dynamics, pitch, duration, timbre, formal structures). Students coordinated their gestures with these large musical features. Bamberger (1999, 49) described these units of perception—"landmarks"—as "highly aggregated, structurally meaningful entities," since we do not listen to music as a progression from one note to the next. She stated that listeners tend to grasp the approximation of the shape and feel of "wholes," sections, or excerpts.

Upon learning or creating their movement sequences over the course of repeated listenings, the students then filled in details of the music, such as subdivision, embellishment, note duration, articulation, melodic rhythm, sequence, thematic material, motives, mood and other gestures specific to affective response. This logically implicates students' experiencing musical excerpts as a "whole" and in terms of general features first, before deeply analyzing and listening at the "part" level in the typical whole-part-whole learning sequence (chapter 1).

In this and the next few chapters, you will read my disclaimers about students' multisensory responses being full of ambiguity. This is not to undermine the meaning embedded in their responses, but to remind teachers that these responses provide only partial glimpses into the students' music listening experiences. Students provide morsels of information through their responses, but they are left to interpretation by researcher or teacher. My observations were analyzed in terms of when the movements occurred in the music and which musical ear anchors the students might be capturing in their movements. While some students' verbal descriptions of their movements were helpful, I could not rely solely on verbal accuracy. Students used words to describe the musical features that they subsequently used to describe different musical features. Students also used musical vocabulary "inaccurately," at least in terms of standard musical vocabulary usage. For example, the words *flute* and *trumpet* were often interchanged. Therefore, in our teaching, we might seize these moments to supply students with the actual term of an event they describe and revisit and experience this and other concepts of confusion and challenge in subsequent music lessons.

As I mentioned earlier in the chapter, the movement task followed the talk-aloud and mapping tasks in the sequence of the individual interview sessions. I would keep this sequence for the individual interviews (talk-aloud, mapping, movement), because the students' comments indicated that the kinesthetic task was difficult even after repeated listenings. If that is the case, then how difficult would it be for the students to create movements after only one listening to a musical excerpt? In a classroom or rehearsal setting that is not a research setting for individual student interviews, however, I encourage you to follow what I believe to be a stronger (and theoretically based) lesson sequence: placing the music listening movement sequence (enactive) prior to the mapping (iconic) or talking-aloud/verbal description (symbolic) experiences (Bruner 1966).

STRATEGIES FOR TEACHING AND LEARNING WITH MOVEMENT

In my teaching and research experience, I have approached classroom movement during music listening experiences with the expectation that everyone will participate. If a teacher goes into the movement portion of a music lesson or rehearsal with that expectation (expressed verbally and nonverbally), then the students will typically participate in some capacity. Invite participation without begging, bribing, or bullying, for these tactics inevitably fail and weaken your position as leader-facilitator. Invite the students to participate in the movement experience by using inclusive language ("Let's..," We're ...," "We...").

As I mentioned in chapter 2, students should have the opportunity to determine whether or not they participate by responding to the teacher's invitation in one of three ways: (1) "Yes, thank you," (2) "No, thank you," or (3) "Not right now, thank you." Designate a "safe space" in your classroom or rehearsal room where students can go to watch and observe without fear of punishment if they decide not participate in the movement experience. Give the option for these students to do the movements by themselves, as they sit or stand outside of the movement area.

The students need to know that not participating in classroom experiences is only temporary. Perhaps they have a valid excuse for not participating on a particular day. Perhaps they want to observe others first. But maybe they refuse to participate each time. The teacher and, most effectively, the students must determine what the protocol is for participating, for not participating, and for returning to the status of "participating student" after observing from the safe space. I have found that the newness of incorporating movement into music classes can be intimidating to students, especially for the often self-conscious secondary school students. As in any music class or rehearsal, developing a culture of respect, courtesy, compassion, and expectation are key to successful lessons.

TEACHER BEHAVIORS

There are three categories of teacher behaviors that can either support or sabotage movement experiences during music listening: (1) verbal language, (2) nonverbal language, and (3) planning. The examples provide a means for you to engage with and motivate your students during their movement experiences (and other musical behaviors).

Language that Supports Movement Experiences

Try using inclusive language to show that you and the students are working together to kinesthetically express musical sound.

> "Let's try something new today. This is new for us in this particular class, but let's try it. We are doing the movement so that we can listen to music in an attentive, meaningful way."
> "We will now explore some ways we can move our bodies in one space and in a variety of spaces in our music room."
> "Let's get into our personal spaces in the room and get ready to put some movements to the music we'll listen to."

Typically, I describe movement experiences as just that—creating movements and gestures that express and represent musical sound. Using the word *dance* to describe movement experiences can conjure up something embarrassing (i.e., something that they are reluctant to do), while the word *free-form* sounds like an invitation in the students' minds to move in a way that is not necessarily connected to the music.

Language that Sabotages Movement Experiences

Teacher language that suggests movement is "silly" or "embarrassing" plants or reinforces doubts that students might have about participating in movement experiences. Similarly, suggesting that the class will return to "doing something they like after the movement experience" erases the possibility that students will enjoy the movement experience. "If, then" statements provide temporary motivation for participation, but rarely intrinsically motivate students as a long-term goal.

> "We'll all look a bit funny, but..."
> "I know this will be a bit strange, but if you do it, we'll do something you like to do afterwards."
> "I know this will be a bit embarrassing, but you'll get used to it after awhile..."
> "I know. I feel funny doing movement like this, too, but let's do it together anyway. We can be silly together..."
> "You must participate; there is no discussion it."

Body Language that Supports Movement Experience

Teachers' body language can send supportive messages that encourage students to take risks and to participate in movement experiences in music class. Positive body language cues that facilitate movement are included in the following list.

- Teacher actively and enthusiastically participates in the kinesthetic tasks with the students.
- Teacher demonstrates the movements and gestures before having the students try them. You might call it "practice time" before you and the students place the movements in the context of the musical example.
- Teacher demonstrates the movements as expressive representations of musical sound.
- Teacher makes eye contact with students while performing the movement sequence.

Body Language that Sabotages Movement Experience

In addition to verbal communication—the words we use—our body positioning and posture can also suggest that we, ourselves, are uncomfortable or not committed to the expectation that all students will participate. The following list illustrates this point.

- Teacher demonstrates hesitancy and timidity in demonstrating the movements.
- Teacher tells students about the movements they will do, rather than demonstrating the movements.
- Teacher does not participate while students do the movements.

- Teacher maintains a "closed" body posture during instruction (i.e., crossed arms, standing at the front of the class, hands on hips/in pockets; lack of energized and committed movements as the listening excerpt is heard).
- Teacher lacks eye contact and does not monitor students' movements/gestures.
- Teacher lacks nonverbal (or verbal) reinforcement and encouragement during the movement sequence.

Teacher Preparation that Supports Movement Experience

Music teachers that implement successful (and fun!) movement experiences in their classrooms or rehearsals make the process look easy. However, the class engaging in the movement experiences is the product of careful planning prior to the lesson. Here are some helpful tips for including movement experiences with your students.

- Teacher clears area of classroom in which movement can occur. Teacher also considers the physical space for movement and plans the type of movement (i.e., locomotor or nonlocomotor) accordingly.
- Teacher selects a musical excerpt that is 1.5 to 2 minutes in length. Age consideration for the length of the movement sequence is essential.
- Teacher plans for the movement sequence portion of the lesson that is age-appropriate (approximately 10 minutes for older students). This time includes learning the movement sequence, placing into the music listening context, and brief discussion per class period.
- Teacher designs movement sequences that include repetition, so that the experience does not seem like dance choreography.
- Teacher firmly knows the movement sequence order.
- Teacher plans for the presentation of the movement sequence (exploration, creation/editing, performance, and reflection/assessment).

Teacher Preparation that Sabotages Movement Experience

There are many elements of the movement and listening experience to consider that are well beyond the actual teaching and learning strategies students experience. Here are examples of small, but significant, oversights in planning that can impede movement experiences in a classroom or rehearsal.

- Teacher is uncertain of movement sequence (i.e., actual movements, order).
- Teacher has not practiced the movement sequence prior to introducing it to the class.

- Room arrangement includes clutter, lack of movement space, or potentially dangerous set-up.
- Teacher has too many movements/gestures in a movement sequence.
- Teacher selects a musical excerpt that is too long.
- Teacher has not carefully thought through the presentation of the movement task (exploration, creation/editing, performance, and reflection/assessment).

FOUR PHASES FOR INCORPORATING MOVEMENT

There are four primary steps in the music listening movement procedure: *exploration, creation/editing, implementation,* and *reflection/assessment.* These procedures for using movement as a pedagogical tool are ones that I have found successful in classroom situations; however, I encourage you to adapt procedures to fit your own style of speaking, questioning, and interacting with students, whether in your music classroom or a rehearsal setting.

Exploration

While students naturally move to music, it is helpful for teachers to work with students to develop a "movement vocabulary" from which they might choose movements or gestures in creating their own kinesthetic expressions and representations. In fact, exploring movement as an introduction to incorporating movement experience in the music classroom helps alleviate or minimize student self-consciousness or fear of the unknown. Thus, students can become comfortable using their bodies for expressive purposes. Note: I approach movement as expressive movement, not as a choreographed dance, although learning actual dances can bring vitality to the music classroom, too. I encourage teachers to present students with opportunities to view recordings or live performances of people moving their bodies in a variety of dances (including popular forms of dance), in a variety of cultural contexts.

Over the course of several classes, perhaps only a few minutes per class and not initially using music, have the students explore:

- Movement planes (high, medium, low)
- Shapes/objects (angular, pointy, jagged, smooth, round, soft, melting ice cream, tree blowing, sumo wrestler, snake, popcorn, raindrops)
- Tempo/speed (fast, medium, slow)
- Space (locomotor—walk, skip, gallop, slide, high-step, dance; nonlocomotor—sit, stand, bend, twist, turn in circle, stretch, jump, pose)
- Body parts: gross motor (arms, legs, knees, waist, symmetrical, asymmetrical) and fine motor (fingers, feet, toes, nose, mouth, head, hand)

I recommend using music soon after introducing the movement exploration stage, for students need to make the connection between music and the expressive movements they perform. The exploration stage sets the tone for teacher- and student-generated movement sequences that are intentional, thoughtful, and musically expressive, rather than random body movements that are disconnected from musical sound and experience.

Creation/Editing

The goal of creating a teacher-generated movement sequence is to highlight a few musical events as they occur in a music listening example. The movements (i.e., plane, shape, tempo, space, body parts) should be appropriately designed for each musical event and include repetition. For example, a fast *legato* melody might best be depicted using small, quick, smooth pointer-finger motions rather than using asymmetrical, nonlocomotor, full-body gestures. The same movement, then, should be used each time the fast *legato* melody occurs in the music listening excerpt.

Movement sequence creation can also be a collaborative process between teacher and students. Invite the students to offer alternative movements, and their musical rationale for them, in order to edit the teacher-generated sequence that you presented. After you and the students perform a "draft" movement sequence, ask, "Were there any movements that did not seem to fit the music? Show me which one(s)." Work with one movement at a time, as suggested by the students. Probe their rationale for wanting a replacement movement: "Why do you think that particular movement did not best express or capture the music?" Together, you and the students decide the best fit for the music and collaboratively shift the movement sequence from being teacher-generated to class-generated.

As you monitor the creation of small-group (student-generated) movement sequences, sculptures, and montages, offer questions regarding the students' movement choices. For example, you might say, "I am noticing quick foot movements in this section of music. Tell me what in the music led you to this decision." Perhaps the students will have specific reasons for their movement decisions. In the event they do not, however, try offering verbal prompts such as, "I wonder if the quick foot movement actually captures the music here. Might there be other possibilities that best capture the music at this point of the listening excerpt? See what you can figure out." In other words, provide students with verbal feedback without making actual suggestions or becoming the decision maker. It is easy for us to jump in and "save the day" when students are puzzled or suggest they "don't know what to do." Instead, encourage them to continue exploring, creating, and editing. Allow them to experience the messiness that can accompany creativity and reassure them that they can be successful.

Implementation

In presenting teacher-generated movement sequences, I use an approach similar to presenting teacher-generated music listening maps (chapter 4). First, have a practice time during which you preview the movements the students will be doing as they listen to music. Without the music, demonstrate a few key movements from the sequence and have the students imitate, similar to echo singing or echo clapping. After the practice time, ask the students to "describe how the music might sound, given the movements we have practiced. What type of music do you expect to hear considering the type of movements that will be used in our sequence to express something about the music?" This gives the students the opportunity to speculate, imagine, anticipate, and practice inner thinking/hearing of sound. Record the students' verbal responses on a chalkboard or white board for a debriefing conversation after the music listening and movement experiences.

Next, pose a focus question to the class immediately prior to performing the music sequence with them: "As you listen to the music, what about our movements shows how the music sounds?" Then, invite the students to join you in "performing" the movement sequence. I use the term "performing" because I want to reinforce the musical flow and connection between the expressive movements and the music, rather than simply "doing" random, disconnected movements.

To implement student-generated movement experiences, provide space for each group to do its movement sequence, sculpture, or montage. As one group performs its movements to the music, the other students observe and try to discern "what about the music the group captured in its movements?"

Students reluctant about the movement experience might simply be fearful of their peers' opinions of them as they attempt to do something new. Therefore, try having the students sit in their seats and close their eyes in order to eliminate some of the self-consciousness and any other distractions that may occur in the class. On the other hand, some students might giggle or laugh while doing the movements, perhaps as "nervous laughter" or because they are enjoying the experience. Reassure the students that it is okay to have fun! Unless the laughter is maliciously directed toward another student, acknowledge it (nonverbally) and continue with the movement sequence.

Reflection/Assessment

Immediately after performance of a teacher-generated or small-group movement sequence, sculpture, or montage, have the class revisit the original focus questions: "What about our movements shows how the music sounds?" and "What about the music did the group capture in its movements?" Compare the students' anticipatory responses to the responses they offer after having performed or observed others perform movement sequences, sculptures, or montages.

Encourage dialog between the student observers and small-group performers. You might act as moderator, depending on the students' ability to initiate discussion among themselves. Of course, the older the students, the easier it is to facilitate a discussion. Yet, even young students are able to compare, contrast, and reflect using their own words.

Another option for initiating discussion among students is to have them jot down what musically they think each group captured in its performance. After all of the groups have performed, have the students create a list of similarities and differences: What about the music did all/no groups depict? What about the music did most/few groups depict? Were there any similar ways in which the groups depicted these musical features? Were there any unique ways that the groups depicted these musical features? Lead the students in speculating why all/most musical groups depicted certain musical features versus the least depicted musical features. Also, take the opportunity to discuss decision making (e.g., what to include/exclude in the movement sequence, sculpture, montage; choice of movement; group member roles) and the reality that every person listens to and responds differently to music. These types of questions and prompts assist students in developing not only their music thinking and listening skills but also their group-learning, metacognition, critical thinking, and reflective thinking skills.

IDEAS FOR MOVEMENT LESSONS

Lesson 1: *Also Sprach Zarathustra*: "Sunrise" (Strauss)

Observe the North Ridgeville Middle School perform a music listening sequence while listening to "Sunrise" (Strauss). Go to the Companion Website and click Video 3.4.

Since I have presented a description earlier in this chapter (see "Observing a Sixth-Grade General Music Class"), only the actual movement sequence descriptions are given here.

- (Organ): Begin in a squat position; fingers tapping on the floor
- (Do-sol-do): Squat (hands on knees), stand, stand with arms extended over heard (feel free to add the do-sol-do hand signs with each corresponding movement)
- (Cymbals): Arms explode upward in a circular motion
- (Timpani): Feet jog and then march

After third repetition (beginning with the do-sol-do movements), continue with:

- Right arm curve, left arm curve
- (Trumpet): Hands move upward following melodic contour

- (Trombone): Arms extended at shoulder-height and descend with arm motions pointing outward; add timpani part by jogging/marching in place
- Arch one arm outward; arch the other arm outward
- (Cymbal, final chord): jump; large, complete body shake
- (*Subito piano*): Small, crouched complete body shake
- (Crescendo): Growing large, complete body shake
- (Organ): End in a squat position, fingers tapping on the floor

Lesson 2: "Saqsahumanpi/Valicha" (Andean Folk Song)

Observe Northwood middle-schoolers perform dance steps while listening to "Saqsahumanpi." Go to the Companion Website and click Video 3.6.

Caitlin Roseum, graduate of the Oberlin Conservatory's Master of Music Teaching program, designed and taught this lesson to a group of twenty-five sixth-grade students in a general music class. The class period lasted for approximately fifty-five minutes. At the time of this lesson, Caitlin was in the secondary school music-methods class that I taught at the Oberlin Conservatory. We visited this class weekly during the spring semester as our teaching laboratory setting for the methods class.

Caitlin used a music listening map and video excerpt (found on YouTube) of the "Saqsahumanpi"/*Valiche* dance as experiences leading up to her teaching the movement portion of the lesson. However, as you will see from Caitlin's lesson, she does not merely teach a movement sequence; rather, she creates and uses an adaptation of an actual Peruvian folk dance. Therefore, notice the deviation from the "implementation" procedure described earlier, since she is not teaching a movement sequence. There was limited area in the classroom for movement experiences, so Caitlin used two rows of risers on which the students executed many of the movements. Her lesson reflection (Roseum, 2011) appears in chapter 2.

Thomas Turino (2008, x) described the "Saqsahumanpi"/*Valiche* music as a "folkloric style of Andean music developed for nightclub, folk club, and festival presentational performance." The music is typically played on the bombo (drum), the guitar, and kena (Andean flute). "Saqsahumanpi"/*Valiche* is characterized as music having sectional contrasts between the various instruments. Here is a portion of Caitlin's lesson plan (Roseum, 2011):

> *Grade Level:*Sixth-Grade General Music*Musical Concepts:* Tone color, instruments of Peru, traditional *Valicha* phrases and movement
> *National Standards for Arts Education* (Music Content Standards):
> ...
> 6. Listening to, analyzing, and describing music

8. Understanding relationships between music, the other arts, and disciplines outside the arts

9. Understanding music in relation to history and culture

Students' Prior Knowledge: tone color, steady beat, movement (at seats), music listening mapping.

Materials Needed for Lesson: Scarves/ties for dance, *charango* (member of lute family) (or picture of it),*Kena* (Andean flute) or picture of it, world map/map of South America, CD of music, YouTube videos of dance, projector (and cords), computer (and cords), speaker (and cords)

Observable Learning Outcomes/Objectives:
Students will be able to:
1. Recognize the different tone colors of the *charango* and the Andean flute.
2. Identify phrasing and "chunks" within "Saqsahumanpi"/*Valicha*.
3. Coordinate gross motor movements required to perform the traditional *Valicha* dance (modified).

Teaching Procedures/Student Active Engagement
Introduction
*This is a very famous dance in Peru. It has been passed down since the Inca people inhabited the area.

*Raise your hand if you have heard of the Inca or the Incan empire.

Question: "Who knows in what time period the Inca people were in power in South America?" (between the years 1200 and 1450)

*As I teach the dance steps, you might notice that not all of them are the same as the video we just watched, but that's because just like the song itself, the dance has many different versions because it's been around for so long.

Teach Dance Movements
*Your feet will be doing this basic step: "Short-short-long, short-short-long." Let's say that together, "Short-short-long, short-short-long." This is the pattern your feet will use for almost the entire dance! (Demonstrate feet.) Instead of saying, "Short-short-long, short-short-long, we will say, "1+2 3+4". Your turn, ready go.

*Our arms will be moving along to the music with these scarves.

Question: "Thinking about the instruments that we learned about today, which instrument would best represent our feet? Our arms?" (feet are rhythmic like the *charango* and arms are flowing like the flute or voice and melody)

*You'll also notice that the phrases in this piece and this dance might feel different than the phrases in songs you dance to at home. Our movements are 12 beats long, usually with a pause in the middle to change to the next move.

Lesson 3: *The Four Seasons*, "Autumn" (Vivaldi)

⊳ Observe Pleasant Elementary School kindergarteners engaged in movement while listening to "Autumn" (Vivaldi). Go to the Companion Website and click Video 3.7.

The focus of this kindergarten lesson is short and long sounds and movements. Have students sit in a circle, on risers, or in chairs (whatever is best in your physical space).

> *Question:* "Who could show me an example of a sound you can make with your voice that sounds 'short' ('long')? I'll take three ideas; remember to raise your hands."
> *Question:* "Who could show me an example of a way to move your body that is a quick, short (long) movement? I'll take three ideas; remember to raise your hands."

• Echo short-short-short-LONG-short-short. (Tap two fingers in palm of hand on "short"; hands clap and top hand is sent forward in front of body.) Practice saying and doing arm/hand motion.
• Teacher demonstrates the phrase shape (i.e., each "short" becoming gradually louder and leading to the "long" then becoming softer on the last two "short" statements). Teacher demonstrates the phrase with each "short" and "long" being equal in volume.

> *Question (before the teacher does the demonstrations):* "What is the difference between the two ways I performed, 'Short-short-short-short-LONG-short-short' "?

• Students and teacher practices saying and performing the rhythm with the phrase shape.
• Perform movement with the music, while also saying "short-short-short-short-LONG-short-short."
• Perform movement with the music, without saying "short" and "long.

Lesson 4: Symphony #7 in A Major, "Allegretto," Movement 2 (Beethoven)

⊳ Observe a Norwalk High School music appreciation class "pass the phrase." Go to the Companion Website and click Video 3.8.

The focus of this elective high school music-appreciation class was how composers build tension and excitement in music through beat/pulse/rhythm, repetition, dynamics, and long, seamless phrases. The rhythmic motive of Beethoven's Symphony #7, movement 2, was used to illustrate how this occurs in music. (This particular movement experience comes from a Dalcroze Eurhythmic training workshop that I experienced.) Since my visit to the music appreciation class occurred early in the school year, this portion of the lesson represented the students' first movement experience in the course.

- Students and teacher tap steady pulse on chest. Focus on maintaining a slow steady pulse.
- Teacher claps quarter-eighth-eighth-quarter-quarter rhythm (the primary motivic rhythm of the symphony's second movement); students echo the rhythm.
- Students stand in two rows facing each other.
- Students practice "passing" the full rhythmic motive to the next person in line, until every person has clapped it. Remind the students that there is no "wait-time" between people. If students have difficulty, have them count out loud (1 2 + 3 4) while clapping and passing the rhythm.
- Students practice passing the motivic rhythm from one student to the next in line; with each person's clapping of the rhythm, the dynamic level increases (*pianissimo* to *fortissimo*).
- Teacher focus directive: "As we listen to the music, raise your hand when you hear the rhythmic motive."
- Listen to the music. (After students raise hands in recognition of the rhythmic motive, invite students to tap the rhythm along with the listening excerpt.)

Lesson 5: "Chugoku-Chiho no Komoriuto" (Japanese Children's Song)

▶ Observe Prospect Elementary students engaged in movement. Go to the Companion Website and click Video 3.9.

In prior classes, the students and teacher had learned a Japanese poem and song. To build upon those experiences, I designed a lesson involving the piece, "Chugoku-Chiho no Komoriuto," (instrumental version) and pictures of the Japanese *koto* and *shakuhachi*. The focus of the movement experience was to highlight the Japanese instrumental timbres and, ultimately, their role in creating texture. We also discussed how performers produce sounds on each of the instruments. The movement experience preceded the students mapping the same piece of music.

- Students are seated for the movement experience.
- Students echo teacher who moves fist from low to high position. Tell students that this movement represents one instrument in the piece of music they will listen to. (Small *koto*)
- Students echo teacher: use pointer finger of one hand and pluck high, then low pluck, low pluck, high pluck (quarter, eighth-eighth, quarter, eighth-eighth, etc.). This movement represents the second musical instrument in the listening example. (Large *koto*)
- Finally, students echo teacher: use pointer finger to draw a high, wavy line. This movement represents the third musical instrument in the listening example. (*Shakuhachi*)
- *Question*: "Which instruments will you be hearing if you see this?" Teacher simultaneously performs the movements for instruments #1 and #3.
- Students practice doing movement for instrument #1 in one hand and instrument #2 in the other hand.
- *Question*: "Which instruments will you be hearing if you see this? Same or different from what we just practiced?" The teacher simultaneously performs the movements for instruments #1 and #2.
- Students practice doing movement for instrument #1 in one hand and instrument #2 in the other hand.
- Students echo teacher performing different combinations of movements to represent the three instruments.
- Listen to music and perform movements with teacher.
- Repeat listening. Divide class into two sections. One side of the class performs the *koto* motion; the other side performs the *shakuhachi* movement. Switch parts.
- Repeat listening. Invite students to show teacher which instrument they are focusing on. Remind students that they can change their focus any time during the music listening.
- *Question*: "Raise your hand if you stayed with the high *koto*, low *koto*, or *shakuhachi* for the entire time. Raise your hand if you listened to two instruments. Raise your hand if you listened to all three instruments at some time or another." (Students often feel challenged to depict two or three instruments simultaneously!)

YOUR TURN

Now that you have read this chapter, reflect on its content, your personal comfort level with music and movement, and the movement experiences you have already implemented in your classroom or rehearsal space. These prompting questions might help you engage and focus your reflective thinking skills.

1. What are at least three theoretical points presented in this chapter that you will incorporate into your use of movement in class or rehearsal? What will they look like in your classroom?

2. What are at least two pedagogical points or shifts of mind that you will incorporate into your teaching? What will they look like in your classroom?

3. What are your personal fears about movement? How comfortable are you moving your body through space and time? How will this comfort level impact your students' willingness to participate and to take a risk in doing something new in the classroom or rehearsal space? What is your plan for infusing small, gradual movement/gestures into your music classroom?

4. Now that you have tried or added to your existing movement experiences, what have you learned by observing your students? How could you learn more about their music listening experiences? What are your wonderments about the connection between the body-mind-feeling-spirit entity and musical sound? How might you explore (i.e., research) your observations and anecdotes in a systematic manner?

REFERENCES

Bamberger, J. (1999). "Learning from Children We Teach." *Bulletin of the Council for Research in Music Education* 142: 48–74.

Black, J., and S. Moore (2003). *The Rhythm Inside: Connecting Body, Mind, and Spirit Through Music*. Van Nuys, CA: Alfred.

Bruner, J. (1966). *Toward a Theory of Instruction*. Cambridge, MA: Belknap.

Chen, J., V. Penhune, and R. Zattore (2008). "Listening to Musical Rhythms Recruits Motor Regions of the Brain." *Cerebral Cortex* 18(12): 2844–54.

Dalcroze, J. E. (1921/1980). *Rhythm, Music and Education* (trans. H. Rubinstein). London, UK: Dalcroze Society.

Dura, M. (2002). *Music Education and the Music Listening Experience*. Lewiston, NY: Edwin Mellen.

Ebie, B. (2004). "The Effects of Verbal, Vocally Modeled, Kinesthetic, and Audio-visual Treatment Conditions on Male and Female Middle-School Vocal Music Students' Abilities to Expressively Sing Melodies." *Psychology of Music* 32(4): 405–17.

Oxford Dictionaries. "Embody" Retrieved February 7, 2012, http://oxforddictionaries.com/definition/embody.

Gardner, H. (1983). *Frames of Mind*. New York: Basic Books.

Joseph, A. (1982). "A Dalcroze Eurhythmics Approach to Music Learning in Kindergarten through Rhythmic Movement, Ear-training and Improvisation." Unpublished doctoral dissertation, Carnegie-Mellon University.

Juntunen, M., and L. Hyvönen (2004). "Embodiment in Musical Knowing: How Body Movement Facilitates Learning within Dalcroze Eurhythmics." *British Journal of Music Education* 21(2): 199–214.

Kerchner, J. L. (1996). "Perceptual and Affective Components of Music Listening Experience as Manifested in Children's Verbal, Visual, and Kinesthetic Representations." Unpublished doctoral dissertation, Northwestern University.

Kerchner, J. L. (2001). "Children's Verbal, Visual, and Kinesthetic Responses: Insight into Their Music Listening Experience." *Bulletin of the Council for Research in Music Education* 146: 35–51.

Kerchner, J. L. (2005). "A World of Sound to Know and Feel: Exploring Children's Verbal, Visual, and Kinesthetic Responses to Music." In *Music in Schools for All Children: From Research to Effective Practice*, edited by M. Mans and B. W. Leung, 21–33. Granada, Spain: University of Granada.

Leman, M., and R. Godøy (2010). "Why Study Musical Gestures?" In *Musical Gestures: Sound, Movement, and Meaning*, edited by R. Godøy and M. Leman, chap. 1. New York: Routledge.

Lindeman, C. (2011). *Musical Children: Engaging Children in Musical Experiences.* Upper Saddle River, NJ: Pearson Prentice-Hall.

Mead, V. (1994). *Dalcroze Eurhythmics in Today's Music Classroom.* New York: Schott.

Merleau-Ponty, M. (1962). *Phenomenology of Perception* (trans. by Colin Smith). London, UK: Routledge and Kegan Paul.

O'Hagin, I. B. (1998). "A Discovery Approach to Movement." *General Music Today,* 12(16), 16–20.

Roseum, C. (2011). "Lesson Plan and Reflection Assignments." Oberlin College.

Silver Burdett Ginn. (1995). The Music Connection, "Chikoku-Chiho No Komoriuta," Grade 8, CD #6, Track 5. Morristown, NJ: Silver Burdett Ginn, Inc.

Turino, T. (2008). *Music as Social Life: The Politics of Participation.* Chicago: University of Chicago Press.

Weikart, P. (1982). *Teaching Movement and Dance.* Ypsilanti, MI: High Scope Press.

CHAPTER 4

Listeners Mapping

Invented Notations

Standard musical notation is a visual (written) metaphor for musical sound in Western societies. It is a codified symbol system with its own syntax and semantics, which provides musical suggestion and direction for those wanting to perform, analyze, or create musical compositions. Yet, many music-making inhabitants around the world do not rely on learning, performing, or transmitting music and musical traditions by reading some form of written notation. Standard musical notation grants privileged status to those who understand it and can interpret it, while providing some people (usually composers) the tools to communicate their musical ideas. It is an externalized (written) analog of a composer's mental conception of musical sound that is, ultimately, given to performers to perform and audiences to listen to. Given the unique nature of musical experience, notation does not, and cannot, embody the complexity of a performer's, listener's, or composer's musical experience—the expressive, emotive, affective, interpretive, or even the technical aspects necessary to produce musical sound.

In my research and teaching, I have repeatedly heard children and adults label themselves as being "unmusical" simply because they cannot read or are not facile in reading standard musical notation. However, standard musical notation is not the only viable form of visually representing musical sound. Take a look at musical scores composed by John Cage, Karlheinz Stockhausen, and Hans-Christoph Steiner. They represent only a few composers who depict musical ideas by providing nonstandard notational, symbolic suggestions of how their music is to be performed.

For developing music students, reading, writing, and performing standard music notation can prohibit them from freely and intuitively engaging in and producing expressive musical sounds. I do not wish to enter the debate surrounding how much of the school music curriculum (if any or what proportion) should be devoted to teaching students to read standard musical notation in order to use this criterion as a marker of knowledge within the music domain. Instead, let me trace connections I have made between alternative notation systems, especially students' invented notations, and music listening mapping. Mapping is a tool teachers can use to focus students' attention while they listen to a music excerpt or to provide students with a means for expressing (at least in part) what they perceive and respond to when they listen to music.

As an intermediary step between learning music by rote (oral tradition) and reading standard Western music notation, a music teacher might ask students to create invented notations of sound in order to remember what they heard in a music listening excerpt or what they composed. This idea parallels the "invented spelling" strategy implemented by some teachers of reading and creative writing. Encouraging children to write holistically as they *hear* verbal sounds and discover actual spellings as needed are two aspects of the whole language approach (Goodman 1986) to reading and writing that re-emerged as a popular philosophy and methodology in the late 1980s and 1990s. "Whole language teachers believe that children *learn to read* [emphasis in original] by writing, and vice versa" (Bomengen 2010).

Students learn to speak by exploring verbal sounds and sound combinations, imitated by those who spend the most time interacting with them when they are babies, toddlers, and preschoolers. Children learn to speak words as whole units, rather than saying consonants separate from vowels or vowel combinations. When young children first attempt to write these sounds, they might create visual representations for word sounds using letters of an alphabet, even if the spelling is not the standard one for the word. Children represent sounds that have visual and aural meaning to *them*, rather than becoming bogged down with "correct" spellings that might inhibit their creative flow. For example, a child might write the letters "chre" on a piece of paper to represent the word *tree*. The child says the word and hears the "tr" consonant cluster as a "chr" actual sound combination. The vowels *ee* might be represented with only one *e*, since phonetically there is no difference in the sound of a single *e* and the double letters *ee*.

Working with the teacher, children are led to discover the traditional way of spelling a word and, thus, they learn to edit their writing. They grow into spelling and creative writing by experiencing a potpourri of sounds, creating symbols for representing sounds, and finding ways to communicate written ideas in a context meaningful to students, so that others who read the writing may share in its meaning.

Encouraging students to create invented notations of musical sound promotes the spirit behind children's being encouraged to first write their linguistic ideas using invented spellings. Thinking holistically, music teachers might similarly prompt young composers and listeners to find solutions for representing musical expression, pitches, rhythms, tempo, instruments, and other performance information related to their compositions or listening experiences. Adopting Bomengen's premise (2010) regarding students' invented spellings leading to learning traditional word spellings, it seems feasible that invented musical notations might be a step-ping stone toward children's learning to read standard musical notation.

Bamberger (1982), Upitis (1992), Barrett (1997, 1999, 2000, 2001, 2002, 2004), and Davidson, Scripp, and Welch (1988) are leaders in researching the relationships between musical sounds and children' (and adults') invented nota-tions of that sound. These researchers found that children composers' drawings, markings, and word combinations frequently depicted musical features that were typically rhythm and/or pitch based. Some (i.e., Bamberger; Upitis; and Davidson et al.) also suggested that children's invented symbol systems appear to progress along a developmental continuum. Children's reflexive reactions to musical sound (i.e., scribbles that young children create when music is heard) later develop into differentiated rhythmic and melodic groupings that approximate standard musical notation groupings of pitches and rhythms.

Bamberger (1991, 52) wrote that invented notations "hold still so that children can reflect on [them]. In a conversation back and forth between playing on the paper and looking back at the trace left behind, the children can learn about their own knowledge, their functioning knowledge, which ordinarily escapes scrutiny as it passes by in action and through time." Further, Bamberger (1991) and Upitis (1992) found two types of rhythmic groupings in children's invented notations of their compositions or other familiar songs—figural and metric. Figural representa-tions (groupings) most closely resemble the depiction of a natural, intuitive sense of musical phrasing and rhythmic grouping according to how the music "sounds." Metric representations, on the other hand, tend to denote actual rhythmic dura-tions, relationships between beat and its subdivisions, and metric groupings indica-tive of a musical measure in standard notation.

To illustrate students' invented notations of their compositions, let us take a look at three musical scores. My former second-grade general-music students were asked to create a brief composition using ABA (tertiary) form—a concept that we had experienced in music listening examples and songs we sang. Students worked in groups of three or four and used classroom rhythm and melody instruments of their choice in creating their compositions. While the students created their pieces, they were to "notate" the music so group members could remember and perform it for their peers in a subsequent class. Notice the developmental differentiation among the three scores. In figure 4.1, we observe nonspecific counting of musical events; figure 4.2 shows groupings, note durations, and expressive qualities; and figure 4.3 approximates standard notation but also includes counting, grouping, and expressive qualities.

First, take a look at the musical score written by Stephanie, Elizabeth, and Mary Kate (figure 4.1). As a part of their score, the students wrote the names of the instru-ments they played—egg shakers and cymbals— and the motion used in playing them. The arrows indicated the alternating hand motion used to produce sound on the various instruments. The number 8, written at the conclusion of the egg shaker

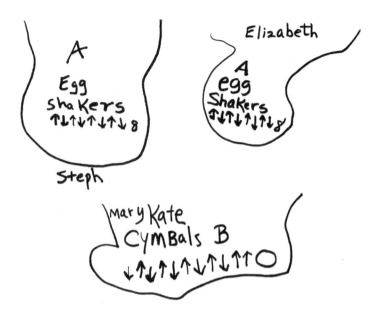

Figure 4.1.
Stephanie, Elizabeth, and Mary Kate's Musical Score.

arrows, indicates the number of times the students shook their instruments—a figural representation of how many times the music "should sound." While the markings did not indicate notational duration, the students did count the number of musical sounds they were to play per section of the composition. Mary Kate's cymbal part had more sound events than the other parts, and it concluded with a loud "bang" on the cymbals.

Jessie, Whitney, and Kelsey created a score in ABA form for two instruments—an egg shaker and cowbell (figure 4.2). Their map is set as a linear score, unlike figure 4.1 in which the students simply labeled who would play which rhythm and instrument in each of the three formal sections of their composition. Figure 4.2 includes the suggestion of metric grouping by the indication of longer and shorter durational note values and the slight separation of those groupings of lines that belong together. Additionally, the students added "S" and "L" to indicate pitch (i.e., sol and la) and tempo differences between the A and B sections of the composition.

Finally, consider Lauren and Catherine's musical score (figure 4.3). While it is set as a linear progression (the A section first, then the B section), the notation of the final A section is not included in the score. But under her name, Lauren noted that the A section occurs twice and is to be played with claves. Catherine's recorder part, like Lauren's claves part, showed the students counting the number of sound events to play, groupings of the sounds, and relative note durations. The students wrote a figural representation of a score using standard notation, yet there was no indication of meter. They also showed expressive qualities (dynamics) and

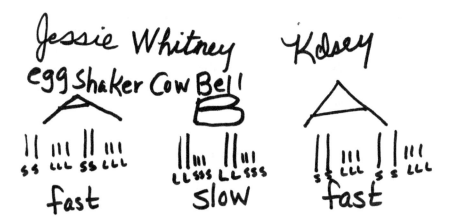

Figure 4.2.
Jessie, Whitney, and Kelsey's Musical Score.

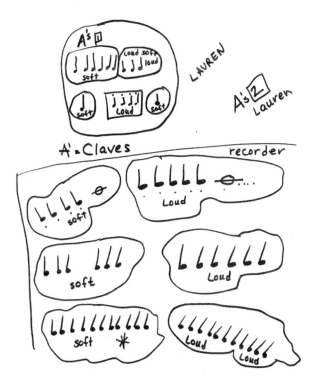

Figure 4.3.
Lauren and Catherine's Musical Score.

articulation (*staccato* markings to indicate short musical sounds). Even though Catherine played various pitches with her rhythms during section B, there was no pitch indication on the score. The students assigned their own meanings to that which initially appeared as standard musical notation; it is semi-invented (counting number of events, relative note duration, and grouping) and semi-standard (using symbols of standard notation and staccato marks).

MUSIC LISTENING MAPS DEFINED

A variation on children's invented notations for their compositions, then, is a music listening map that contains nonstandard, alternative music symbols to represent features of a music listening example. Mary Helen Richards was the early music education pioneer who, in the late 1960s and 1970s, introduced maps to the music education profession. The first maps contained directions for teacher-generated movements and phrase movements for folk-song games that children played in music and general-education elementary school classes. The maps typically captured the melodic flow of folk songs and were used only after students were comfortable singing the song, moving to the song, and playing games based on the song. Children were also encouraged to create their own versions of song maps, thereby creating and pointing to their own symbolic representations as they sang a folk song. About maps, Richards (1978, 29) said, "It is play … It is symbol … It is music."

Observe Oberlin Conservatory Preschool MusicPlay students follow and add onto song maps of "Fly Away Little Birdie" and read music listening maps to "O fortuna" (Orff: *Carmina Burana*). Click on Video 4.1.

Music listening maps consist of pictures, graphs, shapes, words, and lines that are created and "performed" as one listens to music repeatedly and in "real time." I use the phrase "performing a music listening map" to suggest the manner in which students and teachers might consider pointing to their maps as they listen to a musical example. While mapping is an aural and visual experience, it is also a kinesthetic and musical one. For teachers, performing listening maps is not only an opportunity to reflect musical nuance but also a way to guide students' eye-to-symbol coordination in their reading of musical notation. Therefore, I encourage map performers to point to the various symbols in a way that indicates forward motion inspired by the spirit of the musical example, rather than simply dropping a finger on a symbol and letting it rest. Performing a map should be visually and kinesthetically musical, fluid, and continuous, since one can use many visual cues (including the hands and body) to communicate the nature of what he or she might experience during music listening.

Maps cannot, and should not, depict all of the many details of a musical example. Instead, maps show visual chunks of music that do not represent a one-to-one correspondence between sound and symbol. Since music moves through time and space, it is not feasible to create a symbol for every musical event. Therefore, listening maps are considered "conceptual" in content. For example, a picture or shape on a map might represent a section of music or several pitch- or rhythm-related events, instead of a single pitch or note duration. Two broad categories of music listening maps—*teacher-generated* and *student-generated*—will be presented and explored in this chapter.

Miller (1986) described a teacher-generated listening map as "a valuable teaching aid for the music-listening lesson because it visually represents exactly where musical events take place, making it easier for children to understand musical relationships, especially regarding balance and contrast" among other musical features that can be depicted. The younger the music student, the simpler the music listening map should be. I would recommend focusing the students' attention on only a few musical events or concepts per map. For example, suppose a teacher would like students to focus on melodic contour. The teacher might create a music listening map of wavy lines and curves to represent the pitches moving up and down. As the teacher points to the music listening map, students follow the teacher's hand or pencil tracing the symbols that coordinate with the melodic contour of the music listening example to which they are simultaneously listening.

Student-generated music listening maps are students' visual depictions of musical features from their listening experience. Students create pictures, symbols, markings, lines, graphs, or words to represent their unique music listening experiences—what the students are thinking, feeling, and hearing as they listen to music. The process of creating a map and performing it assists teachers in understanding individual students' perceptual and affective responses and what naturally captivates their focus of attention. Students become informants of their listening experiences.

From a constructivist perspective, student-generated maps can also provide teachers insight into "where the students are" in terms of their focus of attention, cognitive abilities, and progress toward developing, refining, elaborating, and reflecting on "new features" that are discovered in the music during repeated listenings. Similar to the whole language approach, teachers can base subsequent curricular experiences on the information students initially provide in their maps: the introduction of new musical vocabulary; a discussion or debate of "mystery" instrumental timbres; an introduction to standard musical notation, melodic contour, harmony, and other properties of musical sound; or a means of comparing and contrasting musical styles and genres from around the world.

The "free-style" (student-generated) mapping process is usually successful only after the teacher provides music-listening mapping models that the full class experiences together. Teachers can create their own music listening maps, use those found later in this chapter, view piano-roll notation in music software such as GarageBand, or utilize maps found in general music basal text series, grades K–6, as mapping resources. Experiencing these mapping models from prior music listening experiences in class provides concrete examples upon which students can draw as they create their own listening maps of familiar or unfamiliar pieces of music or songs.

The two types of music listening maps featured in this chapter are dotting and ideographs. Both could be implemented in general music classrooms or ensemble settings as teacher-generated or student-generated visual representations of music listening excerpts or songs. The use of mapping in ensemble rehearsal settings will be the topic of chapter 6.

Dotting is notation that represents the number of sound events, usually of a children's folk song or other melody that students know or will learn (see Bennett and Bartholomew 1997). Children and teachers point to one dot per syllable of the song or per note of a melody in an instrumental listening example in order to "perform" the map. Figure 4.4 shows a dotting map for "Row, Row, Row Your Boat." Try singing the song and pointing to each dot for each text syllable.

Dotting is an excellent "pre-reading" strategy for pre-school and elementary school students. Teachers can use dotting to introduce students to visual symbols that represent musical sounds and to have students practice coordinating sound, sight, and symbol by reading "the dots." Even for older elementary, middle, or high school students, dotting can be employed as a strategy for introducing the concept of mapping and notation—creating or using any symbol to represent sounds. Dotting a simple song or part of a song can help take the mystery out of reading music notation.

Ideographs consist of pictures or other symbols to represent chunks of sound—patterns, phrases, formal sections. Unlike dotting maps, ideographs represent several sound events or musical concepts rather than individual sounds of a song or instrumental melody. Further, the same or similar musical events are represented by the same symbol on the map. Figure 4.5 is an ideograph for "Row, Row, Row Your Boat"; it indicates phrases and phrase parts (two pictures per phrase).

Ideographs do not only have to show pictures of song lyrics or music program content. They can depict curvy or jagged lines or "graphs" of the music, drawn in a linear fashion (i.e., the chronological order in which the musical events occur), or they can be nonlinear (i.e., invented notations that do not necessarily appear in chronological order, but are "performed" by the student or teacher in the order dictated by the music). Ideograph maps can also contain written words or combinations of standard and invented notations to represent musical sound. Not all ideographs depict the most prominent features of the music. Imagine designing a map that highlights an accompanimental figure or background rhythm. Ideographs

Figure 4.4.
Dotting for "Row, Row, Row, Your Boat."

Row, row...

gently down the stream;

Merrily....

life is but a dream.

Figure 4.5.
Ideograph of "Row, Row, Row Your Boat."

can encourage students to delve into all parts of the music—foreground and background. (For examples of student-generated ideographs, see figures 4.7 through 4.10 in the next section of this chapter.)

Like dotting, ideographs can also be used with PK–12 students. The younger the students, the simpler the ideograph must be. Even for older students, music listening maps must be visually appealing and uncluttered; simplicity is key to creating and following mapping symbols. Ideographs can be used as a "pre-standard-notation-reading" event. Showing different ways of notating (and reading) the same piece or portion of a piece of music can foster students' flexibility in representing and reading notation. Imagine showing students a wavy line to indicate melodic contour on a map and then showing them the melodic contour of the same melody written in standard notation. The comparisons of scores and maps, the amount of musical and performance detail shown on each, and reasons for using different types of notation are important issues for students to explore. Box 4.6 shows the primary features of music listening maps.

MAPPING IN ACTION

Before we consider the "how's and why's" of having students engage in creating music listening maps, let us view individual students' maps and listen to students in grades two, five, eight, and eleven describe the contents of the maps they created

---

Box 4.6
FEATURES OF A MUSIC LISTENING MAP

---

1. Nonstandard music notations that direct students' and teachers' attention to salient features of a particular musical excerpt.
2. Representations of students' (and/or teachers') thinking, feeling, hearing as they experience music by actively listening to it.
3. Visual chunks (groupings) of musical events.
4. Concept representation instead of one-to-one correspondence between notation and music sound events.
5. Invented symbols can include any markings, graphs, shapes, lines, words, and/or pictures.
6. Can be used for any PK-12 student in general music classes or rehearsal settings.
7. Can be teacher- or student-generated, or a combination of both.

---

relative to their music listening experiences. In my investigations, I played the roles of teacher and researcher, since these students were already in my music classes in public school and community music venues. What is presented here is the result of my interviewing individual students during two research sessions. In all cases, except for the group of middle-schoolers who listened to Copland's *Fanfare for the Common Man*, the students listened to an excerpt of the Bach's Brandenburg Concerto #2 in F Major, movement 1 (BWV 1047), approximately 2"20' in length. The first task was for the students to listen without doing any other task (listening to the "whole"). Then, I provided individual students with an 11 by 14-inch piece of paper and asked them to create a music listening map to show "what they are thinking, feeling, and hearing" as they repeatedly listened to that Bach excerpt (listening for "the parts" of music). With each listening and mapping experience, students used a different colored crayon or pen to draw, so that I could track their listening (and mapping) development over the course of repeated listenings. After the completion of the mapping task, I asked the students to describe verbally the content of their maps and then to "perform" their map (i.e., point to the markings) as they listened to the music (placing the symbols in the context of the "whole").

In this section are samples of the rich information embedded in the children's music listening maps and the developmental trends contained in these maps across grade levels. The individuals tell their stories, and I provide my interpretations of their maps and words. As you view the maps and read the students' music listening portraits, consider the wealth of information that might have remained unearthed if students only had the opportunity to describe the music listening example in verbal terms. Furthermore, ask yourself: What are the students telling us about how to teach music listening skill development? What rationale do the students' responses provide for implementing music listening mapping as a pedagogical strategy in classrooms and rehearsal settings? Would students respond in a similar manner if other musical styles and genres were presented? How might students' mapping and verbal responses be dependent on their musical abilities or musical training in or outside of school? Let's read, listen, and learn.

Listening to Margaret

Observe Margaret perform her music listening maps. Go to the Companion Website and click on Video 4.2.

Margaret was a second-grade female, age seven, who had been a student in my music class during her first- and second-grade years (Kerchner 1996). At the time of the interview, she had not received any extracurricular music performance instruction. Margaret's parents stated that she enjoyed listening to most styles of music, although she preferred classical and folk musics only slightly less than other musical styles. She typically listened to music each day, especially Broadway musical tunes. Margaret's musical preference might have been influenced by her familiarity with Broadway music, since her family reported that they frequently attended musical theater performances. As she listened to recordings of music, her parents noted that Margaret usually sang along with and danced to the songs. In fact, they explained that Margaret tried to sing along with the songs, even if she did not know the words. She also liked to "act out" scenes depicted in the songs' lyrics by dancing while she sang.

Margaret's focus of attention seemed captivated by instrumental timbres not only in the mapping task but also in her verbal reporting. On her first map (see figure 4.7), she drew a violin, trumpet, and flute. She also drew a drum and keyboard, even though these instruments were not part of the instrumental ensemble. Initially, I thought these instruments reflected Margaret's concept of beat or the continuo accompaniment; she might have incorrectly named the harpsichord as a keyboard, for example.

At the beginning of the pointing and listening task, however, Margaret's explanations of the instruments dismissed my original supposition. She told me that she would not be pointing to the drums, the keyboard, or the guitar because those instruments were not found in the musical excerpt. She explained that she included them on the map because she "just thought [she] wanted to make other instruments." Furthermore, she stated at the conclusion of the pointing and listening task, that she "forgot [to point to] the piano. I like the piano." When I asked her if she had heard the piano, she shook her head, "No," and replied, "But I wanted to point to it anyway!" Margaret was captivated by the nature of the mapping task and her preference for and perception of musical instruments. She consciously determined which instruments she would or would not include on the maps.

On her map, Margaret also included eighth-notes, a bow, a violinist, a guitar pick, and a conductor. Although she did not know the term for a bow, she used

Figure 4.7.
Margaret's First Music Listening Map

other means of verbally describing its purpose and how it was used. "It is the stick that makes the noise on the violin," she said. With that statement, Margaret placed a pretend violin under her chin. She continued, "This is the girl playing the violin." The eighth-notes did not correspond to a particular rhythm, but were Margaret's way of depicting musical sound produced by the instruments. As for the conductor, Margaret explained, "He's doing those things with the baton." Once again, she was at a loss for specific musical terms, yet she communicated her musical insight in her own terms.

Margaret's map from the second interview recounted the Christmas images (tree, carousel, ballerina, and presents) she had presented in her talk-aloud earlier in the second interview (see figure 4.8). There was no new information about the musical experience that she included in the actual drawings on the listening map. The verbal descriptions and performance of the map, however, shed light on Margaret's musical perception.

Margaret explained that she drew the ballerina because the musical excerpt reminded her of *The Nutcracker*, and she associated it with Christmas. During the final mapping session, Margaret continued to search for and compare the musical example to music she had encountered in prior listening experiences in order to determine its musical style.

The carousel also embodied musical significance. Margaret said she "drew the merry-go-round because in the music it sounded like going round and round." I interpreted this statement to reflect Margaret's awareness of the repetition of thematic material that occurred throughout the musical example. She supported

Figure 4.8.
Margaret's Second Music Listening Map.

this assumption when she sang the primary theme of the musical example as she attempted to explain the meaning of the carousel—an object moving in a circular direction, or music that "returned" throughout the musical example.

The role of various instruments was associated with the Christmas images contained in Margaret's second map, but I uncovered this relationship only as she performed her map. Since Margaret had not depicted any instruments on her second map, she pointed to the ballerina when she heard solo instruments and the carousel during *tutti* (full ensemble) sections of the music.

Perhaps the amount of information contained in Margaret's maps coincided with the fact that drawing was her favorite task. Her maps, and performance of and explanation of them, provided more tangible musical information than I gleaned from her verbal or kinesthetic representations. According to my observations of Margaret, she exhibited nonlinear thinking as she listened to the music. She primarily relayed pieces of global information, but not as they necessarily occurred sequentially in the music. Instead, she determined when to divulge information during the music listening tasks.

Comparing her maps from the first and second sessions, it appeared that the repeated listenings allowed Margaret to fill in the mental schematic gaps with perceptual detail that was ignored or unreported in her initial listenings and mappings. On her initial map, she included pictures of instruments, while in her performance of her second-session map, Margaret demonstrated her perception of music form. She pointed to her drawings in a manner that suggested her recognition of musical patterns, especially solo instrument and full ensemble sections, and thematic material that repeated throughout the musical example. About the repeated listenings, Margaret said, "Last time [the first interview session], I was thinking about the music. This time [second interview session] I was thinking about the music, but like the pictures of the music." To me, this statement confirmed that the musical elements Margaret perceived and depicted were closely related to the pictures and associations she had created on her second map. Additionally, her statement reinforced the notion that we listen with fresh minds and ears, recreating the music listening experience anew even with repeated listenings of the same musical excerpt.

Listening to Maribeth

▶ Observe Maribeth perform her music listening maps. Go to the Companion Website and click on Video 4.3 and Video 4.4.

Maribeth, the precocious fifth-grader we met in chapter 3, described the music she heard by creating elaborate stories related to the music (Kerchner 1996, 2001, 2005). Yet within the story plots was perceptual and affective information that connected the stories to the musical excerpt. Maribeth imagined herself as an integral character in each story—one of being royalty attending a ball and the other being a conductor of an orchestra. She mentioned that the music engaged her imagination as she created these stories verbally, visually, and kinesthetically. In fact, she said her imagination temporarily "removed her" from the interview setting and placed her in the actual stories she was creating while listening to the music. When I asked Maribeth what in the music helped her decide which story to create, she explained that "most of the things in the stories I've seen or done. Like I've been in a ballet. I've seen a ballet. I've seen a conductor on television. Most of this had to do with dancing." It seemed that she created the stories, in part, based on her personal life experiences, particularly her musical and dance experiences.

In the first mapping session (see figure 4.9), Maribeth wrote the word *classical* on her map; she later told me she had described the music that way because the rhythm of the melody reminded her of "running." She drew curved lines, a table and bowl, a lady, and musical notes, along with dots that she drew in conjunction with the steady beat of the music. In addition to the figures that related to her story, Maribeth's focus on the beat of the music became especially apparent during the presentation of primary thematic material in the listening example. Furthermore, she wrote the word *rhythm* on her map during the repeated trumpet figure. She also wrote the words *notes bunched* on the map.

Her second map from the interview (see figure 4.10) captured the mood of the music and displayed hints of affective response. She drew smiling, neutral, and sad faces and wrote words describing laughter and happiness. She also wrote the word

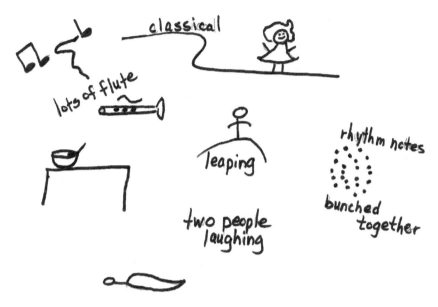

Figure 4.9.
Maribeth's First Music Listening Map.

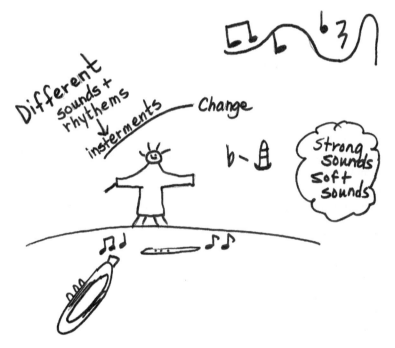

Figure 4.10.
Maribeth's Second Music Listening Map.

feeling on her map in the midst of the listening episode and *sadness* after the musical example had concluded. At the conclusion of the mapping, Maribeth told me that some of the music was sad, while the music in the beginning of the example (the primary theme) sounded like two people laughing. Similar to her first map, Maribeth noted that "some parts are stronger" as she listened to the trumpet solo and primary theme, an indication of rhythm and solo/*tutti* sections. She also reported that she heard a flute.

Before Maribeth performed the pointing and listening portion of the mapping task, she explained that she did not remember why she drew the horizontal lines. In order to remember, she "needed to hear it one more time." Furthermore, her comments reflected new musical events or associations that captured her attention with each additional listening. She remarked, "Some parts are mixed together 'cause when I heard it like twice, I heard rhythm the first time, and then the second time I heard people laughing as well." Her statement also suggested that rhythm was one of the musical features that evoked her imagination. During her verbal description of her map, she said, "You can actually hear the leaping and imagine leaping while it's [the sixteenth-note rhythm is] going on."

By observing Maribeth during the pointing and listening portion of the mapping task, I realized that her affective response was closely intertwined with the formal musical events that she depicted on her map. She differentiated between solo and *tutti* sections of music. It appeared that the primary thematic material and the *tutti* sections corresponded to Maribeth's notion of laughter, "notes bunched," and "stronger parts." Maribeth appeared to associate each solo instrumental part as having unique characteristics. She pointed to the word *sadness* during the flute solo, but pointed to the laughing people during the violin solo. During the oboe solo, she pointed to *notes bunched*. When the trumpet was the featured instrument, Maribeth pointed to the lady on the "classical path."

Although Maribeth said that the verbal, visual, and kinesthetic tasks might have interfered with her music listening experience, she also noted that mapping allowed her to "think on paper" more easily than when she was talking aloud or moving to the music listening excerpt. The following is what Maribeth had to say about performing her map. Notice that even though she found mapping to be an easy and efficient method for representing her music listening experience, she found that the map also required her to provide verbal explanations of her drawings and markings. She enjoyed the social—teaching—aspect of the mapping task.

> I'm not an artist, but I just think that I like drawing the map, because you can explain it by just motioning your hand. And . . . when you explain it, it's fun to teach someone what you're trying to do. But when you dance [create motions], they [the observer] understand it already. Most of the time they get it. And when you talk, they know what you're saying. So, I like drawing [the map] instead.

Maribeth continued to tell me that mapping best captured the essence of music "because you can really think. It's harder for me to think out loud. So when I, I can think and write it down and then talk about it, it is better." She conceded, however, that the talk-alouds and movements permitted her to describe specific musical events and create story details that the mapping task did not. Indeed, Maribeth's verbal descriptions of her map illuminated new perceptual and affective information that was not explicitly presented in the representations on her map.

When she heard unfamiliar music, Maribeth said her imagination was called into action. She said the music prompted her to concentrate more than she would have while listening to familiar music. Repeated listenings also imprinted the music into her mind, a fact about which she was displeased. She said that the music "stuck in her head" during the hours following the interview sessions. Additionally, she mentioned that she dreamed about similar music during the evening prior to the interview sessions.

Listening to Groups of Middle-Schoolers

▶   Observe the middle-schoolers perform their collaborative music listening maps. Go to the Companion Website and click on Video 4.5.

This is a tale of students at a middle school in rural Ohio (Kerchner 2009, 2010). The school hosts students who have parents affiliated with the local college and the 48 percent of the community designated as living in poverty. Although it is a small-town school district, it also demonstrates academic and social challenges indicative of larger, urban education settings.

I was asked to teach a secondary school general-music class at this school, a class of students not wanting to be in or not being wanted in the three existing musical offerings (i.e., the traditional band, chorus, and orchestra). There were forty-five students (forty-one of which were males) in the class that I ultimately divided into three sections of the course called Music Workshop. The number of students changed constantly, for students were suspended from school or were moved to a different town with a parent or guardian. School special services labeled most students in these classes as academically, socially, and/or behaviorally challenged, yet one or two were identified as gifted. For many, English was a non-native language. These students had nowhere else to go in the school, and there was no other supervising teacher for them for this particular time period in the school's daily schedule.

Midway through the academic year, I asked the students to participate in a small-group mapping project. The task was to listen to Copland's *Fanfare for the Common Man* and, as a group, create a listening map that would be performed for the class (Kerchner 2009, 2010). The students were in charge of selecting their group members, videotaping the process of mapping and performing, and listening and relistening to the *Fanfare* as many times as needed in order to create their music listening maps. The students had four days in which to create the maps and practice performing them before they would perform them in class for each other.

The students were eager to work together on the mapping task. Within the groups that became their communities of learners, they negotiated roles and procedures: who would draw and in which order; who would ask for edits, which edits would be approved or rejected by the group; how they should represent what they heard in the *Fanfare*; and, who would perform the map.

After three days and countless listenings to the Copland, editing their maps, and practicing for the performance, the students taped their music listening maps, colorfully drawn on large pieces of plastic banquet-table coverings, onto the walls of the school cafeteria. While I had invited school administrators and administrative assistants to the students' mapping performances, I had not anticipated that the students would invite some of their teachers. The students, who were not musical performers in the traditional sense, took seriously their roles as performers of their music listening maps, as they practiced for and performed their maps for the class and audience.

As the mapping performances progressed, I observed the students taking turns performing their maps. Students tended to perform only those portions of the map they had drawn during the previous days. It was as though the students "owned" their contributions to the group music listening map. Occasionally, several students performed the map simultaneously, since the map consisted of stacked, vertical markings to depict more than one musical event occurring at the same time. Students seemed comfortable helping their peers who did not point accurately to the markings on the map or who were "lost" and wanted to get back on track.

Comparing the groups' maps, I saw a few trends emerge in terms of what the students perceived and chose to include in their drawings and markings. The maps primarily consisted of pictures of instruments, people playing instruments, musical form, repetition and contrast, phrases, texture (solo and duet trumpets), melodic and rhythmic contour, beat and beat subdivisions, figural groupings (counted and grouped notes indicating some durational value), and pictures of musical associations and stories (Kerchner 2009). Students seemed to group the musical events as they heard them, rather than how they might be grouped in standard musical notation; this was especially true of the students' notion of phrase length and melodic contour.

The students appeared to be thinking in sound as they performed their group music listening maps. Occasionally, students commented out loud that they were pointing to the map incorrectly or that the symbol they pointed to had not yet occurred in the music. Following their listening maps was challenging, especially for those students whose maps were created as nonlinear graphs of the music. Yet when students became temporarily "lost" while performing the group map, they waited for "ear anchors"—familiar musical events—to occur. Students remembered and anticipated those key musical moments that they knew would eventually arrive in the musical excerpt and lead them back on track in their mapping performance.

Listening to Chris

▶ Observe Chris perform his music listening maps. Go to the Companion Website and click on Video 4.6.

Chris was an eleventh-grade male who sang in the community high school choir that I conducted (Kerchner 2005). He studied voice privately, participated in his high school choir, and played several leading roles in high school and community theatrical productions. He described listening to music as something he did regularly. When he spoke, Chris was animated and used a plethora of hand gestures to give emphasis to words in his sentences.

During his first mapping experience, he listened to the Bach and drew a large, blue, wavy form across the top of the paper. At times, Chris seemed to be creating his map in a nonlinear fashion—he drew one object and then another without appearing to represent detailed musical events. However, from the midpoint of the musical excerpt until the end, his hand movements, and consequently and drawn wavy lines on the paper, appeared to correspond to individual musical events as they occurred in real-time (linear representation). When Chris had the opportunity to add onto his first map, he did not add anything, until the arrival of the middle of the excerpt. At that time, he added representations of phrase segments that repeated in the music. Chris explained his map:

> Right away I do this [he points to the large wavy object atop of the music listening map]; the music kind of goes up and down and up and down. It does that for a large chunk of the music. That's why there are so many lines. That's why the [large blue object] form at the top. Right here [the music] changes; it gets thicker [he points to the right side of his map]. All the parts of the music are going back and forth, trading sections of the music. [His drawings of the blue and red lines] represent all the parts moving in and of each other going back and forth. [The primary theme stated in the minor mode] feels like it needs resolving. On the map it is blue [the lines at the bottom of the map and moving upward on the left side of the page]. All the parts keep moving, but it hasn't gotten to the resolve yet. Thick parts move to the return of the main theme; it resolves at the very end of the music.

From an analytical standpoint, it appears that Chris perceived and drew representations on his first map that indicated: melodic contour, accompaniment contour, sectional form (ABA), the musical tension that arose in the B section and needed resolution as the music moved into the primary musical theme, sixteenth-note accompaniment figures, repetition, full ensemble (*tutti*) and solo sections of the music, and textural changes. Because of his ability to describe and give hints about the mapping content, I was able to understand much more than what I would have without his verbal descriptions. The pointing and listening task corroborated Chris's verbal descriptions of his map and the inferences I made regarding the relationship between his drawings and musical events.

During Chris's second interview session mapping experience, he created a completely different style of map. Instead of capturing formal sections and the repetition of melodic and rhythmic figures, he created a story inspired by the music. Chris described the scene:

> The sun just burst out in the meadow, from the very beginning. All of a sudden it happens. At this point, the high part [trumpet] trills and this person just daintily prances out into the meadow. And the soft part is the butterfly and bird just talking back and forth, and then it flutters away, and then she walks farther (*tutti* section). And then another little animal (solo section), and it resolves to another part [*tutti* section], very joyful[ly]. I can see the person picking a flower and smelling it and enjoying it. She's carried away by this part [in the music]. The high fast parts (accompaniment and sixteenth-note scalar passages) are the wind in her hair. She is dancing and enjoying the scenery. This minor part (statement of the primary theme in the minor mode), she sees the cloud (red cloud). She's contemplating the echoing back and forth. Should I head back? Should she give up enjoying the scenery. It [the music] builds, and it's a bit happy again, so she keeps going. She's enjoying the entire scene and taking it all in. This is the wind (transition) going to the main theme . . . joy again.

Clearly, the music engaged Chris's imagination during the second interview, such that he created a story closely related to the musical events he perceived and to which he responded. In his descriptions of the map, he confirmed the affective responses he had experienced, based on the changes in the music: the sunshine and joyful nature of the beginning section, changing to the minor statement of the primary musical theme depicted by clouds, and ultimately returning to the sunshine and joy of the statement of the primary theme in a major key. His depiction of musical transition, its intensity, and its wandering statement of the main theme appeared as the female character of her story questioning whether she should continue on her joyous journey in the meadow or turn back. Chris's verbal description of the story was stated in a rather dramatic manner, as though he were actually telling a story of himself and what he felt during that particular music listening experience. How was Chris related to the main character of the story? Were the characters' emotions also Chris's emotions?

STUDENTS INFORMING TEACHERS: IMPLICATIONS FOR MUSIC LISTENING PEDAGOGY

From my research (Kerchner 1996, 2005, 2009, 2010), I found the *process* of drawing maps during music listening provided the students with a venue to depict more musical detail than they were able to or chose to relay verbally. The mapping *product* itself, however, did not necessarily shed light on detailed perceptual and affective information. Therefore, I relied on reviewing videorecordings of the students' mapping processes—their verbal descriptions of their maps and the pointing and listening tasks—to clarify my inferred meanings of the maps. Therefore, student-generated mapping processes used as a pedagogical strategy must include consideration of the mapping process, product, performance, and the students' verbal descriptions in tandem. Teacher-generated maps should also include the sequence of students performing, describing, adding markings to the teacher's map, and performing again.

According to the students, mapping allowed them, regardless of grade, to provide more detailed musical information than they could verbally. The second- and eleventh-grade students drew the most number of pictures on their maps, while fifth-grade children used more words on their maps than the other students. Eighth-grade students tended to draw graphic, linear maps of the melodic contour, repetition, sections, and the style of thematic material. Eleventh-grade student maps tended to capture the most detailed musical information. Their mapping content increased in detail (differentiation) per interview session, and the means of depicting that information was stylistically different in each of their interview sessions. For example, eleventh-graders' first maps might consist of perceptual and or affective information about the music, while the second sets of maps might depict a story with drawings having embedded musical meaning.

Drawing pictures or stories on listening maps represents a key aspect of these students' music listening experiences: creating associations and connections while listening to music. Students related current music listening to their prior music (and life) experiences. In this visual culture of learners, they created stories and images as they listened to music. As teachers we should acknowledge the story and picture references, but not stop the conversation there. We might probe students' responses by asking, "What in the music made you think of . . . ?" so that students can think in sound, recall, discern, and reflect on the musical structures and relationships that evoked perceptual and affective responses vis-à-vis stories or pictures.

From my analyses of the students' mapping responses, the following might serve as rationale for including music listening mapping as a pedagogical strategy for teachers and learners in PK–12 general music classes and rehearsals. These same principles equally apply to moving to music as described in chapter 3. Mapping:

1. Honors the unique perceptual and affective responses and musical, discrimination, recall, memory, and cognitive abilities of each student.
2. Provides an aural, visual, and kinesthetic way for students to "know" music.
3. Validates the unique nature of students' music listening experiences, especially during repeated listenings.
4. Fosters active music listening and thinking in musical sound.
5. Focuses students' attention on musical features to be noticed and remembered.
6. Provides students with a nonverbal entry point to access music and create and communicate personal musical meaning.

7. Provides students who are developing language skills or who have difficulty communicating in words with a musical "voice."
8. Provides a "holding pond" for remembering students' perceptual discoveries and affective responses.
9. Facilitates students working individually, in small groups, and as a class of meaning-makers.
10. Appeals to a variety of learning style preferences (aural, visual, kinesthetic).
11. Allows students to become informants about their music listening experience (students become teachers; teachers become students).
12. Provides teacher-directed and student-directed opportunities in the teaching–learning partnership.
13. Does not rely on traditional, "standard" notation, and reading or writing skills, since maps primarily consist of alternative notation systems to represent musical sound.
14. Provides a tool for internalizing musical sounds through repeated listening, practicing, and performing the maps.
15. Engages students' imaginations and problem-solving skills as they create concrete symbols for abstract musical sound.
16. Provides "performance" opportunities for those students who are not in ensembles.
17. Provides evidence for student progress and skill development and the accumulation of musical information as a product of repeated listening.
18. Enlists students' inner hearing, metacognitive, and reflective thinking skills as they trace and retrace their music listening experiences captured in their maps.

PROCEDURES FOR MUSIC LISTENING MAPPING

Here we will explore the three primary steps in the procedure for music listening mapping: *creation, implementation,* and *reflection/assessment.* The procedures for using music listening maps as pedagogical tools are ones that I have found successful in classroom situations; however, I encourage you to adapt the procedures to fit your own style of speaking, questioning, and interacting with the students *you* teach in *your* music classroom or rehearsal setting.

Creation

Any music lesson planning procedure begins with taking inventory—of students' and the teacher's interests, abilities, and prior teaching–learning experiences. There are other considerations, too, such as available resources, the point where you and your students are in your curricular journey, and the curricular path that lay ahead. In order to design a music listening map, the teacher must first reflect on what musical concepts and experiences the students have had. From that point, the teacher builds on these foundations and takes the students into new musical territory. The first question to ask is, "What musical concept(s) do I want the students to encounter while using music listening maps?"

The next questions to ask yourself are: Is this an appropriate time in the scope and sequence of teaching this concept for me to incorporate a music listening map? and, Do I need to create a music listening map for this music listening example? You might be wondering why I would encourage you to consider these questions. Creating music listening maps can be time-consuming, and while it is an extraordinarily effective pedagogical tool that is designed specifically for your classes, I do not believe it is necessary to incorporate mapping into every listening experience. In fact, I discourage overusing them, for in a creative music classroom there are a variety of multisensory tools that can work in developing students' music listening skills. Further, if you have basal text series resources, see if they include music listening maps that serve your teaching-learning goals according to the types of music and concepts you want the students to experience.

The next step in the mapping creation process is crucial: choose a piece of music that you and your students will enjoy listening to repeatedly. If you are excited by the musical example, the students will probably catch your enthusiasm. Consult your school recording resources. Download a listening example from the Internet. Check your own listening library and mp3 player. Any music can be age-appropriate. It is the pedagogical sequence and tools that make the music accessible to your students.

Regardless of style, genre, performers, or historical period, the music must clearly illustrate the concept(s) you wish to highlight for the students. This is tricky, since teachers' musically trained ears might hear something in the music—a pattern, repetition, a rhythm, an instrument—that is easily discernible to them but obscure and abstract to the students. Listen to the musical example several times, and maybe even find a score, to help you verify the concept in question. Confusion may ensue if students' ears cannot readily find the musical concept or formal property—the "ear anchor"—you are attempting to illustrate.

Now that you are ready to create your map, try the following steps:

1. Map a music listening segment that is only 1 to 2 minutes in length.
2. On an 8 by 11-inch blank piece of paper, create signs, symbols, drawings, and markings to represent what you hear. No editing, quite yet. Just let your pencil flow.
3. Pick and choose what musical information, other than the musical concept(s) you wish to highlight, to include on and exclude from your map.
4. Consider using colored markers in order to highlight repeated patterns and possible "mystery features" to which you wish to draw students' attention.

5. Re-listen, re-listen, and re-listen to the musical excerpt and follow your map. Make edits accordingly. If you cannot follow your map, your students will not either.

6. Transfer your map onto a larger piece of paper. Hint: plastic banquet-table covering works beautifully for creating maps that you wish to place on the walls of your classroom; they also store easily. Or, retrace the map with a dark marker or a variety of colored markers for use with an overhead projector or document camera.

7. Practice performing your map, until you are comfortable performing it *musically* with the music. Hesitancy or getting lost while performing your map can ruin an otherwise fun mapping experience for you and the students.

Implementation

If your students are new to using music listening maps, then the teacher must find ways to *introduce* them in class. The idea is to take this abstract thing (the map) and relate it to something concrete or familiar that the students have already experienced. As visual aides, have a globe, map of your state, map of the school, or roadmap on display for the students. Try the following questions to prompt brief discussion:

> "Why do we use a globe or a map?"
> "What kinds of information does a globe or map give us?"
> "What kinds of signs or symbols might we find on a globe or map?"
> "What does a map's legend tell us?"

For older students, ask if they have seen a GPS (global positioning system), why it is used, and what signs and symbols it displays.

Show the students your music listening map. "How might a music listening map be like a road map?" After soliciting students' responses, explain that a music listening map guides the ears from the beginning to the end of a musical excerpt, while providing signs and symbols along the way to highlight what is happening in the music as we listen. Obviously, if students are familiar with music listening maps and why they are being used in your classroom, simply skip the mapping introduction.

Before teachers perform a music listening map, ask the students to think in musical sound and *anticipate* musical sounds the map might be representing. In other words, what do the students expect to hear in the musical excerpt, based on the types of symbols and invented notations that appear on the music listening map? Record all student responses, without interjecting any evaluative comments, on a chalkboard or white board for subsequent reference. This is an exercise in students' thinking in musical sound, inner hearing, and setting up expectations that can be affirmed, edited, or challenged as the music listening occurs. Meyer (1956) suggested that musical surprise challenges listeners to reformulate current mental representations of musical sound (in this case, their *expectations* for musical sound) and, therefore, learning occurs.

The final step in the anticipation phase of the mapping process is for the teacher to say something like, "As we listen to the music, see if you can figure out what about the music has been captured and shown on my map." When teachers state a directive or pose a question immediately prior to the actual listening and mapping performance, the students' attention becomes focused, and they are ready to listen with their musical ears and mind.

The teacher *performance* of the map is followed by a return to the anticipatory response list the students created prior to the listening. These *questions* might facilitate discussion with your students:

> "What about the music was represented on the map?"
> "Was that idea on our original list? If not, let's add it."
> "On your list you mentioned that you expected to hear…because of this symbol on the map. Did you hear it? If not, what did that symbol actually represent?"

In many cases, students will have different responses to these types of questions. In fact, they might disagree about what they heard. What an excellent opportunity to listen to the music excerpt and perform the map again, specifically listening for the musical event (i.e., instrument, dynamic level, texture, etc.) in question! If students are unable to describe what they are hearing, listen to the musical excerpt yet again, have them raise their hands when they hear the "mystery" something in the music. Together, this experience can become a puzzle to solve, especially since the teacher and students are working collaboratively to discover "what is." Let the students grapple, wonder, and "get messy" with what the music has to offer.

Let your students inform you when they are ready to finish the mapping in any single class period. Observe their body language and facial gestures in order to gauge when to move onto the next experience in class. You can create opportunities to work with the map and music over the course of several class periods.

What might be the next procedural steps in subsequent music classes or rehearsals? As a review, ask the student to "re-view" the map and recall three facets of the music that are displayed on the map. After this, perform the map with the students remaining at their seats and using their pointer fingers to perform the map in the air. Discuss where the students might have become "lost" while performing the map or what it felt like to be performing the map with the teacher. If there is time in the class period, have individual students attempt to perform the map for the class, while other students continue to perform the map in the air while remaining at their seats. Assist the students only as needed. Let them have a chance to find their own ear anchors to get back on track with the map, should they stumble a bit.

Another idea for subsequent classes is for the students to have the opportunity to add features to the map that were not included on the teacher's maps. While the music listening mapping may have begun with a teacher-generated map, the experience can easily become a shared and co-constructed listening experience. Distribute copies of your map to each student or groups of students. Encourage them to add markings, graphs, words, shapes, pictures of musical features that are prominent to *their* ears. Have the students take turns performing their *additive maps* for a partner. Another option is to copy the teacher map onto one or two overhead transparencies. Distribute the maps and markers to one or two students, who will place their additions directly onto the transparency. Then, have the students with the transparencies perform their additive maps for the whole class. It is important that the students who are observing also try to discern "what about the music" the performer has represented on her or his map. In these ways, students are encouraged to remain active listeners.

Additional Mapping Lesson Extensions

1. Have students create their own maps (student-generated maps) and take turns performing them for a partner while listening to music. Have one partner add markings (representing something musical) to the other's map.
2. Based on the markings from a teacher-generated or student-generated map, have the students create a composition. The composition may or may not have qualities similar to the original music listening example, but the invented notations can provide a frame for organizing students' compositions.
3. Cut photocopies of the teacher's (or students') map into large chunks. In small groups, have students rearrange the segments of the maps (the pieces can be in an order different from the original map). Create a composition based on the "new" map.
4. Have students create a vocal improvisation based on maps. Encourage students to compose using a consonant in a repeated pattern, a vowel sound, or combination of vowels and consonants (not necessarily words) using a variety of pitches. The vocal improvisation can also consist of whispers, tongue clicks, whistles, sirens, vocal swoops moving up and down, and other expressive vocal sounds.
5. Create class/rehearsal graffiti boards. Place large pieces of paper, butcher paper, plastic table coverings on the walls of the cafeteria, your classroom, or on the floors of your room. One student at a time adds something to the music listening map. One person, perhaps initially the teacher, places the first symbol on the paper. When the other students choose, they go to the paper and add their marking at the appropriate place on the map. Large, thick, colorful markers work well with this project.

REFLECTION/ASSESSMENT

Reflection occurs throughout the mapping process (creation and implementation). Reflective thinking not only occurs retrospectively—after teachers and students have listened to the music and performed their maps—but also as in-flight decision making when students determine which visual representations adequately describe features of the music listening experience that they wish to highlight on the map. Teachers and students determine, consciously or unconsciously, when to allow their hands to flow with the music, when to draw a picture, and when to create another symbol. Students and teachers also reflect as they re-create their maps by performing the map; they think about their own thought processes (i.e., metacognition) that led them to draw particular symbols that coordinate with specific musical events.

Teachers might facilitate students' reflective thinking when they pose questions for students' discussion during the mapping experience. By using "prompting questions," teachers can lead the students to think deeply about their music listening experience and to think in musical sound by providing explanation and rationale for what they heard. Prompts might include:

"What in the music made you think of...?"

"Tell me more about..."

"I think I am hearing you say... Tell me what I should add or change in that description."

"Help us understand more about your response."

"Did anyone else hear it that way? Could you add to the description of what was going on in the music?"

"Keep going with that description. Let's hear more."

"If my symbol on the map does not quite fit what you are hearing, then how would you change it?"

Yet another level of reflection is that of teacher reflection: when to insert musical vocabulary that seems to capture the essence of students' descriptions, when to listen to the music again, when to pose prompting questions, when to move on to another musical experience in class, what about the music listening map does or does not "work" effectively, and the degree of aural discrimination and music cognition that students demonstrate before, during, and after the music listening experience. Teachers' keen observational skills enable them to assess students' perceptual skills that require additional reinforcement in subsequent classes. Use students' perceptual and affective mapping depictions and descriptions as teacher prompts of that which students are ready to learn musically. More on teacher assessment of students' multisensory music listening responses can be found in chapter 7.

STUDENT-GENERATED MAPPING PROCEDURES

As a teacher's research project or an assessment tool, student-generated maps can empower students to be informants for their teachers and student peers. Earlier in this chapter, I shared a procedure for individual mapping interviews that I conducted with my former students; however, this is an impractical procedure to implement frequently in the music classroom. Therefore, a modified procedure is necessary.

1. Select a musical excerpt (the teacher can do this, or the students can choose one excerpt from three pieces the teacher offers).
2. As a class, have the students listen to the complete excerpt (one to two minutes in length). No discussion or mapping, yet.
3. During the next listening of the same excerpt, encourage the students to show on a piece of paper those markings, pictures, graphs, lines, and/or words that indicate what they are "thinking, feeling and hearing" as they listen to the music. Students choose one color crayon or marker to draw on the map per musical listening (i.e., first listening, students use red crayon; second listening, students use blue crayon). Have students place an asterisk (*) at the beginning of their map, and an X at the end of their map. These markings help the teacher understand the progression of markings on the paper.
4. Ask the students to choose another crayon or marker of a different color. Invite the students to "add anything new to the map, perhaps something you did not hear or did not have time to add during the first mapping." Students listen to the music and provide additions to the map. Again, have the students place an asterisk (*) at the beginning of the mapping and an X at the conclusion of the map.
5. At some point during the next music classes, have one or two students perform their music listening maps for the class and for each other. The teacher and students can try to discover what the students represented on their maps. The teacher and students observe the map performers while inferring possible meaning from symbols that seem to coincide with specific musical events. The teacher also assesses whether the map is linear or non-linear, if the map includes global or differentiated musical events, and how the maps are refined (additions, deletions, repetition, etc.) during each repeated listening. Ask the student performers to describe their maps ("Lead us through your map. Tell us what you included"). If students are older, they can provide written descriptions of their mapping symbols. Both the teacher and students are responsible for posing questions to the performers: "What in the music made you draw this?"; "Why did you decide to include this marking on your map?"; "How did you know how to follow your map?"
6. Individual student-generated maps can be created at least twice during a school year—once at the beginning and once at the end of the school year. The teacher can compare the maps for the number and types of responses the students provide in order to show evidence of their music-listening skill development (see chapter 7).

MAPPING ADAPTATIONS FOR STUDENTS WITH VISUAL IMPAIRMENTS

Music listening maps are typically posted on a bulletin board or white board or projected onto a screen from an overhead projector, computer, or document camera. However, these display options can be problematic for students with moderate to severe visual disabilities. Projection screens often contain the glare of bright light that can overpower the mapping symbols. Adaptive mapping modifications can include copying and enlarging the music listening map for the student. Having moderate to severe visual disability, the student should become acquainted with the copy of the map before it is used in class. This strategy provides the student with a one-on-one preview of the mapping lesson by giving the student a visual referent that will be presented "at a distance" in the classroom. Another idea would be to work with the student's one-on-one aide, so that she or he can perform the map with the student's pointer finger while you perform the map for the other members of the class.

One of my colleagues told me about Miguel's music listening mapping story. He was a member of her seventh-grade music appreciation class and had a severe visual impairment. In fact, he was almost completely blind, except for the ability to discern the presence of light (i.e., whether the lights of the room were on or off). So that Miguel could fully participate in the mapping experience, the teacher copied her maps onto 8 1/2 by 11-inch white paper. Then Edward, Miguel's one-on-one aide, traced the mapping markings with "puffy paint," two-dimensional fabric paint that when applied to a surface creates an embossed design. Edward also translated musical terms (e.g., *fine, da capo, coda*) and formal sectional markers (e.g., ABA, ABACADA) into Braille symbols.

Prior to class, Edward guided Miguel's pointer finger over the map in order to preview the raised notation for the music listening excerpt that he would later experience in music appreciation class. Then Edward guided Miguel's pointer finger over the map, but this time as they listened to the musical excerpt. Once Miguel came to class, he had had two prior experiences with the music listening map. Eventually, Edward and other peers only helped Miguel perform the map only as needed. Furthermore, Miguel participated in creating his own maps. He sketched his representations onto a piece of paper, Edward used the puffy paint, and Miguel was ready to share his map with his peers.

IDEAS FOR MAPPING LESSONS

Following are several music listening maps that you can (1) use in your classroom or (2) use as models for creating and implementing your own music listening maps. By going to the book's Companion Website, you might also use the videorecorded classroom demonstrations as a resource for your own pedagogical information, or you might project the video clips onto a large screen in your classroom and use the mapping performances and questions to lead a music listening lesson, prompt student discussion about music listening and mapping, introduce mapping, or show models of mapping. Realize that the lesson ideas stated below are to be used as guidelines only. Make teaching and learning come alive in your own classroom situation! Adapt the questions or sequence of learning to suit your curricular and student learning needs. While students of any age can listen to any of the musical pieces demonstrated on the website or in this chapter, not all of the lesson suggestions presented are suitable for every grade level. Again, please adapt accordingly.

Go to the Companion Website to observe teachers and students interact with the following music listening maps and music:

VIDEO 4.7.	"Row, Row, Row Your Boat"*
VIDEO 4.8.	Handel: "Hornpipe" (*Water Music Suite #2*)*
VIDEO 4.9.	Vivaldi: "Autumn" (*The Four Seasons*)*
VIDEO 4.10.	Liszt: "Un Sospiro"
VIDEO 4.11.	Strauss: *Also Sprach Zarathustra**
VIDEO 4.12.	"Saqsahumanpi" (Andean Folk Music)*
VIDEO 4.13.	Glière: "Russian Sailor's Dance" (*The Red Poppy*)*
VIDEO 4.14.	Duruflé: "Sanctus" (*Requiem*)

"Row, Row, Row Your Boat" (Dotting for Pre-school and Kindergarten Children)

Go to the Companion Website and click on Video 4.7 for a mapping demonstration of the dotting map for "Row, Row, Row Your Boat."

Together with your students, say the song lyrics: "Row, row, row your boat gently down the stream. Merrily, merrily, merrily, merrily, life is but a dream." Now, hold one of your hands out (palm facing upward) and tap each syllable of each word of the text in the palm of your hand with the pointer finger of the other hand. Together with your students, tap and say the words. Notice that there is one tap for every syllable that you speak. Sing the lyrics of "Row" and tap the song in the palm of your hands (students do this, too). After the students are comfortable singing the song and tapping it, have them point in the air and follow your performance of the dotting maps. The notation would look as shown in figure 4.4.

Remember to point to one dot per each sung syllable. Also, observe that there is no duration differentiation specified—each dot looks the same. Instead, it is the performance—pointing to the dots in the rhythm of the song—that makes the map fit the song.

*Lesson ideas appear in this chapter

In another class period, distribute a copy of the dotting map to each student. With a closed marker (i.e., cap of marker is still on), have each child sing the song and point to each dot on her or his map. Finally, ask the students to think the song in their heads (i.e., inner musical hearing) while they point to their maps.

During yet another class, distribute a clean sheet of paper to each student. Invite each child sing the song and tap her or his map with a closed marker. Next, ask the students to use open markers to draw actual dots on a clean piece of paper (one dot per sound they sing). Ask a few students to sing the song and perform their dotting maps for the class.

For an extra challenge during another class period, change the map to look as shown in figure 4.11. Ask the students if this dotting map fits the song, "Row, Row, Row Your Boat." Sing and perform the new map together. Show the original map and ask:

> "How are the maps the same/different?
> "How can the maps look different and yet fit the same song?"
> "Why are some dots grouped together?"
> "Which dotting map was easier to follow? Why?"

These questions prompt the students to think of multiple ways to represent sounds that "belong together" in a group (i.e., a figural map) while still representing one sound per dot.

• • • • •   • • • • •

• • • • • • • • • • • •   • • • • •

Figure 4.11.
Phrase Dotting for "Row, Row, Row Your Boat."

Handel: "Hornpipe" (*Water Music Suite No. 2*)

▶   Go to the Companion Website and click on Video 4.8 for a mapping demonstration of "Hornpipe."

Background Information

- Handel was King George I's court composer.
- King George I wanted to gain popularity in his home country, so he hosted parties, some of which occurred on a barge that sailed up and down the Thames River.

- Small groups of instrumentalists performed suites (collections of dance music) onboard the barges.

Focus Question

"What instrument do you expect to be featured? Why?"

Play Recording/Perform Map
Debriefing Questions

"What instrument was featured?" [French horn]
"What instrumental family?" [Brass]

Anticipation

Show "Hornpipe" map (A section only).

Questions

"What do you notice about the markings or symbols on the map? Do you see any symbols/markings that repeat?"
"Raise your hand if you would like to come up to the map and point to places where symbols/markings repeat."
"What else do you expect the music to sound like, given the type of symbols on the map that represent musical sounds?"
"Notice there are some broken, dotted vertical lines. What do you think the music might sound like at this spot on the map?" (These show that there is an echo. The part to the left of the lines is echoed by another group of instruments on the right side of the lines.)
"See if you can identify which instruments are echoing one another as you watch me perform the listening map."

Play Recording/Perform Map
Debriefing Question

"Which instruments did you hear echoing each other?" [On the second line of the map, the trumpets play the first part and then are echoed by the French horn. Next on that same line on the map, the full orchestra plays first and is echoed by the French horn again. Finally, on the third line of the map, the trumpets play first and are echoed by the French horns.]

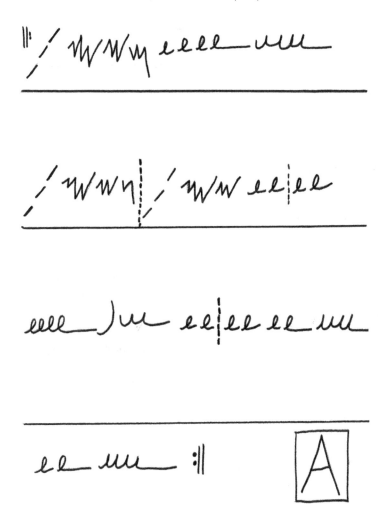

Figure 4.12.
Map for Handel: "Hornpipe" (*Water Music Suite No. 2*).

Play Recording/Perform Maps

"As we listen to the musical excerpt again, use your pointer finger in the air to perform the map with me."

Reflection/Assessment

Lesson continuation/extensions in subsequent classes as needed.

Vivaldi: "Autumn" (*The Four Seasons*)
Background/Anticipation

- Vivaldi's music for "The Four Seasons" was written to tell a story, based on words that he, himself, wrote. This is the sonnet on which the music for "Autumn" was based (Vivaldi).

> The peasant celebrates with song and dance the harvest safely gathered in.
> The cup of Bacchus flows freely, and many find their relief in deep slumber.
> The singing and the dancing die away as cooling breezes fan the pleasant air,
>> inviting all to sleep without a care.
> The hunters emerge at dawn, ready for the chase,
>> with horns and dogs and cries.
> Their quarry flees while they give chase.
> Terrified and wounded, the prey struggles on, but, harried, dies.

Initial Question

"What do you think the words *quarry, slumber,* and *harried* mean? Can you tell by looking at them in the context of the poem?"

Anticipation Questions

"Now that we have read the sonnet, what might you expect the music for "Autumn" to sound like? Why? What are your clues?"
"Let's take a look at a music listening map that I have for this piece. It is very simple. What do you see?" [four small leaves, a large leaf, and two small leaves]

Figure 4.13.
Map for Vivaldi: "Autumn" (*The Four Seasons*).

"This is a rhythmic pattern that you will hear repeatedly in the music. As I point to
each small leaf, say 'Short'; when I point to the large leaf, say 'Long.' Let's try the
whole pattern." [short, short, short, short, LONG, short, short]

"This time, tap the rhythm in the palm of your hand and say the shorts and longs of
the pattern. For the long leaf, send your hand sailing forward to show the longer
sound of the pattern. Let's try."

Play Music/Perform Map

"As we listen to the music, join me in performing the map with the tapping and saying the words 'short' and 'long.' "

▶   Go to the Companion Website and click on Video 4.9 to view children doing
the movement for "Autumn."

Debriefing Question

"Was it easy or difficult to perform that pattern as you listened to the music? Why
or why not? What made it easy/difficult?"

Anticipation

"Here's a copy of my map. It's your turn to point to the leaves and say the 'shorts' and
'longs' as we listen again to the music."

Play Music/Perform Map

Debriefing Questions

"Did anyone get lost during the mapping?"
"How is it different pointing to the map and saying the 'shorts' and 'longs' versus tapping the rhythm pattern in your hand?"

Extensions

"On the board I have paper cut-outs of small and large leaves. What happens if I take the rhythm pattern of shorts and longs and change the order of the leaves? Could we tap a new rhythm? Let's try."
"Who would like to rearrange the leaves to create another pattern? First, the 'composer' of the pattern will perform it for us and then we will echo the pattern. Let's try."

Reflection/Assessment

Lesson continuation/extensions in subsequent classes as needed.

Strauss: "Sunrise" (*Also Sprach Zarathustra*)

Background

- Richard Strauss was a German composer who wrote some of his musical compositions as "tone poems"—a piece of instrumental music based on a piece of literature (in this case, a book by Nietzsche) or art work. *Also Sprach Zarathustra* (*Thus Spoke Zarathustra*) is such a tone poem.
- Zarathustra is a fictitious teacher who could foretell the future. In Nietzsche's book, he comes down from a mountaintop to be with the humans.

Pre-Teaching

Sing the ascending pattern do-sol-do, and simultaneously use Kodály-Curwen hand signs. Students echo-sing with hand signs. If time, have students demonstrate the do-sol-do on an Orff xylophone.

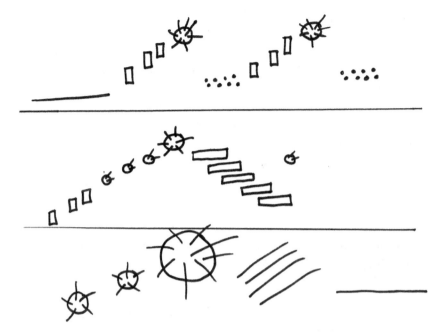

Figure 4.14.
Map for Strauss: "Sunrise" (*Also Sprach Zarathustra*).

Anticipation Questions

"Where on the map might you expect to hear do-sol-do?" [Teacher sings and does hand signs without saying the pitch symbols] "Could someone show me?"
"How else might you expect the music to sound, given the symbols on the map? How about here?" [Teacher points to a symbol; students respond] "Or here?" [Teacher points to another symbol; students respond] [Teacher records students' responses on chalkboard or white board]

Play Recording/Perform Map

"As we listen to the music, let's see if what we thought the music would sound like actually happens in the music. Follow me as we listen and I perform the music listening map."

▶ Go to the Companion Website and click on Video 4.11 for a mapping demonstration of "Sunrise."

Debriefing Question

"Let's look at our list. Did what we thought would happen in the music actually happen? Should we delete or add anything?"

Focus Question

"As we listen again, think about what is missing from my map. What do you hear in the music that we might want to represent on the map?"

Play Recording/Perform Map
Debriefing Questions

"What is something we could add to the map?"
"Where does that belong on the map?"
"How might we represent that on the map?"
Student volunteers add onto the teacher map.

Reflection/Assessement

Lesson continuation/extensions in subsequent classes as needed.

Glière: "Russian Sailor's Dance (*The Red Poppy*)
Background

- Mikail Glière was a son of Jewish parents of Belgian decent. He was born in 1875 in Kiev, Russia, and began studying violin at a very early age. In fact, he was considered a prodigy.

Question: "What is a "prodigy"?" [A child who is an extremely talented, in this case as a musical performer]

- At a young age, he studied violin and piano at the Moscow Conservatory.
- "Russian Sailor's Dance" was music written for the ballet, *The Red Poppy*.
- *The Red Poppy* was written in 1926/1927 and is about revolutionary activity in China and the rise of communism; however, Glière himself was not interested in supporting those perspectives.

Anticipation

Show a listening map of "The Russian Sailor's Dance" melody. The music begins with an "introduction." Ask:

"What's the musical term that describes the music becoming gradually louder?" [A crescendo] "There's even a crescendo symbol on the map under the word *Introduction*."
"Are there any spots on the map that suggest that the instruments slide from one note to another? Do I have a volunteer to show us on the map?"

"Let's listen for the first time this melody is heard." /

Play Recording/Perform Map

▶   Go to the Companion Website and click on Video 4.13 to view a mapping performance of "The Russian Sailor's Dance."

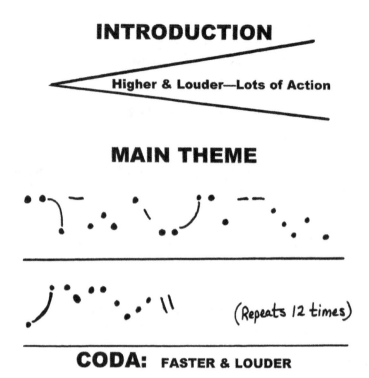

Figure 4.15.
Map for Glière: "Russian Sailor's Dance (*The Red Poppy*).

Debriefing Question

"Where on the map did the instruments slide from one note to another? Could someone show me where that occurs on the map?" [There are lines connecting some markings]

Focus Directive

"Let's listen to the whole piece. As you listen, count how many times you hear the main melody repeat. Be careful! Sometimes the melody is disguised by different instruments playing it and notes that were added. Pointer fingers in the air as we perform the map together and count."

Play Recording/Perform Map
Debriefing Question

"How many times did the melody repeat?" [12 times]

Focus Directive

"As we listen again, listen for instruments/families of instruments other than the basses and celli that play the melody. Pointer fingers in the air as we perform the map together and count."

Play Recording/Perform Map
Debriefing Questions

"Did any other instruments/families of instruments other than the basses and celli that play the melody?" [Yes, sometimes the brass instruments and woodwind instruments take turns playing the melody.] "The form of this piece is theme and variation."

"What kind of symbols or markings could we add to the map that shows the changes in the music during each repetition of the melody? What should we add, and why?"

Reflection/Assessment

Lesson continuation/extensions in subsequent classes as needed.

YOUR TURN

Because of the nature of the qualitative research methodology and constructivist approach that frame my research and pedagogical procedures presented in this book, I do not presume that the findings reported here represent all students' music listening mapping processes or products. Instead, I ask you to consider music listening mapping as a pedagogical strategy in your classroom (teacher-generated maps) and then as means for asking the students to inform you about their listening experiences (student-generated maps). View and review your students' music listening maps in order to compare their responses to the children's responses presented in this chapter. Then, reflecting on the mapping processes and products, ask yourself:

1. What type of markings are included on students' maps in each grade level?
2. How did the information on the maps change or develop during repeated listenings?
3. What perceptual or affective information was included on the students' maps?
4. How are the maps of one grade level same/different from those in another grade?
5. How specific (differentiated) or general (global, undifferentiated) is the information presented on the maps?
6. How do your students' verbal descriptions of their maps challenge or corroborate the information you inferred from observing the students create or perform their maps?
7. What information did you gather when you observed the students perform their maps?
8. What did you notice to be the primary mode of mapping among students in a particular class—linear? nonlinear? both?
9. Were the students able to follow (i.e., perform) their maps while listening to the music? Why or why not?
10. What, if any information from the students' stories and my research observations, seems to resonate with your observations of your students' mapping experiences?
11. What are your wonderments about music listening mapping?
12. How might you investigate your wonderments?
13. What is your plan for this investigation?

REFERENCES

Bamberger, J. (1982). "Revisiting Children's Drawings of Simple Rhythms: A Function for Reflection in Action." In *U-shaped Behavioural Growth*, edited by S. Strauss and R. Stavy, 191–226. New York: Academic.

Bamberger, J. (1991). *The Mind Behind the Musical Ear: How Children Develop Musical Intelligence*. Cambridge, MA: Harvard University Press.

Barrett, M. (1997). "Invented Notations: A View of Young Children's Musical Thinking." *Research Studies in Music Education* 8(1): 2–14.

Barrett, M. (1999). "Modal Dissonance: An Analysis of Children's Invented Notations of Known Songs, Original Songs, and Instrumental Compositions." *Bulletin of the Council for Research in Music Education* 141: 14–20.

Barrett, M. (2000). "Windows, Mirrors, and Reflections: A Case Study of Adult Constructions of Children's Musical Thinking." *Bulletin of the Council for Research in Music Education*, 145, 43–61.

Barrett, M. (2001). "Constructing a View of Children's Meaning-making as Notators: A Case-Study of a Five-year-old's Descriptions and Explanations of Invented Notations." *Research Studies in Education* 16(1): 33–45.

Barrett. M. (2002). "Invented Notations and Mediated Memory: A Case-Study of Two Children's Use of Invented Notations." *Bulletin of the Council for Research in Music Education*, 153/154, 55-62.

Barrett, M. (2004). "Thinking about the Representation of Music: A Case-study of Invented Notation." *Bulletin of the Council for Research in Music Education* 161/162: 19–28.

Bennett P., and D. Bartholomew (1997). *SongWorks I: Singing in the Education of Children*. Belmont, CA: Wadsworth.

Bomengen, M. (2010, September 23). "What Is the "Whole Language" Approach to Reading?" *Reading Horizons Happenings*. Retrieved October 24, 2011, http://www.reading-horizons.com/blog/post/2010/09/23/What-is-the-Whole-Languagee-Approach-to-Teaching-Reading.aspx.

Davidson, L., L. Scripp, and P. Welsh (1988). "'Happy Birthday': Evidence for Conflicts of Perceptual Knowledge and Conceptual Understanding." *Journal of Aesthetic Education* 22(1): 65–74.

Goodman, K. (1986). *What's Whole in Whole Language*. Berkeley, CA: RDR Books.

Kerchner, J. L. (1996). "Perceptual and Affective Components of Music Listening Experience as Manifested in Children's Verbal, Visual, and Kinesthetic Representations." Unpublished doctoral dissertation, Northwestern University.

Kerchner, J. L. (2001). "Children's Verbal, Visual, and Kinesthetic Responses: Insight into Their Music Listening Experience". *Bulletin of the Council for Research in Music Education* 146: 35–51.

Kerchner, J. L. (2005). "A World of Sound to Know and Feel: Exploring Children's Verbal, Visual, and Kinesthetic Responses to Music." In *Music in Schools for All Children: From Research to Effective Practice*, edited by M. Mans and B. W. Leung, 21–33. Granada, Spain: University of Granada.

Kerchner, J. L. (2009). "Drawing Middle-schoolers' Attention to Music." In *Musical Experience in Our Lives: Things We Learn and Meanings We Make*, edited by J. Kerchner and C. Abril, chap. 11. Lanham, MD: Rowman & Littlefield.

Kerchner, J. L. (2010). "Mapping Performance as General Music Informance." *General Music Today*, 23(3), 15-19.

Meyer, L. (1956). *Emotion and Meaning in Music.* Chicago: Chicago University Press.

Miller, S. (1986). "Listening Maps for Musical Tours." *Music Educators Journal* 73(2): 28–31.

Richards, M. H. (1978). *Aesthetic Foundations for Thinking*, Part 2. Portola Valley, CA: Richards Institute of Music Education and Research.

Upitis, R. (1992). *Can I Play You My Song?* Portsmouth, NH: Heinemann.

Vivaldi, Antonio. "Autumn" Retrieved from http://www.baroquemusic.org/vivaldiseasons.html]

CHAPTER 5

Listeners Speaking

Thought and Word

In many Western societies, written and spoken language is the primary cultural tool for transmitting and conserving histories and idealisms. The oral tradition, mentorship, and cultural apprentices are ways for adult members of a community to share with younger members crucial information about cultural structures, histories and traditions, skills, mores, expectations, and beliefs, in addition to familial narratives, histories, and expectations.

Educational communities have stakeholders—teachers, parents, administrators, students, and community members—who value verbal and written forms of teaching and learning, thereby maintaining the oral and linguistic tradition of transmitting information from one generation to the next. Speaking, reading, and writing are the predominant and pervasive learning modes that students experience during their years of PK–12 and collegiate instruction. Students' language abilities are measured not only as determinants of their linguistic intelligence (Gardner 1983) but also in formal educational systems, in conjunction with mathematical skills, as signs of one's general intelligence. The designation of "intelligent" or "not intelligent" leads to society granting privilege and opportunity to some people, while simultaneously creating social stratification and limited opportunity for others. Therefore, having command of linguistic tools (speaking, reading, writing) is a powerful societal tool for determining the "haves" and "have nots" in schools and in later life.

That which is valued about language is its appeal as reason- or logic-based "objective" knowing. But just as thought and emotion permeate any action or movement, words are also imbued with feeling, emotion, and sensory (i.e., bodily) "subjective" knowing. Language is "a bridge between inner thought and shared understanding: the past and the present, the world of the senses and the realm of thought" (John-Steiner 1997, 111).

Winner (1988) wrote that language is full of metaphors that are used to clarify, illuminate, or explain the facets of objects, events, and experiences by comparing them to something else (i.e., a referent) that has similar features or characteristics. Metaphoric descriptions are nonliteral and require the person using the metaphor and the listener to have mutual understanding of the referent's features in order to determine the similarity to the new "something." Students' descriptions of music are filled with vivid metaphors from their prior musical and nonmusical experiences, in order to convey the abstraction of what they hear during music listening.

Language might also be considered a metaphoric representation of a thought or concept. Vygotsky and Kozulin (1986, 256) stated that a "word is a generalized reflection of reality," instead of a direct translation of a thought. Young children learn to speak by uttering one word that conveys a complete sentence or several thoughts. A child's statement "Drink!" might encompass multiple thoughts and sensations, such as those indicated in this complete sentence: "Mommy, may I please have more of the juice in that cup...now? I'm thirsty!" The child's one-word statement is an abbreviated language containing myriad cognitive reference points to sensations, thoughts, feelings, personal needs, and desires. Interestingly, adult inner speech is analogous to children's compressed language representations. One does not hold meanings as mental essays comprising logically and linearly constructed sentences and paragraphs. Ultimately, adult language develops into complete sentences articulated with carefully crafted semantics and syntax, and yet even then, words and sentences only metaphorically represent the general essence of a person's thoughts and feelings. Externalized language is intended for the purposes of communicating and sharing with others.

The processes of thought and speech development do not occur concurrently (Vygotsky and Kozulin 1986). Prelinguistic development includes a child's intentional exploration of his or her physical environs, which leads to symbolic function. Piaget's findings corroborate this notion, since the basis of his theory of cognitive developmental is that physical and mental processes precede the development of children's understanding and use of symbolic representation. Bruner (1966) also described children's sequence of cognitive development as moving from enactive (action), iconic (representation), and symbolic (language) ways of knowing—physical experiences being the precursors to symbolic conceptualization. Children (and adults) understand—through the body, feelings, and mind—much more than they are able to communicate at any point along the lifespan developmental spectrum. Therefore, educators cannot falsely assume that because students cannot verbalize an idea or concept that they do not know or understand it.

MUSIC AS A LANGUAGE

Music is a universal *experience*. Music notes are equated to letter sounds, and words, sentences, and paragraphs to musical formal sections. Students typically learn a music symbol system in a sequence similar to learning language by experiencing sound before symbol through exploration, experimentation, word formation, sentence formation, complex sentence and paragraph creation. Henkjan Honing (2009) explained, however, why music is not a language per se, let alone a universal language. I have summarized and expounded upon his main discussion points:

1. *Music has no syntax.* The rules for creating and performing music are not as confining as those of language formulation (i.e., sentence structure, verb-noun agreement). Languages throughout the world have different grammatical rules that cannot be understood by those who do not speak specific languages. If I do not understand the grammar (syntax) or combinations of letters (semantics) of the Russian language, for example, I will not be able to gain meaning from something I read that is printed in Russian. Listeners can certainly appreciate and even understand elemental facets of musics from cultures different from their own; however, truly grasping the musical rules and performance subtlties might prove exceedingly challenging.

2. *Music has no semantics.* Unlike letters and combinations of letters in the alphabet, musical notes have no inherent meaning. A word itself is embedded with meaning; however, a group of notes do not represent specific meaning. Instead, listeners and performers bring their own meanings to the notes and their structural values related to the entire composition. A musical score, unlike an essay, contains notes and directions that suggest how to perform a piece of music; however, the performers give the music life with nuance, subtlety, and expression. Furthermore, there is usually no "guide" for how to listen to piece of music. Listeners are responsible for creating their own personal meaning and musical experience.

3. *Music speaks to the emotions.* "Music…seems to appeal much more directly to the emotions than language" (Honig 2009, 42). Honing states that melodic and rhythmic structures are the bearers of the emotional import of a musical composition. That is, these structures transmit emotional meaning to the musical listeners and performers. If we relate this discussion to other discussions in this book, music needs no translation. It directly impresses upon the bodies, spirits, feelings, and minds of listeners and performers.

While teachers might choose to "say less and do more" as an effective classroom strategy, Reimer (1989, 97) suggested that it would be a mistake for music educators not to use language as a means for bringing students closer to understanding and "designating precisely the important components of musical events, making helpful generalizations about how music works," and pointing to structural and elemental relationships in the music. People engage with music, and other art forms, as an experience that is ineffable—having words insufficient for capturing the quality of perceptual and emotional impact. Yet, teachers and students rely on finding words to describe music and its meanings, even though the language they use has limitations. Therefore, developing verbal descriptive abilities relative to music listening (and other musical behaviors) is key in communicating "what about the music" is perceptually meaningful and emotionally gripping. Learning to express with clarity, even developing and using music vocabulary, helps students (and later, adults) to communicate with others about the nature of their musical experience and to grow in their understanding of the multiple possibilities for creating musical meanings.

ABOUT VERBAL REPORTING

In their book *Protocol Analysis: Verbal Reports as Data*, Ericsson and Simon (1993) contend that concurrent and retrospective verbal reports are viable data for researchers investigating people's cognitive processes. At the time during which people provide simultaneous verbal accounts of the phenomena they experience, their "streams of consciousness" or "think alouds" reflect the mental operations set into action in order for the information to be processed cognitively. Yet, the authors also recognize the limitations of verbal reporting.

Despite the information presented during verbal reporting, a person includes only those details of the phenomenon that is in the range of her or his conscious focus of attention. Verbal reporting is indicative of the mental processes that permit the "bringing [of] information into attention, then when necessary, converting it into verbalizable code, and finally, vocalizing it" (Ericsson and Simon 1993, 16). Cognitive processes necessary for the verbalization of the phenomenon, therefore, represent only a subset of the total number of cognitive processes employed during the perception of and response to a phenomenon. According to Ericsson and Simon (1993, 109), "the processes underlying behavior may be unconscious and thus not accessible for verbal reporting, or at least may be reportable only very incompletely."

Ericsson and Simon (1993) alerted researchers that presenting research participants with repeated think-aloud tasks could prompt them to think differently about a phenomenon itself. Verbal reports reflect the participant's creation of a solution to a task in a particular moment of time. It should not be surprising, then, that subsequent verbal reports might conflict with previous verbal descriptions of the same piece of music, since with each repeated listening, a person's familiarity with the music affects the nature of the music listening experience. Listeners create and re-create unique realities of the music listening experiences they have with each repeated listening of a piece of music.

There are two types of verbal reporting—concurrent and retrospective— that seem to reveal cognitive information about a person as she or he performs a task—in this case, music listening talk-alouds. The verbal data presented here were procured from students' concurrent verbal reports (i.e., talk-aloud tasks) and retrospective verbal reports at the conclusion of the interviews.

Concurrent verbal reports, also referred to as "protocols," "talk-alouds," "think-alouds," and "level 1 processing," consist of a researcher's asking individual participants to "verbalize the information they attend to while generating the answer" to a specific problem or experiencing a particular phenomenon" (Ericsson and Simon 1993, xiii). In the case of the talk-alouds presented here, students were given the following directions prior to the verbal reporting tasks:

> We're going to listen to the same piece of music you just heard. While we are listening to the music, I would like you to talk loudly and clearly and tell me what you are thinking, hearing, and feeling as you listening to the music. Remember to keep talking as you are listening. Do you have any questions?

Once the concurrent verbal reporting begins, the researcher can remind and encourage the participants to "keep talking" or "tell me more," should there be a lull in the participant's commentary.

Retrospective verbal reports (level 2 processing) require a research participant "to observe his or her own internal processes or overt behavior" while perceiving, processing, and responding to a phenomenon (Ericsson and Simon 1993, 18). This type of verbal reporting occurs upon the completion of a task, such as listening to a musical excerpt. When participants engage in this metacognitive exercise, information about a phenomenon is not procured as immediately as it is during concurrent verbal reporting. Since retrospective reports rely on memory, participants must recall what they encountered and how they encountered it—yet another layer of translation not found in concurrent verbal reports. Retrospective reports are useful in the investigation of general cognitive processes, however, for they deal with traces of the task-procedure awareness that remain in short-term memory. Cognitive processes engaged during retrospective reporting include recoding information, scanning, filtering information, and inference processes, in addition to memory and recall.

The longer the task (e.g., music listening), the more difficult it is to retrieve and verbalize the actual sequence of cognitive processing. To assist with the retrieval process, it is often necessary for the researcher to offer verbal prompts such as, "Can you tell me what you were thinking about during...?" or "Let's see how much you can remember about what you were thinking when you were...." These verbal cues help the participant recall specific and relevant information pertaining to the music listening experience, especially if they are presented in a manner that does not impose on the participant's thought processes and willingness to offer verbal information.

LISTENING TO STUDENTS

In this section, we will explore verbal protocols—talk-alouds—offered by Peter, David, Molly, and Alexis. Each student has his or her own mini-portrait: a general description of the student's musical involvement in and out of school; music listening preferences and habits; transcripts from each talk-aloud (one from each interview session); and my observations, speculations, and interpretations based on the talk-alouds relative to the music listening excerpt—an approximately two-minute (2′20″) excerpt from Bach's Brandenburg Concerto #2 in F Major, movement 1 (BWV 1047). The talk-alouds represent the second music listening in the sequence of the individual interview sessions. The verbal reporting followed an initial listening to the musical excerpt, during which the students completed no other task.

Each student's verbal reports were analyzed using verbal protocol analysis procedures (Creswell 2008; Ericsson and Simon 1993; Rubin and Rubin 2005). After transcribing the verbal reports and reading them many times, I coded individual statements that represented a specific topic. A code represents a concept, "a word or term that represents an idea important to [my] research" purpose of investigating the nature of students' music listening experiences via words, drawings, and movements (Rubin and Rubin 2005, 207). In the case of verbal data analysis, a sentence or phrase in a complex sentence represented the unit that I labeled with a single or multiple codes. While they were not predetermined, the codes represented terms and concepts found in the existing music-listening research literature in tandem with key words from the students' verbal reports.

Only after reading and rereading the transcripts did the codes become clear and consistently defined. For example, a student's statement such as, "The music's like really low, then it gets real high, then low. Like a pattern—low, high, low, high" constitutes two units (the first sentence and the second sentence). I considered the first sentence indicative of musical register as one topic, thus one code was ascribed. The second incomplete sentence seemed to represent musical pattern and register (two codes). In the case of students who provided a story without mentioning specific musical details (i.e., musical elements, affect, mood, formal structures), several sentences might be tagged with a single code such as "imagery and association."

Eventually, I looked for patterns among the various codes in order to determine students' focus of attention in the music and perceptual and affective responses while listening to it. Some of the codes were subsumed into larger categories, clusters, or themes. For example, a student's verbal report might include three separate codes—contour, register, and melody—that could be subsumed by the theme "pitch recognition." Similarly, themes were clustered to form "macro-themes." Using the same example, the "pitch recognition" theme was combined with other themes (i.e., instrument, pattern, duration, and dynamics) in the "perceived musical elements" macro-theme.

As you read the students' mini-portraits, consider the following questions:

1. Can you visualize the vocal tone and body language the student presented during her or his verbal talk-alouds?
2. What follow-up questions would you ask in order to clarify the verbal information presented in the talk-aloud?
3. How might a student's verbal information be affected by a researcher familiar (or unfamiliar) to the student?
4. How might the students' talk-alouds differ if they had provided concurrent verbal reports for their favorite recorded music, jazz, or non-Western music?

5. What additional or different verbal analysis codes would you expect the researcher to use if the students provided verbal talk-alouds for their favorite song, jazz, atonal, or non-Western music?

6. How might researchers' preconceptions about music-listening skill development influence verbal data analysis?

7. How might a researcher ensure her or his coding schemes are valid and consistently applied?

8. How might verbal data inform your understanding of an individual child's or a whole class' music listening experience? How might this knowledge influence your music listening teaching strategies and materials?

Listening to Peter

Peter, a second-grade male (age eight), was a dramatic and creative personality. He was a child who displayed much energy and enthusiasm in music class. He was quick to share his newly composed songs and sing songs from Broadway musicals or theatrical presentations he had created. He had begun flute lessons at the time of the interview and participated in a community children's choir, but reported that he really wanted to be an actor.

About Peter's interaction with music, his mother wrote:

> Peter *loves* music! If he's not talking, he's singing. I don't think he's even aware of when he's singing. He's very attentive to music and will usually hum or sing along and/or move to the music. Music is calming for Peter. It's almost hypnotic at times. He hears music that I [am] unaware of, and [he] will comment [on it].

His mother also noted that music was incorporated into Peter's daily routine. He listened to music as he traveled in the car with his parents and as he walked around the house with his portable music player and headphones. He and his parents attended theatrical productions, dance company performances, and recitals throughout the year. Therefore, Peter had had many musical and theatrical experiences—either attending them or performing in the productions.

Talk-Aloud #1

> Peter: I heard this... Hmm, what first pops into my head? Well, I haven't thought of anything yet. Got it. I'm thinking why are those cow, dog, goose, chicken, pig, sheep, horse, and donkey [pictures] hanging there [on the wall in the interview space].
> Jody: So what does the music make you think about? What do you hear? [Trying to redirect Peter's focus]

Peter: Instruments. I'm hearing flutes. I'm hearing trumpets. I'm hearing trombones. I'm hearing violins. A lot of stuff. The music makes me feel like ... I'm at this giant castle in a party room, 'cause I've heard that all the time on TV. [Peter sings Theme 1 of the Bach.] I'm thinking, "Why am I listening to this?" I am hearing, it sounds like music from a castle probably. It sort of sounds like a bunch of bugs roaming around, like the violins have the beat sort of. And right now, sounds like ants marching. And, "Hurrah, hurrah!" [Peter sings the end of Theme 1 restated at the end of the music listening excerpt.] [After the music stops, Peter continues] The flute makes me think of birds. It sounds like birds. I'd really like to play the flute like that someday.

Talk-Aloud #2

Peter: Hmm, I guess, hmm, maybe it makes me think about a parade or a lot of toys or something. This part, I guess [Peter says this during Theme 1] ... it sounds like a parade when it's loud. And when it's soft, I think it can, I think that when it's soft it's sort of like a lullaby or something. It sounds like a giant like a long, long, long time ago at the President's house. It sounds like when people were dancing with like those white wigs on and those gigantic gowns. When it goes a little bit fast like this part, it sounds like it's a parade and really dancing.

The music makes me feel like *The King and I* when they're dancing. [Peter sings the first line of the song, "Shall We Dance."] I also think it makes me think about a TV show called *Little Boy Volcano*. There's a castle there and royal people and stuff. It sort of sounds like Bugs Bunny when he's conducting something ...

The castle ... [the music] was going fast, and the violin especially. Usually on TV shows or in books on TV, there's music and everything, it sort of sounds like they usually make it in a castle. It sort of sounds like a castle.

Interpreting Peter's Words

From the beginning of the first talk-aloud, Peter showed that he could be easily distracted by his visual surroundings. In the interview space, posters of composers, and pictures of song lyrics were affixed to the walls. At first, he did not describe the music but, rather, the interview environment. His response was a valid one, since listeners' minds move in and out of musical focus, regardless of personal musical preference, attention span, interest, or music listening space.

Peter's initial attention was focused on the timbre of the instrument that he was learning to play—the flute. His private lessons probably heightened his sensitivity toward the flute timbre, thus allowing him to discern it from other instruments in the ensemble. Peter mislabeled the instrument he had identified as the "trombone" with another instrument having a similar low timbre, since there was no trombone in the musical excerpt. While he listed specific instruments in his first talk-aloud, Peter did not list any instruments in the second talk-aloud.

Peter's perception of instruments played a vital role in each of his interview responses—verbal, visual, and kinesthetic. They consisted of programmatic associations that, when he verbally described them, seemed closely linked to instrumental timbres. Peter also recalled information from prior musical and television experiences and then associated it with the Bach excerpt. Although Peter did not label the listening excerpt as music from the Baroque period, he stated that the music belonged to a time period during which people wore powdered wigs and long dresses. Some of his statements suggested that Peter tried to establish a musical, stylistic time line on which he could place the Bach excerpt.

Curiously, at the completion of the interview tasks, Peter described the music as "barbeque" music. During a "sharing day" in music class, one of Peter's classmates brought in a CD of Vivaldi music. I had referred to it as music from the Baroque period. It seemed that Peter attempted to recall the term used in class and apply it to the Bach excerpt. This task required him to discriminate musical features of the Bach and cognitively maintain and manipulate them in order to compare it to a musical example he had heard only once during music class (i.e., the Vivaldi music).

Peter also described the music in terms of kinesthetic associations—dancing and a parade marching. He clearly responded to the strong sense of beat in the music, in addition to the piece's possible dynamic shifts based on thick and thin textural structure changes. His other descriptions, while not verbally detailed, included rich musical information Peter had committed to memory. He sang the first part of the primary theme in the beginning of the first talk-aloud. Peter was able to place quickly into his short-term memory parts of the primary thematic melodic material that repeated and captured his attention.

Peter's responses indicated his global, nonlinear music listening style. While differentiated detail was missing from his verbal responses, his imagination and creativity seemed activated by listening to the musical excerpt. The melodic detail was absorbed into Peter's memory after only one listening to the musical excerpt; therefore, I have to wonder about the levels of musical information that remained inside Peter's mind and body—information that he could not or did not choose to convey in his verbal descriptions.

Listening to David

David, a reserved fifth-grade male (age eleven), had had four years of cello instruction and had participated in the fourth-grade recorder ensemble at school. According to the written questionnaire completed by his parents, David had an affinity for musical theater, but he was open to listening to a variety of musical styles. His family attended an average of two musical theater productions each year. His parents noted that one of David's favorite activities was to go to a prominent local bookstore where he could explore new musical releases. They also stated that David listened to music each evening before his bedtime.

About David's music listening skill, his parents described:

[He] hears better and differently than most of us in the family. It is almost as if he is hearing something else—keener. He is also able to figure out patterns in music. He…made musical sounds as a baby before he talked.… The [sounds] were an early language.

Talk-Aloud #1

David [conducting the music while listening and speaking]: Well, I'm thinking, OK, now I'm thinking, "How do they get themselves together?" How did they like, it makes me feel a weird feeling. It's nice. Weird, It's like…nice music, it really is. I'm wondering how they got it all together. I mean, like, it sounds like, it's not really, well, it sounds like it's *impossible* to do. It sounds like, well, I'm not so sure—difference. It's like most music is classical, so um, rock is fast, this is.…What is this? Um, I can't really tell what kind of music this is. What is this? *What is it?* I'm thinking…like how do they get it this high? How do they get it this low? How do they.…It does go pretty high. And it's going…I wonder how they get it all together? Like how the composer can keep it all together. How *do* they keep it all together? Sounds like a climax is rising. A climax.…That's pretty much it.

Talk-Aloud #2

David: Well, it kind of reminds me of fantasy-like. It kind of reminds me of, this instrument that plays the part, like in *Peter and the Wolf*. Like the flute. They're using a lot of the flute, trumpet, and violin. I'm not sure if that's trumpet or flute. But I know they use a lot of blow things. They mostly also use a lot of strings. Right now, I'm not sure if it's trumpet or flute. Either one. And flute. It kind of makes my mind go blank. It kind of seems like a climax there.

Interpreting David's Words

Most of David's verbal comments were phrased in the form of a question. It appeared that David attempted to place himself in the role of conductor and/or performer, as he grappled to understand how the ensemble was able to perform the Bach piece. His verbal accounts reflected his thinking aloud about the musical product (i.e., the orchestral musicians performing) rather than listing, labeling, or reporting specific musical events as they occurred. Since he played an orchestral instrument, David could have been comparing his performance experience and skill level with the level of achievement demonstrated by the professional musicians performing on the musical recording.

Further, David externalized his mental comparison and evaluation processes. While he did not identify the Baroque style, David searched his knowledge base of classical and rock music, only to realize that these styles did not fit the criteria for the Bach excerpt. David became emphatic as he attempted to label the musical style of the excerpt: "What is this? *What is it?*"

Mingled among the questions David posed during the talk-alouds were his descriptions of affect, musical mood, form, and register. He described the music that was "high" and "low," which might have reflected his perception of register or the scalar virtuosity displayed by the performers of the musical excerpt. David also described the "musical climax" during both talk-alouds. He consistently noted the climax during the moments in the musical structure when the tonality was unstable, the dynamics gradually became louder, and there was harmonic movement toward the statement of the primary theme in the key of the dominant.

During the post-interview, David provided additional detail about the musical climax he perceived.

> At the end, near the end, it's kind of the same notes over and over although it's getting, it starts out with one instrument—the violin—then it goes to the flute, then it goes to the trumpet, and it ends up with all of them, and then it goes into a different thing [David tries to sing that which he is trying to describe—the melodic material at the conclusion of the second transition section]. And it's there where the climax is.

David's words indicated his focused attention on the solo-*tutti* concerto form—at times the full group played the music, while at other times there were featured instruments (i.e., violin, flute, and trumpet). In the second talk-aloud, David also referred to the oboe in his reference to *Peter and the Wolf*, even though he named the instrument, with uncertainty, as the flute. Structurally, David "felt" the tension created by the unstable harmonic progression that was leading somewhere—to the point of arrival of the primary thematic material stated in the key of the dominant.

Although he said the music was "weird," David turned to me and said, "It's like... nice music; it really is." This statement was offered apologetically, in the event he had offended his music teacher's (and researcher's) musical preferences. The first verbal report contained the only hint of affective response; none was explicitly represented in his visual and kinesthetic responses.

David's verbal responses were presented in a linear, nonlinear, and global manner. That is, he presented verbal commentary about specific instruments when he heard them in the musical example, but he interjected questions regarding the ensemble's performance proficiency which seemed to take precedence over any musical information he might have perceived, especially in the first talk-aloud. Further, the information about the instruments that he did present remained at the level of identification. There were few musical details that David included in his verbal talk-alouds.

Listening to Molly

Molly, a thirteen-year-old in the eighth grade, was quite involved in extracurricular and school music activities. At the time of the interview, she had participated in a community youth orchestra for two years, and a community children's choir for four years, and played clarinet for two years in her school's band. She reported that she enjoyed listening to classical music and the Beatles, especially while riding in the car with her parents. Molly stated that she had attended many concerts with her family and that, while classical music was her favorite, she enjoyed listening to many different types of music.

Talk-Aloud #1

Molly: The group of people are marching towards somewhere important. And marching, and marching. They're still marching. And now, here comes the violin, ah…and they answer back—the group that is marching does. Then the oboe asks something. They answer back. The flute asks, is going to ask something, too. And they answer back. The trumpet…he wants to ask something, too. Answer back. And…now they're all talking about what they learned when they asked a question. And the trumpet wants to announce what he learned. And he's so happy about it. And then…then they talk about it some more. And they keep talking. Talking. And the trumpet wants to know, wants everyone to know what he thinks. And, um…the other instruments are whispering to each other. And they're still whispering about something. It becomes more important. And the trumpet, of course, wants to tell everyone what he thinks again. Even though he's whispering at times.

Talk-Aloud #2

Molly: Um…it's like a loud section where everyone's dancing. It seems like a dance. It's sort of like a ball. The violins are telling everyone something, and they keep dancing, and then they keep dancing. The flute wanted to say something about how they danced, and then they keep dancing. Then the trumpet thinks he's the best dancer around, and then they agree with him. Um…and they keep dancing. The trumpet is still talking about himself. And they keep dancing, but the trumpet keeps talking about himself and keeps dancing. And then…they're whispering a rumor about how somebody dances. And they keep dancing, and thy whisper about someone again. They keep whispering, and now they're dancing again.

Interpreting Molly's Words

A primary feature of Molly's talk-alouds was the number of story associations she depicted. Her descriptions included kinesthetic imagery—marching (talk-aloud #1) and dancing (talk-aloud #2)—and imagery of instrumental "conversations," such as the instruments whispering, answering, telling, asking, and saying. In fact, Molly's main characters of her stories were the instruments themselves, a personification of the solo instruments and those serving as accompaniment in the musical example. She repeatedly mentioned that there were individual instruments that had something to say; these instruments were also the solo instruments in the Bach excerpt. She also stated that "they"—the other instruments of the orchestral ensemble— answered, talked, or danced in response to the solo instruments. These descriptions indicated that the concerto solo-*tutti* formal structure was the primary focus of Molly's attention, with a secondary focus on individual instrumental timbres.

Inherent in Molly's stories were also clues about her perception of dynamic contrasts, beat, musical climax (tension and repose), musical style and mood. In each of the talk-alouds, Molly's main character was the trumpet player. She depicts "him" as the instrument that has the most to say and that captures the attention of the other instruments that respond to "him." Whenever Molly perceived the primary thematic material first heard in the musical example, she mentioned the trumpet. During the post-interview, Molly also told me that "he"—the trumpet—was the main character, since it was the loudest and most obvious instrument in the musical excerpt.

She also described the "whispering" portions of the music during the point of the musical excerpt where there was tonal instability, increased musical tension, and building transition toward the restatement of the primary thematic material in the key of the dominant (musical repose). It is also during that transition section that the trumpeter performs the highest pitches of that particular musical excerpt. Could Molly have confused dynamics with pitch levels?

Molly depicted the musical style of the excerpt by comparing it to dancing and marching. Both have prominent, regular, and rhythmic pulses to which people dance or march. That she thought people in her story were marching to some place "important" or that they were dancing might indicate her perception of the light, yet regal, nature of the piece. During her first talk-aloud, Molly says the trumpet is "happy" about talking to the other instruments. Might the trumpet's personified emotional state be somehow connected to Molly's perception of or affective response to the musical mood and style?

Both of Molly's talk-alouds provided similar information couched in undifferentiated story images. While the first talk-aloud provided reference to more specific individual instruments than the second talk-aloud, neither talk-aloud had a plethora of specific musical detail. This was also true of Molly's mapping (visual) and movement (kinesthetic) responses during the interview sessions. In fact, she continued to provide representations primarily of solo-*tutti* formal structures and instrumental timbres. Molly offered new information about her music listening experience during the mapping sessions in which she drew symbols for ornamentation (trumpet trill) and the melodic contour of the ensemble's responses to the solo instruments. Thus, cognitively, Molly appeared to be a linear listener that employed visual and kinesthetic metaphors during the music listening process.

Listening to Alexis

Alexis, an eleventh-grader (age sixteen), participated in the community youth choir that I had conducted. In addition to that choral experience, she was involved in her school's choral program: symphonic choir, chorale, show choir, musicals, and solo and ensemble contests. She was even named "Outstanding Female Vocalist" during a show choir competition. Alexis described herself as a "jamming singer," one who liked to play the piano, improvise, and sing. Instrumentally, she played bassoon, piano, oboe, clarinet, and tenor and alto saxophone in the school jazz band. Additionally, she performed with a community musical theater troupe.

Alexis's responses to the questionnaire indicated that she enjoyed listening to any music, except country music. Punk rock was her favorite style of music because she could "let out all of the emotions and dance." She mentioned that she listened to music and played or sang music everyday and that she usually listened to music by herself or with her friends.

Talk-Aloud #1

Alexis: I can see the bows going over and over the strings. And their fingers flying all over the strings of the violins and cellos. The flutes go up. And I kind of see a meadow and a young girl dancing and talking to birds. . . . It's happy and uplifting. It kind of makes you feel tranquil and peaceful, like I'm in the meadow with the young girl. Um, the flutes prance all over the place. The birds flying, the sun shining down . . . very bright and peaceful. Makes me think of a light wind uplifting and airy. It's a little strong there. I can see fingers up and down on the trumpets, very high. And, I can feel the strange faces of the brass going up to the high notes, and the repeating, and the echoes of the parts going back and forth. And the change in the piece there . . . a little chill there, some goose-bumps 'cause it switches to the minor key for just a second and then back to the happy again. And, I can see the entire orchestra going crazy with this! The bows are flying all over the place, playing all the notes. And I feel the director going everywhere with it [the music], keeping them in mind, keeping the orchestra all together. And ah, I can see the wind picking up in the meadow as it gets louder and louder and the sun comes out again as it calms down for a second. And it picks up and down, and you see branches of trees swaying back and forth.

Talk-Aloud #2

Alexis: It starts off with a very happy sound—bright and cheerful. Fast moving, a nice speed, so it keeps the spirits up. You can hear the entire orchestra playing and all the movement with that. And then it slows down a bit, calming. And then it picks back up and pushes forward. Here you hear the oboist playing, and I can see the trumpeters playing, and then the flutists playing with their fingers moving all over the place. It still keeps the happy tone. I see lots of people moving around, like a bustling city. And I can see the director directing all the people all over the place. I can see the trumpeter's face turning really red at the high part. And this kind of gets angry and back and forth, the people in an argument or something. I can see the bows of the violins and cellos going all over the place and different instruments. And here it turns back happy again. The fight is resolved. All the people going forward with their lives in the city. It gets a tiny bit sad there, but then it goes right out of it again. Kind of like how it is every day with a person's life. And I can see all the instruments playing wildly.

Interpreting Alexis's Words

Musical features that captured Alexis's attention included imagery/story associations, affect, instruments, and performance process. She provided numerous responses that were kinesthetic (movement) references: "prancing," "wind moving and increasing," "dancing," and "talking to the birds." These references also seemed to contribute to Alexis's perception of musical mood, style, and perhaps affect: happy, uplifting, dancing, bright, makes you feel peaceful, tranquil. She equated the pattern of musical mood changes, whether a function of texture, tonality, dynamics, or melodic/rhythmic contour, to the ebb and flow of a person's life cycle—a metaphor used in philosophical theories of music representing the movement of life itself (see chapter 3).

As was also evident in David's concurrent verbal reports, Alexis's talk-alouds focused on the instruments she perceived in the orchestral ensemble, particularly the *process* of performing the musical example. While listening to the music, she visualized the performers' bows moving across string instruments and the players' fingers playing the flutes and brass instruments. Additionally, she noted that "lots of notes" were being played by the orchestra, saw the brass players' facial gestures as they played the high notes, and observed the role of the conductor in bringing the ensemble together during the performance. Alexis actually conducted a four-beat pattern as she listened to the musical example and provided her talk-aloud during the first interview session. It seemed that she was internalizing aspects of the music by moving to it, yet another reference to musical movement and the kinesthetic response mode.

Much of what Alexis perceived musically was presented in the form of a story or framed by her wonderments about the performance process. Yet her descriptions, if considered *when* she said them relative to the musical example, seemed closely linked to specific musical features. Additional information that Alexis reported or that I inferred from her talk-aloud included: *tutti*/solo formal sections, repetition and contrast, dynamics, minor modality, and harmonic tension and resolution ("the sun comes out again") when she heard the primary theme stated again at the conclusion of the musical example. In the second talk-aloud, Alexis repeated information included in the first talk-aloud, but added descriptions of the oboe and cello, affect ("keep the spirits up"), tempo ("nice speed"), orchestra and movement, ornamentation (during the trumpet trill), harmonic tension and resolution ("fight is resolved"), and musical mood with musical material presented briefly in the minor mode.

Alexis's verbal talk-alouds indicated a "mixed mode" of focused attention and listening style. She moved in and out of describing formal musical elements and the story images associated with those and other musical elements and structural details. Similar to Molly's talk-alouds, Alexis's verbal reports were linear and minimally more differentiated than Peter's and David's reports.

LEARNING FROM STUDENTS

The verbal response mode enabled the students, regardless of grade or age, to provide information about their thinking processes that was not evident in their visual and kinesthetic responses to the music listening excerpt. It was also in this mode that the participants best exhibited their evaluative and comparative skills. Additionally, students frequently compared the Bach excerpt to other pieces of music familiar to them.

The concurrent verbal reporting task allowed the participants, regardless of grade or age, to indulge in stories, images, and associations related to their music listening experience. The level of story and imagery detail provided during the verbal descriptions, although mostly depicted in terms of global musical features, was more replete with information than that which the participants' presented in their visual and kinesthetic responses.

The students' verbal reports (and drawings and movements) were full of ambiguity. The youngest participants tended to use limited musical vocabularies in comparison to the older participants. Despite age, however, the participants frequently applied incorrect adjectives in their descriptions of musical events. They tended to confuse terms for high, low, loud, quiet (soft), fast, and slow. In some cases, students created their own terms for describing musical features. Many of these verbal terms or phrases remained mysteries until I observed the students' responses offered in the visual and kinesthetic response modes.

Students presented information during the talk-aloud tasks that served as schematic foundations for information depicted in their mapping and movement tasks. The verbal reports typically contained global (i.e., undifferentiated, general) descriptions of musical events, while the visual and kinesthetic modes contained descriptions of more differentiated musical events that the participants did not or could not describe verbally. It seemed that the children held mental schemes of the music that remained relatively rigid over the course of several repeated listenings, at least in terms of the broad topics the students presented in their responses. While the students provided more details about the topics they represented, there were typically no new musical topics, features, characteristics that were added to the second verbal reports. The students' verbal responses gained depth rather than breadth with repeated listenings.

Perhaps the most striking difference in the verbal reports among the students in grades two, five, eight, and eleven was the number of perceptual and affective responses students provided. For example, the youngest students (grade two) provided the fewest number of verbal responses related to musical features, structure, affect, or mood. Among the older the students, the number of different topics or categories they addressed increased in their talk-alouds. Additionally, the younger students (grades two and five) provided the highest number of musical associations, stories, and images in their verbal descriptions. Eighth- and eleventh-graders tended to include associations, stories, and images with the addition of descriptions of musical elements, mood, and formal properties. Often, these adolescent students also gave musical rationales for including stories and images in their descriptions. In other words, the students verbally connected their stories to elements of the music.

As one might imagine, the older the student participants, the more specific the musical detail in their talk-alouds became. This seems a natural developmental occurrence, since older students have had more experience with music and language, so they articulated features of their musical experiences with a broader range of descriptors. Younger students appeared frustrated at times, as they searched for words to describe the music. It is not surprising that, regardless of age, student participants provided few descriptors of affect other than musical mood. Music, as an ineffable product of performance, can stir emotions and feelings in its listeners that cannot be completely or accurately described. Or, perhaps the students did not know exactly what they felt, if they were even conscious of affective responses.

For some participants (including Alexis, Peter, and David), providing verbal descriptions of the music was not adequate for representing their music listening experience. Instead, these students reverted to musical means of expressing that which they heard, thought, or felt during the interview sessions. Singing was the primary alternate response mode that students used in their attempts to describe music. They used musical descriptions to depict musical sounds when their words could not capture what they were trying to convey verbally in their interview talk-alouds. This was particularly true of students' descriptions of embellishments (i.e., trill), repeated thematic material, instrumental performances, and some programmatic features or associations.

In addition to singing and other vocal sounds, participants used a variety of kinesthetic and visual images in describing the Bach musical excerpt. Most students reacted to the beat of the music. I observed them either tapping their fingers or their feet to the steady beat, even thought they did not verbally describe the pulse of the music in their talk-alouds. Furthermore, students incorporated action (movement) verbs in their descriptions that indicated their listening to the music in terms of kinesthetic responses and imagery. Words such as *dancing, swirling, swingy, bouncy, flow, running, jumping, wigglier, walking, shaking, hopping, floating, playing,* and *shivering* suggested the listeners' innate kinesthetic connection to the musical experience. Even though they verbalized "what they were thinking, hearing, and feeling" as they listened to the music, the student participants' experiences were linked to kinesthetic aspects of their visual imagery and musical explanations.

How might these observations inform our music pedagogy? Perhaps the beginning level of fostering students' verbal descriptions is for them to provide descriptive verbal stories, since the visual and kinesthetic components of the music listening experience were so vivid in their talk-alouds. However, to stay at this level is not enough. Teachers must ask clarification questions to prompt students to uncover how the musical elements, structures, and characteristics relate to their "extra-musical" responses. It is also the music teacher's responsibility to lead students to acquire new vocabulary terms and deeper levels of musical perception and analysis based on the information the students give in their multisensory responses.

Repeated listenings in class provide opportunities for the students to listen beyond that which they initially tend to describe verbally—instruments, melodic contour, and beat. A teacher statement such as, "This time as we listen, let's focus on the instruments that do not play the melody, but seem to be in the background," can point students to listen to something new by bringing the musical feature into their conscious focus of attention. Of concern, however, is that music education (i.e., private lessons, ensembles, or general music classes) might not move students beyond instruction that is perception-based—learning about music notation, elements, and formal structures, history, and performance technique and craft. Do we make concerted efforts to help students connect possible feelings, moods, and emotions resulting from music listening to inherent musical relationships that evoke affective responses?

Children's talk-alouds could be categorized into three types: (1) reporting; (2) engaging the imagination, creating stories, and connecting with past musical and life experiences; and (3) reflecting on musical performance processes. Talk-alouds as a pedagogical tool seem to be cognitive (perceptual and affective) essays that are the results of listening to music, situating the current experience among numerous prior musical experiences, and articulating metaphors in one's personal style of communicating to self and community "others." Furthermore, talk-alouds are translations and metaphors, not mirrors, of thoughts and feelings. Students also know music much more deeply than they can articulate. Therefore, teachers must take talk-alouds for what they are: incomplete representations that, when considered with other multisensory responses, are windows into students' musical minds (Davidson and Scripp 1988) and their music listening experiences.

CLASSROOM AND REHEARSAL STRATEGIES
Talk-Alouds

The students' verbal reports in this chapter were presented as a part of research project participation. You might be wondering how the talk-aloud methodology can be implemented in the music classroom or ensemble rehearsal. As a part of a music learning center, individual students can use digital recorders or computer software programs (e.g., GarageBand) to record their talk-alouds while listening to a musical excerpt. Of course, it will be important that the students' verbal reports *and* the music are recorded simultaneously. Teachers can analyze (and infer) the student's words in relationship to the musical events, features, and formal structures. Additionally, the learning center setup will need to be located in a space where students' speaking aloud does not interfere with other learning centers or classroom experiences.

If students have difficulty finding words to describe what they hear in the music, have a Word Choice Chart available for them (see figure 5.1). This chart includes standard musical vocabulary and students' "own words"—common descriptors students in my research used in describing music listening excerpts. This chart can assist students by prompting specific terms they might seek or features of the music they might wish to describe in their talk-aloud (or mapping and movement) responses.

Written Essays

A variation on talk-alouds is having students write an essay about what they are thinking, feeling, and hearing while listening to music. Realize that writing requires an additional level of thought "translation" beyond verbal reporting. Teachers will need to determine the form of the students' written responses: narrative/essay? Incomplete sentences? Single-word bullet points? Students need to provide enough information to be informative to the teacher; however, writing essays might interfere too much with the music listening process. Teachers could also have students jot down ideas and "notes" as they listen to the musical example, and then have them transform the notes into sentences and paragraphs.

For illustrative purposes, let us examine two essays written by Charlie, a ninth-grade bassist who plays in his high-school orchestra. Charlie represents an orchestral member with "average" musical performance skill. Throughout the

Figure 5.1. WORD CHOICE CHARTS

Music Listening Word Choices

Melody/Tune/Theme	Rhythm	Instrument						Bright
Pitch	Short notes	Voice	Plucked	Short (*Staccato*)	Getting slower (*ritardando*)	Very soft (*pianissimo*)	Lots of instruments or voices(thick texture)	Dark
Up	Long notes	Brass	Bowed	Smooth (*Legato*)	Getting faster (*accelerando*)	Soft (*piano*)	Few instruments or voices (thin texture)	Blue
Down	Jazzy	Woodwind	Struck/Hit	Short/sharp	Very slow(*largo*)	Medium (*mezzo forte*)	Solo instrument or voice	Red
Contour	Syncopated	Strings	Blown into	Accented	Slow(*adagio*)	Loud (*forte*)	Instruments/voices play or sing together(*tutti*)	Yellow
Shape	Steady Beat	Keyboard	Ornamented	Jagged	Medium(*moderato*)	Very loud (*fortissimo*)	Accompaniment	Happy
Repeated notes	Uneven beat	Percussion	Decorated	Curvy	Fast(*allegro*)	Getting louder (*crescendo*)	No accompaniment (*a cappella*)	Sad
Same	Pulse	Choir	Embellished	Whirling	Very Fast(*presto*)	Getting softer (*diminuendo*)	Background music	Funny
Different	Quarter notes	Band	Elaborated	Jumpy			Foreground music	Relaxing
Scale	Eighth-notes	Orchestra	Additions to the melody	Spinning				Exciting
Leaps	Sixteenth-notes	Small group	Additions to the rhythms	Running				Calm
Steps		Large Group		Continuous				I like because…
Major/minor/modal				Constant				I don't like because…

school year, Charlie's orchestra teacher presented the students with listening examples (approximately seventeen listening essays per academic year), some related to pieces the students rehearsed for performance and some for the sake of exposure to a variety of musical soundscapes (Western and non-Western). The students listened to the music, provided brief written reflections of the music, and subsequently analyzed the music in full-group discussions.

Charlie's first essay was written during the first week of the academic year (August), while listening to Ippolitov-Ivanov's "Procession of the Sardar" (*Caucasian Sketches*). He wrote the second essay during the final listening assignment nearing the completion of the academic year (May). This essay was a reflection on the Sultans of Strings's "El-Kahira" (*Luna*). As you read both essays, try analyzing the data with verbal protocol analysis codes in order to track changes between the music listening essays. Additionally, consider the following questions: (1) What progress in music listening skill do you notice from the first listening assignment to the last? (2) What progress in verbally describing the music do you notice from the beginning to the end of the school year?

Essay #1

There are several instruments at work here. The main one is a flute. There is also a bass, cymbal, violins, drums, and cello. Overall, it includes most types of instruments. Through the whole piece you can hear the flute. The cymbals stuck out in several places as well. The tempo was pretty fast, but it slowed down in some parts. The piece was mostly loud, but it got quiet in some parts. It [the piece] was pretty long. It was also exciting and almost as if music from a renscanse [*sic*] [Renaissance] fair. As far as I can tell, it's one whole piece and does not have a separate [*sic*] ending. This song reminds me of a renissance [*sic*] fair or something like that. I thought this piece of music was OK, but it didn't thrill me. It didn't have enough bass.

Essay #2

This piece of music is performed by a small, full orchecstra [*sic*]. Throughout the whole piece, you can clearly hear a pan flute and violins and violas. This piece is about *moderato*, but it does slow in some places. This piece never really gets all that loud, but in some spots it gets very quiet. This piece is defanately [*sic*] short and lively. This piece kind of reminds me of the movie *Avatar*, when the crippled guy uses the avatar body for the first time and explores the jungle. I think this piece is closest to contemporary music than any other genre in our [orchestra] folder [that we are performing]. The piece would be closest to "Arabian Dreams." I really like this piece. It used old style instruments and yet created something cool and current. I like it.

Charlie's first essay reflected written description of general musical occurrences, without much musical detail or differentiation. He primarily listed the instruments that he heard in the music—strings, percussion, and a flute. As a string bassist, I would have imagined Charlie to list members of the string family; he listed bass, violin, cello, but did not mention viola. Notice that Charlie's description of instruments did not include any brass instruments or specific percussion instruments other than the cymbal. He stated "most types of instruments" performed the music, but did not identify or use the term "orchestra." The piece of music actually included a full orchestra of strings, brass, woodwind and percussion instruments (i.e., timpani, tambourine, triangle, snare and bass drums, and cymbals).

Charlie's descriptions were void of standard musical terminology, although he wrote about tempo and dynamics in his own words. Instead of using the term "movement" of an orchestral piece, Charlie stated that the music is a "whole piece" and that it did not have "a separate ending." The one time he attempted to use a term the students had learned in the ensemble class, "Renaissance," he associated the music with a fair. Yet, the musical example was from the Romantic era, a style the students had not yet studied in class. Finally, Charlie provided his opinion of the piece ("Okay, but it didn't thrill me"), even though he described the style or mood of the music as "exciting."

In Charlie's second essay, he provided a more detailed account of the musical excerpt than in his first essay. He identified the ensemble as an orchestra and its size. Charlie correctly identified some of the specific instruments found in the musical excerpt, such as violin and viola, and even the more exotic pan flute. He also identified the tempo of the piece using a musical term (*moderato*) then returned to using his own, nonmusical terms to describe the tempo, dynamics, and musical style/mood. These statements suggest that Charlie's attention was captured by similar musical qualities in both listening sessions, but he incorporated musical terms and specific instruments, albeit incomplete, along with a non-Western musical instrument that he must have encountered in some prior musical experience.

Perhaps the most specificity is found in the second half of Charlie's essay. He explained why the music reminded him of a specific part in the movie *Avatar*, but unless the readers know the movie storyline they still might not understand Charlie's rationale. While he described the movie sequence, he did not write about "what in the music" made him relate to the movie. Finally, Charlie stated that he "really like[d]" the musical example, and he provided a bit of rationale for his judgment, something not revealed in his first essay.

Charlie also related the musical excerpt to a piece he was learning to play in orchestra rehearsals. Although he did not divulge why the piece sounds like "Arabian Dreams," one can infer that Charlie is hearing the Middle Eastern influence in both pieces. In the first essay, Charlie tried to attach an historical period term to the piece (i.e., "Renaissance"), but without concrete evidence to support the musical description. However, Charlie's statements in the second essay show musical comparative skills, juxtaposing at least two different pieces of music and comparing musical features and styles ("contemporary music").

What information did you glean from Charlie's essays? What feedback would you have provided Charlie on each of his music listening essay assignments? What prompting questions might you have used to clarify or gather more information from Charlie? If you gave Charlie the opportunity to rework his essays, to which of your questions would you ask him to respond? According to the musical descriptions that Charlie offered, what new vocabulary might you introduce to him and/or the ensemble? What musical concept(s) might you wish to review in class?

Venn Diagrams

A tool used to engage students' critical and comparative listening skills is the Venn diagram (see figure 5.2). It is a structure familiar to most students in upper elementary, middle, and high school, albeit from mathematical contexts. Nonetheless, students understand that Venn diagrams show numerical sets, subsets, and intersections (shared elements among sets). Applying these same principles, Venn diagrams can be used in describing, comparing, and contrasting characteristics of two or more music listening excerpts.

Venn diagrams can also be used to compare (1) two or three performances of the same piece music, (2) music from different historical periods or world cultures, or (3) music having different instrumental/vocal configurations, arrangements, meters, tonalities, rhythms, dynamics, or formal structures. For example, I have used three recordings of "Amazing Grace" in a listening lesson presented over the course of several class meetings: the students singing the song in class and two field

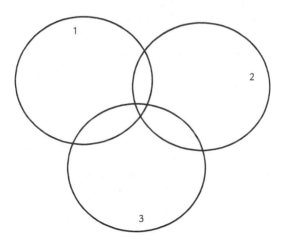

Figure 5.2.
Venn Diagram for Comparative Music Listening.

recordings of "Amazing Grace"—one in four-part hymn style and the other of a worship leader with congregational response (Titon 2002). As the students listen to one of the versions of the song, they write descriptive words in the larger, open space of the first circle. Each musical example is heard at least twice. Then, the students listen to the second version of the song and write words describing the music in the second circle. The process continues with the third musical excerpt.

After the students listen to all the musical examples, they circle words or ideas that are common among the first two pieces of music and then draw a line from the circled words to the overlapping areas of circles one and two. Similarly, they find common musical characteristics between examples two and three and between one and three, drawing lines from the descriptors to the intersecting portions of the respective circles. Finally, as a class or individually, students find those musical features common among all three pieces of music and draw lines to that intersection of the three circles on the Venn diagram.

When the students have described the musical excerpts and found commonalities and differences among them, class discussion can take place. Student participation in class discussion seems to be enhanced by first revisiting a musical excerpt and then immediately discussing it. For example, re-listen to the first musical excerpt and then have the students present their descriptors. This sequence would also occur with excerpts two and three, before discussing "intersections" among the pieces.

Fill-In Charts

Fill-in charts (see figure 5.3) provide a structure by which teachers and students can track their listening perception and affective responses during repeated listenings to the same musical excerpt. For example, during the first listening of Ravel's "Bolero," students write a single verbal descriptor in each box under the heading "Listening #1." During the same or different class period, students listen again to "Bolero" and write down anything new in the spaces below "Listening #2." The idea is for students to add new information and/or specific detail during each of the listenings.

A second use for the fill-in chart is as a call chart. Certainly you have seen call charts found in basal text series books: the teacher (or a person calls a number on the music recording) and the students circle the words on the chart that describe what they are hearing. In each box of the fill-in chart, students provide their own words to describe what they hear in the music when the teacher calls out a number. Upon repeated listenings, the students write their descriptions in the second and third columns of the chart and at each number called by the teacher. Similar to the Venn diagram tool, teachers and students are encouraged to compare descriptions of the music and revisit sections of the music that are challenging to describe. Community description, analysis, and comparison lead to co-constructed understanding of the musical excerpt.

Figure 5.3. MUSIC LISTENING FILL-IN CHART

Call Number (Optional)	Listening #1	Listening #2	Listening #3
1			
2			
3			
4			
5			
6			
7			
8			
9			
10			

Listening Webs

Years ago, I attended a workshop that dealt with whole language strategies for teaching children to write stories. The clinician spoke of story "webs" as one such strategy. The webs hold the main theme of a student's story in the center oval of the web and related details, plots, character action, and scene descriptions in the outer ovals of the web. I began thinking how to make this tool relevant to music teaching and learning.

One of my solutions was to create a music listening web. This tool (see figure 5.4) seems to work best when there is a musical formal structure that is the focus of the music listening lesson, such as theme and variation, or melodic and rhythmic motives. For example, listening to a piece of Polynesian drumming music, one hears a repeated rhythmic pattern that forms the crux of the piece (quarter-note, quarter-note, eighth-eighth, quarter-note). While listening to the music, students find the pattern by tapping it in the palm of their hand and then create ways of notating the rhythm in the center of the web. Some students use standard musical notation while others draw long and short lines, large and small circles, or some other form of invented notation. Since the rhythm is varied in the number of instruments playing the rhythm, volume, and tempo, students describe these variations in each of the outside ovals connected to the central oval. The web provides an organizational scheme in which students can keep track of theme and variation, rondo (if the web ovals were numbered), motives, and texture (i.e., the addition of voices and instruments—think "Bolero").

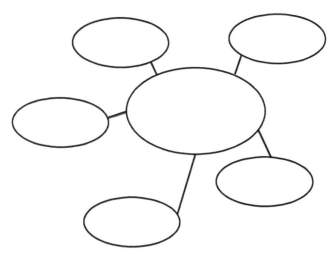

Figure 5.4.
Music Listening Web.

After the listening and subsequent discussion of the students' webbing descriptions, the web can serve as a springboard for compositional experiences based on the music listening excerpt. For example, students can create their own theme and variation. They can plot the theme in the central oval of the web and then determine in each of the surrounding ovals how they will vary the theme. Then, they can compare the original music listening excerpt with their own composition. The students could also compose a piece based on a piece they had just listened to in class—listening to a theme and variation, completing the web structure, and composing a new piece based on the theme and variation descriptions in each oval.

Question Pathways and Idea Pathways

A "question pathway" and "idea pathway" are strategies for collecting students' questions and points of interest, respectively, for subsequent class or small-group discussion. I refer to these repositories of ideas and questions as "pathways" because they reflect students' cognitive paths in their quest to understand the musics they encounter. Their externalized wonderments, information from prior experiences, perceptions, affective responses, and reflections contribute to the students' personal and community construction of musical meaning. Furthermore, since the entire class has the opportunity to contribute to the pathways, every student is given an individual "voice" in the learning community.

Imagine a middle-school class listening to Duke Ellington's "Giggling Rapids" from the suite *The River*, written in 1970. This piece, in Ellington's jazzy big-band style, was originally choreographed and performed by the Alvin Ailey Dance

Troupe. On a white board, chalk board, bulletin board, or a sheet of paper acting as a "graffiti board" (inclusive of words, drawings, cutout pictures, listening map segments), students place questions (on a question pathway) or observations and comments (on an idea pathway) that are the result of listening to "Giggling Rapids."

Students' questions placed on the question pathway might include:

1. What is a suite?
2. Why is this piece called "Giggling Rapids?"
3. What is a rapid?
4. Why did the composer write this piece?
5. Who was Duke Ellington?
6. What type of group plays this piece?

Students' ideas placed on the idea pathway might include:

1. I noticed the music moving slowly, but then moving more quickly.
2. There are two main ideas in this music.
3. I hear a pattern repeated: short-short-long. Then the whole group answers it.
4. This is jazz.
5. Ellington was a bandleader.

From these questions and ideas, teachers and students can enter discussions based on the inquiries and knowledge the students bring to the music listening experience. The students' responses on the pathway lists initiate the direction of the discussions and future musical experiences. Pathways can also prompt students to research the questions posed by themselves or other students; therefore, the teacher is not expected to "answer" the questions but, rather, facilitate learning experiences so the students can discover the "answers" to their own questions. If students place "inaccurate" information on the idea pathway, it presents an opportunity for students and teachers to explore and discover the "accurate" information about their perceptual understandings (i.e., descriptions of musical elements). Teachers can keep the question and idea pathways posted in the classroom as a reminder of the students' main questions and ideas, and as an opportunity for the learners to add new questions, observations, and comments as they become familiar with a musical excerpt through repeated listening.

YOUR TURN

Teachers and students communicate through verbal interactions, although nonverbal behaviors add to the context of what is being said and heard. In this chapter, we explored the connection between language and thought development and how teachers can effectively use language-based tools to facilitate students' verbal descriptions of music. As you reflect on the content of this chapter, consider the following question prompts:

1. What type of language-based experiences do you and your students experience in music class?
2. What have you learned about the students' music development based on these experiences in class?
3. How did/will what you learn from students' verbal descriptions of music listening excerpts inform your teaching for music-listening skill development?
4. From your teaching observations, which musical elements or expressive features do students have difficulty describing verbally? How does this vary per grade level?
5. How might you incorporate verbal reporting (concurrent or retrospective) in your music class?
6. What are some ways that you would assess students' writing or talking-alouds?
7. How do you/would you guide students in their development of musical vocabulary?
8. In your music classroom, what percentage of the class time is devoted to the teachers and students talking relative to the percentage of the class time making music? How might you vary these percentages (musical vs. verbal)?

REFERENCES

Creswell, J. (2008). *Educational Research: Planning, Conducting, and Evaluating Quantitative and Qualitative Research* (3rd ed.). Upper Saddle River, NJ: Pearson, Merrill, Prentice-Hall.

Davidson, L., and L. Scripp (1988). "Young Children's Musical Representations: Windows on Music Cognition." In *Generative Processes in Music: The Psychology of Performance, Improvisation, and Composition,* edited by J. Sloboda, 195–230. New York: Oxford University Press.

Ericsson, K., and H. Simon (1993). *Protocol Analysis: Verbal Reports as Data* (rev. ed.). Cambridge, MA: MIT Press.

Gardner, H. (1983). *Frames of Mind: The Theory of Multiple Intelligences.* New York: Basic Books.

Honing, H. (2009). *Musical Cognition: A Science of Listening.* New Brunswick, NJ: Transaction.

John-Steiner, V. (1997). *Notebooks of the Mind: Explorations of Thinking.* New York: Oxford University Press.

Kerchner, J. L. (1996). "Perceptual and Affective Components of the Music Listening Experience as Manifested in Children's Verbal, Visual, and Kinesthetic Representations." Unpublished doctoral dissertation, Northwestern University.

Reimer, B. (1989). *A Philosophy of Music Education* (second edition). Upper Saddle River, NJ: Prentice Hall.

Rubin, H., and I. Rubin (2005). *Qualitative Interviewing: The Art of Hearing Data* (2nd. ed.). Thousand Oaks, CA: Sage.

Titon, J., ed. (2002). *Worlds of Music: An Introduction to the Music of the World's Peoples* (CD#1, tracks 22 & 23). New York: Schirmer.

Vygotsky, L. and A. Kozulin, ed. (1986). *Thought and Language* (original book by Lev Vygotsky). Cambridge, MA: Massachusetts Institute of Technology.

Winner, E. (1988). *The Point of Words: Children's Understanding of Metaphor and Irony.* Cambridge, MA: Harvard University Press.

CHAPTER 6

Listeners Rehearsing and Performing

U p to this point, we have primarily considered music-listening skill development of students in preschool, elementary school, and secondary school general-music settings. This chapter, however, is dedicated to highlighting multisensory pedagogical tools—mapping, moving, and verbally describing—that can be utilized in school choirs, bands, orchestras, and other performance-based classes. We will consider ways of nurturing student musicians who are learning to demonstrate their understanding of musical intersections—of musical knowledge, affective sensitivity, technique, imagination, and musical craft—in their performances. As a foundational skill, music listening is at the heart of our discussion.

Most music teacher/conductors embrace the goals of developing students' love for music and performance and for helping students become lifelong, independent, informed music performers and connoisseurs. The voluntary Music Content Standards stipulated in the *National Standards for Arts Education* (Consortium of National Arts Education 1994) provide music educational pathways for achieving these student musical outcomes and habits of mind. In addition to nurturing students' musical technique and expressivity, ensemble curricula provide students with experiences in at least four music content standards: singing, playing, reading notation, and listening to music.

Cultivated music listening skills provide the groundwork for performing as a soloist or ensemble musician. Listening is a complex process that exists on several functional planes as individuals perform within the ensemble community. First, ensemble members must develop the ability to discern their individual musical instrumental or vocal sounds from those produced by others in the group. Ensemble members should track not only the features of their own unique sound production but also their sound relative to other performers' musical sounds. Next, there is the process of listening to the sound of the entire group in order to feel and hear the unified ensemble sound. As an ensemble member, it can be powerful, if not profound, to be surrounded by nuanced musical sound being produced by an entity greater than any single individual performer. On yet another level of listening, ensemble members employ individualistic and communal listening to feel the musical pulse, produce sounds of emphasis and de-emphasis within a phrase, and hear oneself relative to the pitch, volume, timbre, diction, phrasing, and breath inhalation that other ensemble players or singers produce. Musicians collaboratively sense musical spaces, including silence and those spaces between pitches (i.e., rhythmic intricacies), and the intensity with which the group gives life to each tone. When a group of "understanding" individual musicians work together as performing musician/listeners, audiences are given the gift of hearing music as artistically and aesthetically interesting interpretations that bring novelty to their body-mind-feeling-spirit selves as listeners.

How, then, do students gain knowledge and understanding of the literature they rehearse and perform? How do students' enhanced focus of attention and music discrimination skills transform their music performance experiences? How do teachers lead students to become independent, understanding, and informed performers? In an educational setting that is intended for musical performance, what is the purpose of including music listening lessons in rehearsals?

LOOKING IN ON LISTENING

Reimer (2000, 186) defined an "understanding performer" as "one who, while approaching music from the particular perspective of a performer of it, is able to incorporate within that musical role a host of relevant connections to the wider musical/cultural world in which performance resides." To summarize, he is concerned that, although music teacher/conductors do a fine job at tuning up their students' technical skills, student performers might leave their ensemble experiences without an authentic sense of and personal satisfaction in knowing what it means to be an understanding artist/performer. His concern is what students are *not* learning in and experiencing from performance ensemble instruction if rehearsals are focused on students knowing the music literature only from purely technical and notational perspectives. When music educators focus solely on the instruction of notes and vocal or instrumental technique, students can lack the full range of musical sensitivities, imagination, and decision making that is inherently linked to performance, because the music is not situated in authentic cultural, artistic, stylistic, and historical contexts—bodies of knowledge important for performing as musical musicians.

Learning about the repertoire they perform vis-à-vis music listening and analysis tasks assists young musicians in finding ear anchors or musical cues that inform them of their entrances or starting pitches, help them get back on track if they somehow lose their place in the music, or model interpretive possibilities. Granted, teachers/conductors continually encourage ensemble members to watch the conductor's *visual* cues during performance, but developing students' independent musicianship skills also requires individual performers to use their peers' vocal or instrumental sounds and their own hearing in order to identify and respond to *aural* cues as they perform.

Providing young ensemble musicians opportunities to learn about musical structure, along with its historical, cultural, socio-political contexts, is crucial in any comprehensive ensemble curriculum. However, equally important is leading students to make connections between that musical knowledge ("knowing about") and their musical performances ("knowing with"). In other words, students must become aware of how factual musical information and music listening experiences, for example, inform and transform the quality of their musical decision making, technique, and listening during performances. Listening to musical exemplars during rehearsals, particularly to diverse musical interpretations and presentations including students' own performances, gives them fodder to apply their musical knowledge and prior experiences to familiar and unfamiliar musical contexts. By discussing and analyzing stylistic features, techniques, performance practices, musical formal structures, and interpretive decisions made obvious in music recordings, students (individually and as a group) bring into their awareness the "best choices" and "best practices" for their own performances. The process of building co-constructed, comprehensive musical knowledge and skill bases as an ensemble can empower individual students to explore musical interpretations on their instruments or in their voices, thus building a bank of possibilities and rationales for future interpretive, musical choices.

LOOKING IN ON SCHOOL MUSIC ENSEMBLE CURRICULA

To nurture informed student performers, there would need to be relatively radical curricular paradigm shifts in current music-performance program curricula, especially in the content knowledge students experience. Figure 6.1 depicts a typical model for school music curricula. There are general music classes, if the students are lucky, in kindergarten through the eighth grade. (Unfortunately, many schools offer general music options only in elementary grades K–5, if they offer them at all. This travesty is yet another topic worthy of continued debate and action in educational policy and curricular development.) As a part of the general music circle, there are those musical skills that students typically exercise—reading notation; learning about historical, cultural, and artistic contexts of music; and listening and describing music. Innovative classes might even include lessons or full courses devoted to composition, improvisation, singing, music technology and engineering, and playing instruments (e.g., recorder, drumming, guitar, keyboards). The focus of traditional general music classes, however, tends to be "learning about" music.

On the other hand, the second circle represents school ensemble programs (e.g., band, chorus, orchestra, steel drums, world drumming, show choirs, jazz band, mariachi, etc.). Notice that the circle is a disparate entity, occurring separately from those experiences provided in the general music realm. In addition to performance (singing and playing), students naturally experience other Music Content standards such as reading notation, and perhaps improvisation.

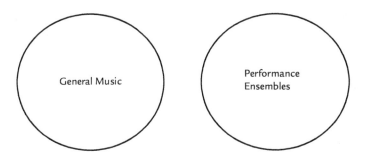

Figure 6.1.
Traditional School Music Curriculum Model.

In a comprehensive musicianship model for school music curriculum, however, the two circles overlap in terms of the musical behaviors in which the students are engaged. Figure 6.2 shows that, ideally, all school music offerings would facilitate the development of a variety of student musical behaviors while maintaining the unique focus of each class. We expect ensemble instruction to focus on performance. We expect general music classes to focus on experiencing a potpourri of musical behaviors and experiences. The difference between figures 6.1 and 6.2, then, is that both circles provide opportunities for all students to experience a variety of musical behaviors while preserving the primary musical focus that makes each class a distinct type of student learning opportunity.

To illustrate this point, purposeful, sequential, and authentic music listening experiences would occur as a part of every general-music *and* every ensemble curriculum. In performance ensemble curricula, listening experiences would occur regularly in class, or as homework, small-group work, or weekly class listening

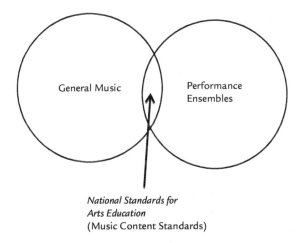

Figure 6.2.
Comprehensive Music Curriculum Model.

opportunities. In a rehearsal, the amount of time devoted to listening would be proportionally appropriate, so that performance remains the focus of the class. The same would be true for students experiencing composition, improvisation, or learning of cultural, historical, and artistic connections in rehearsal. A five- or ten-minute listening episode, for example, could mean the difference between a shallow musical performance of musical repertoire and one being performed by students who are cognitively connected and informed.

RESPONSES TO THE SKEPTICS

At this point, you might be thinking, "I don't have time for extra activities in my rehearsals. We have a lot of music to learn before our concert performances. Besides, my students learn how to develop their listening skills by singing or playing concert literature, or during the sight-reading exercises they perform during warm-ups. They have to listen carefully in order to play or sing as a group and be in tune."

I have several responses to these sorts of comments. The first is simply to question what we are attempting to teach—yes, *teach*—in our ensembles and why. For instance, is an ensemble program valid as a "cognitive" or "core" subject if its only purpose is to have students perform music for a concert or contest adjudication (i.e., short-term learning)? Or is there a broader vision for our students' well-being and musical engagement, knowledge, and performance experiences? It is possible that the time teachers invest up-front in providing comprehensive musicianship experiences that enable students to become independent musical thinkers and performers ultimately gives depth to the students' performances now and in future musical engagement (i.e., long-term learning).

My second response includes several wonderments: How can teachers be certain that students' listening skills automatically develop just because they are able to sing or play a piece of music? Does ensemble performance necessarily reflect the refinement of musicianship skills needed for independent, informed musicianship? Remembering the different types of listening engaged during performance, is each type given practice in the ensemble?

To equate individual listening (and performance) skill development to the musicianship portrayed by an entire group is presumptive at best, if not completely erroneous (Broomhead 2001; Hendricks 2010). It is deceptive, perhaps delusional, to equate the quality of music teaching and individual learning in ensemble classes to the quality of the ensembles' performances on a particular day and at a particular point along the teaching–learning continuum. Ensemble members who possess weaker musicianship skills are easily masked by students who demonstrate stronger musical and technical skills. Furthermore, it is relatively simple to copy what another performer does or to learn by rote throughout the course of rehearsals, instead of truly learning a particular skill and demonstrating it independently and confidently. Unless teachers take great effort to teach for individual skill development, there is no guarantee that each person within an ensemble possesses the degree of skill development demonstrated by the ensemble as a whole.

Teachers cannot assume that students actually discern those particular musical features the teacher verbally highlights. Teachers can tell students "what to listen for" in the music, but how do we know they hear what we have highlighted? Drawing student musicians' attention to the interplay of musical parts, involving them in score study (at the level of the ensemble musicians' technical skill and musical understanding), and prompting them to take co-responsibility in determining musical interpretation are strategies for building strong communities of ensemble learners.

Pierce (2007) purports that music performance calls for technical mastery and precise hearing, both the intellectual and the imaginative. Without listening to choirs, orchestras, bands, African drummers, recorder players, marimba ensembles, and jazz quartets playing a potpourri of possible musical interpretations of that which they are performing, students will have a narrow focus for their own ways of sounding and being with the music in their own performances. By listening to others perform music and having different interpretive solutions, students might be imaginative in their own interpretations, thinking in musical sound to determine how the music should be performed. They can also begin to make choices about which performances they prefer, while also developing their critical listening skills and asking, "Why do I like this performance better than that one? What is it about this performance that is more compelling technically and artistically?"

Finally, teachers know the reality of time spent with their students. Some schools offer longer class periods than others. No matter what the case may be, time is a valuable commodity in the teaching profession. There is never enough of it. The only option, then, is to maximize teaching and learning within the time frame that is available.

Presenting quality performances throughout the school year is also a reality. Public stakeholders expect to see and hear performances that are polished and primed. In fact, it is not objectionable to expect performance ensembles to play or sing their music well, since valuable school resources and time are dedicated to rehearsing the music. However, there is no way for people outside of the classroom to know what is involved in teaching music comprehensively and from a constructivist stance through ensemble participation unless they have also had these types of experiences in their own school music-ensemble instruction. Therefore, it is the music teachers' and students' responsibility to educate those same stakeholders about the processes and products that arise from comprehensive music ensemble curricula.

Time spent on listening, improvising, composing, and learning about historical, artistic, and cultural contexts of the music that the ensembles will perform is not wasted time, nor is it superfluous to facilitating the performance process (rehearsal) and product (concert performance). On the contrary, if teachers value these musical behaviors, they will find time to include them in their ensemble curricula. The key, then, is to hold performance technique development and learning to perform musical literature (i.e., "the notes" and interpretations) as the primary musical behaviors experienced in ensembles, while also including learning segments that involve other musical behaviors such as listening, composing, creating, and learning about historical, artistic, and cultural contexts of the music the students rehearse.

METAPHORS AND MUSIC MAKING

The process of perceiving and processing musical sound is closely linked to bodily experiences—what the body perceives in visual, aural, tactile, and kinesthetic ways. Because of this embodiment, Godøy and Leman (2010, 106) purport that music perception is multimodal, since "we perceive music with the help of both visual and kinematic images... in addition to pure sound." Ideally, music educators lead student performers to find out how they can best "inhabit the notes" of the music (Keller 2004). Therefore, music listening strategies that engage students' verbal, visual, and kinesthetic learning modalities can serve as nontraditional, multisensory tools for students to develop score analysis and aural skills. This is especially true, since mapping, movement, and verbal strategies make otherwise abstract musical sound concrete by highlighting the musical structural elements that are key in analyzing and, ultimately, performing musical literature.

In chapter 1, we considered music listening processes and products as an act of creativity, since music listeners create and re-create pathways unique to their thinking and feeling selves as they listen to music. The acts of creating music listening maps, movements, and verbal descriptions serve as students' externalized metaphors for their thinking and feeling processes and products during the music listening process. Yet, we also recognize that these external forms of student thinking and feeling pathways provide only partial glimpses into the complex process we call music listening. But even these morsels can illuminate how we teach, what we teach, and to whom we teach as we facilitate student music-listening skill development.

Mentioned earlier in this chapter, there are generally three types of listening that occur within performance ensembles: (1) listening to one's self in relationship to others in the group; (2) listening to the ensemble or group sound; and (3) listening to recorded music of student or professional performances in order to analyze a particular stylistic feature, music structural or elemental facet (i.e., rhythm, form, melody, harmony, dynamics, timbre). In the next section, we will look at the role of verbal, visual, and kinesthetic metaphors as means for engaging student performers in multisensory ways of knowing the music they rehearse and perform.

The multisensory metaphors and pedagogical experiences discussed in this chapter are primarily those that address these three types of listening in performance ensembles; however, the lists are hardly exhaustive. Metaphors that teachers and students use to enhance performance technique will not be included in the following sections, although there is often no clear separation between technique and expressive interpretation. Instead, metaphors will be featured that can be used by full ensembles to become informed about the musical characteristics, concepts, and expression of their musical repertoire (as they listen to themselves and others).

Kinesthetic Metaphors

In chapter 3, we considered the body as a holistic unit with which we experience and make meaning—cognitive, physical, emotional, and intuitive/spiritual—of our surroundings. For music performers, movements can result from being responsive to sounds, producing sounds on an instrument or voice, and at times, being showy for audience members.

Performers' gestures and movements are culturally learned, individually devised (consciously or unconsciously), and biomechanical in nature. Body movements can also serve to comfort and free performers from the stress of performance or reflect their personal enjoyment of sound produced in the moment. Similarly, movements can become acts of communication between performers and audience members, as the latter can detect subtleties of timing, pitch, dynamics, and emotional intent originating from the performers' body movements as they sing or play music (Davidson and Correia 2002). Consequently, student performers should move beyond "learning" movements simply to accompany a musical excerpt or section. Instead, they must become aware of the effectiveness, rationale for, and contribution the movements have to the overall expressive nature of the music they perform.

Whether executed by solo performer or ensemble member, body movement is vital to the performance itself. "Movement processes...[are] especially beneficial for both kinesthetic re-education and awakening awareness of the particular qualities of the musical elements" (Pierce 2007, 6). Where is the epicenter of movement awareness? On the one hand, music is physically heard—listened to, processed, and responded to—by performers. On the other, movement awareness begins in the body, not as a responsive act but as the genesis of human knowing and intent to produce musical sound in a particular fashion. By involving the full body or portions of the body, ensemble musicians can feel the speed and space needed to execute a particular kinesthetic gesture they will ultimately place into a musical gesture using the voice or an instrument. Using body movements to explore shape, size, path direction, effort required to produce a physical gesture in time and space, and the nature of musical beginnings and endings makes musical concepts and interpretations concrete that might otherwise remain obscure, inaccessible, and abstract to young ensemble musicians.

Students should have opportunities to listen to and move with audio or video recordings of their own performances, as well as others performing the same repertoire or music stylistically similar to the repertoire rehearsed in class. Isolate patterns, articulations, dynamics, and textures in the listening excerpts to highlight that which a passage in the repertoire demands. Listening to brief excerpts is fine. Listening to excerpts that are obvious in their illustrations of a musical characteristic or concept is necessary. Sometimes showing students "the opposite" in listening examples is the best way to illustrate a point (i.e., "If not this style, then its opposite. What would that sound like?"). Video and audio recordings of student rehearsals and performances might best illustrate the "before and after" movement moments, so students can listen critically for differences in their sound as a result of engaging in movement experiences. Hearing and seeing generally mean believing. Helping students increase awareness of their own sound and develop their critical listening skills are giant steps in facilitating the students' independent, informed musicianship.

Developing kinesthetic experiences within a rehearsal need not take much time or space. Sometimes extra space might be desirable—the gym, cafeteria, hallway, or an outside area—for walking with intent and direction, walking in mixed meters (feeling the groupings), or engaging in other Dalcroze Eurhythmic movements. Logistically, finding larger spaces within and outside of the rehearsal space might not be possible; therefore, movements may need to be adapted in order to work within the space allotted for the rehearsal. Most movement opportunities in an ensemble will likely be nonlocomotor movements or gestures—those that involve standing or sitting without moving out of a defined space while moving the upper body parts or full body along planes of different levels (i.e., high, medium, and low). Students should also have the opportunity to participate in small-group or sectional work, exploring and creating movements to illustrate their understanding of a concept being highlighted in a music listening example.

Most important is that movement opportunities grow organically from the music literature being rehearsed. Movement should highlight not only broad musical concepts but also expressive nuances and even the muscles engaged in controlling an instrument or supporting the vocal sound. Very little rehearsal time is required for engaging an instrumental ensemble in nonlocomotor movement, such as singing a melodic or harmonic line and pointing forward to indicate the movement and energy required to maintain the phrase through to its completion. Key is having all students participate in the movement, regardless of whether the movement highlights a musical feature in all instrumental parts or only in one section. This strategy enhances student awareness of what parts other than their own are doing, what they sound like, and what their roles are within the overall musical scheme.

An obvious, but sometimes overlooked, place to begin movement experience in rehearsals is with posture and alignment. Teachers might use the following kinesthetic metaphors with students to develop their technique, since alignment issues are directly related to healthful, efficient production of musical sound. Students should be encouraged to monitor themselves as they listen to themselves in relation to others in the ensemble.

Teachers/conductors provide students with reminders regarding the need to sit up, sit straight, or stand tall. All too often, however, these reminders need repetition because the students are not given the responsibility for monitoring their own alignment. Ask your students to "check your body readiness for singing or playing" or to monitor "how your body alignment is supporting sound production". We must help our student performers think as musicians think. I tend to use the term *alignment* rather than *posture*, for *posture* seems to instill the notion of body rigidity, stretching, and contortion, rather than what a naturally aligned body requires. Therefore, making students aware of proper alignment is at the heart of balancing the body (for instrumentalists and vocalists) while maintaining flexibility, centered breathing, and effective and pleasing sound production.

Teachers have used the metaphor of "pretending there is a string attached to the top of your head and pulling yourself upward" as a strategy for students thinking about alignment, but it is not accurate. Alignment begins not at the top of the skull but at the atlas occipital ridge where the skull rests on the spine. At first glance, this might seem like an unimportant and irrelevant detail. But experiment with your own body, focusing on a string attached atop of your head versus one attached to the atlas occipital joint. What is the difference in the way the two body positions feel and look? Also, realize that the look and feel of body alignment varies per individual.

Have the students pretend to "yank the back of their shirt collars" to remind them of their body position. They should practice feeling the differences in the body when standing as a "singer, soldier, or slob." And they can practice sitting using a toned "body core," perhaps if they pretend there is a glass tube supporting their upper body (place flat hands parallel to each other, one at waist level and one at shoulder level), and then they sit with a "broken glass tube." Asking students to stand "as a tripod with suction cups attaching their feet to the ground" might serve to give them stability in standing or sitting. Invite the students to play or sing a scale while sitting or standing in unaligned body positions, and then have them describe the differences. These awareness exercises gradually become natural extensions of the musical performance process.

There are kinesthetic metaphors and experiences for students to determine *collaboratively* the phrase length and energy exerted throughout the duration of the phrase. They include "passing the phrase," a technique I experienced in a Dalcroze Eurhythmics workshop, and "moving the phrase."

"Passing the phrase" requires students to stand in a line or on choral risers, or to sit or stand in their instrumental sections, to perform this movement task. The teacher isolates a repeated rhythmic figure from a recorded musical excerpt. All students of the ensemble learn to clap the rhythm. Using the third movement of Beethoven's Symphony #7 as an example, the rhythmic figure is motivic (i.e., quarter-note, eighth-note, eighth-note, quarter-note, quarter-note), and it unifies the formal structure of the movement. Students pass the rhythmic figure from one person to the next in line, until everyone has clapped the rhythm individually and the rhythm reaches the end of the line. The idea is for the students to seamlessly pass the clapped rhythm from one person to another while maintaining the tempo and building the rise and fall of the rhythm within the phrase through the intensity with which the students clap.

A variation on this experience is to isolate a melodic rhythm of a specific phrase. Have the students each clap one measure of the phrase, experimenting with its beginning, climax, and repose in terms of dynamics and energy levels, while maintaining seamless phrases. Yet another variation includes having students each clap only one note of a melodic rhythm before passing it to the next person in line. In the Beethoven examples, an individual student would clap the quarter-note, another student an eighth-note, yet another student an eighth-note and so forth down a row of students.

▶ Observe the Norwalk High School music appreciation class "pass the phrase," as they explore the seamless and regular phrasing of Beethoven's Symphony #7, movement 3. Go to the book's Companion Website and click on Video 3.8.

The second collaborative kinesthetic task is "moving the phrase." This task is particularly effective when the students have the opportunity to listen to a performance of a piece they are rehearsing, especially a new piece that has just been introduced in rehearsal. "Moving the phrase" can require additional space if students are instructed to stand in one large circle or several small-group circles. If large areas for movement are not available, students might otherwise sit or stand in rows in the regular rehearsal space setup.

Using either space configuration, students raise their arms to shoulder height and place the palms of their hands against the palms of the persons on either side. If school policy is one that prohibits any type of touching, then simply have the students raise their hands shoulder height and pretend to be touching the palms of their neighbors on either side. The task objective is to prepare the phrase by leaning to one side (left) and inhaling, before moving the phrase in the opposite direction (right) by pushing against the neighbor's palm, and then repeating throughout the music listening excerpt. Students are to place pressure evenly on the palms of the other person until the phrase ends. Then the students prepare to move the phrase in the opposite direction (left), thus pushing against the other neighbor's palm to indicate the beginning of each new phrase. Each time the students hear and feel that the phrase ends, the phrase movement shifts to the opposite direction from which it was moving in the circle or line.

The fun part is when different people in the circle or line hear the phrase in longer and shorter chunks, and therefore try to change the phrase direction at different times. Students must work together to provide reason and rationale for having longer or shorter phrases, until the group members agree on the phrase beginnings and endings. One group's interpretation of phrasing may, of course, differ from another group's interpretation, which sparks discussion within the entire ensemble. The transfer of learning occurs when the students describe the energy and length of the phrases and translate it to their performance of phrases that are sung or played. Because the students had these concrete movement experiences, the teacher can easily refer back to them and the students' decisions for phrasing and maintaining energy in subsequent rehearsals.

▶ Observe singers of the Oberlin Youth Chorale work in small groups to determine collaboratively the beginnings and ends of phrases and maintaining energy throughout the duration of the phrase as they move the phrase to Rutter's "Magnificat" (Magnificat). Go to the book's Companion Website and click on Video 6.1.

In chapter 3, we explored movement sequences as a pedagogical tool for use with music listeners in general music classes. On occasion, however, I used movement *sequences* in my students' choral rehearsals. Sometimes, the singers and I would procure additional space in the school, on the playground, or in the parking lot for larger, locomotor-movement experiences. One of the students' favorites included listening experiences that helped develop their inner hearing (aural memory) and feeling the pulse and phrase. The following is one such experience.

Irving Berlin's song "Steppin' Out With My Baby" became a popular tune as a result of its appearance in the 1948 movie musical *Easter Parade*, and it served as the music for this kinesthetic and inner-hearing task. Invite the students to stand in one large circle, in concentric circles, or in small-group circles for this exercise. A less desirable, yet possible, adaptation would be for the students to do the movement sequence "in place."

The teacher and/or students create an eight-beat movement sequence, which is later "performed" by the group. On the video recording of this book's Companion Website, you will notice the students executing the movement sequence, but gradually parts of the music are removed from the recording, leaving only the pulse and then only silence. During the silence, however, students are expected to continue the movement sequence until the music fully returns. The challenge is to maintain the inner pulse and inner hearing, so that when the music returns, the students are doing the movements that begin the movement sequence and are in synch with the music.

▶ Observe the Oberlin Youth Chorale experience a version of "Steppin' Out With My Baby," a locomotor movement sequence in which students are exercising their internal hearing and maintaining musical pulse. Go to the book's Companion Website and click on Video 6.2.

If you do not have a recording of this music or another piece that gradually eliminates its parts, then you might wish to create your own version of this piece. For example, using GarageBand or some other software in which you can record individual tracks, enter a section of a score that is being rehearsed by the group. Create a loop of all the parts playing, and then gradually remove a track from the performance until there is silence. At the end of however many measures or beats of silence (enough to accommodate the completion of two or three cycles of the movement sequence), "paste" all the parts back into the software to conclude the altered composition.

Students might also enjoy using music software that facilitates their arranging, performing, and recording of a piece of music from their repertoire or from a popular tune. If there is a limitation of recording space, time, and software, simply use the students' music recordings brought from home, create a brief movement sequence, eliminate the music for several measures or beats, and then bring the music back into the movement exercise.

As another idea, the teacher could also record the students performing a piece of music from their repertoire to be used with a movement sequence and the inner-hearing experience mentioned above. Assign ahead of time the order in which parts or sections would stop playing so that eventually there is silence. Again, determine how long or how many beats (i.e., four, eight, twelve, or sixteen beats) the silence will last. At the point of the silence, the teacher and students will count silently the number of beats and then enter the music with the full group without the conductor's cue. What alternative movement strategies can you think of for maintaining the goal and essence of this experience without using technology to eliminate parts of the music? What other forms of technology could enhance this movement task?

Regardless of which version of the task the students experience, ask the students how they maintained the beats during the silence, what was challenging about the task, what they needed to think about and do to prepare for reentry into the music, and what they heard differently when parts dropped out of the musical texture that they had not heard while listening to the full ensemble. Students' responses can inform you as to the nature of their music listening processes and focus of attention.

Another example of a full-group, full-body musical movement experience is having the students feel the primary pulse and its subdivisions. Find a piece from the ensemble's repertoire or a recording of music and determine the largest pulse and the smallest subdivision. Perhaps the smallest note duration in the piece is an eighth-note, or perhaps it is a sixteenth-note. The object of this movement experience is for students to feel subdivided pulses "in the body" while not moving faster or slower than the original macro-pulse.

This task can be done as a nonlocomotor or locomotor task, depending on space availability. The body parts involved are feet/legs, thighs/lap, and hands. To begin, the teacher plays a steady pulse on a hand drum. The students simply walk one step in place or in a circle with each pulse. Then ask the students to clap an eighth-note—subdivision of the primary pulse—while continuing to walk/step the primary pulse. When everyone demonstrates the ability to do this portion of the task, bring the primary pulse into the feet (walking) and hands (clapping). Next, have the students clap the basic pulse (quarter-note) and place the subdivisions in their feet (eighth-notes). Then, have the students tap the next level of subdivisions (sixteenth-notes) on the thighs while their feet maintain eighth-note subdivisions. While maintaining sixteenth-notes on their thighs, have the students return to primary pulse in feet, ultimately returning the claps to eighth-notes and then to the primary pulse in synch with their stepping.

There is no mystique in creating kinesthetic-movement metaphors and experiences for your ensemble. In fact, asking the students for their assistance in creating gestures and movements that highlight or remind the students to perform in a certain manner is even more effective than those generated by teachers. The students "own" their movement suggestions. For example, a choral ensemble was challenged by uniformly placing consonants (i.e., *t, k, d, s*) at the conclusion of phrases. The teacher-conductor asked the students, "How will we remember to listen for the exact placement of consonants at the ends of phrases, so that it sounds like one group doing this, instead of individuals placing the consonants all over the place?" After the students suggested several gestures, they decided that they would use the pointer fingers of each hand and tap them together at the ends of phrases exactly where the final consonants belonged. Simultaneously, they watched and listened to each other in order to coordinate the motion with the conductor and each other. The teacher also had students listen to several musical phrases sung by professional choral ensembles, highlighting the unified consonant placement and asking the students to do the "pointer finger touch" when they anticipated and heard the final consonant. If in future rehearsals students returned to scattered final consonants, the teacher/conductor simply incorporated the "pointer finger touch" into his conducting.

Simple gestures can be most effective. Most important, be creative and design physical metaphors that make sense to students in your ensembles. Here is a list of gestures that could prove to be effective in your rehearsals and during music listening opportunities (recordings of the ensemble's or professional ensembles' performances). Of course, there are many more kinesthetic gestures that relate only to performance technique that are not included here.

1. *Recognition standing*: Students stand when they hear the main theme of a musical section in a musical recording. Then ask students to stand only when their voice part or instrumental section has the main theme of the musical section.

▶ Observe singers of the Norwalk High School Choir standing only when they sing the main theme of the piece. Go to the book's Companion Website and click on Video 6.3.

2. *Steering wheel*: Students move the wheel in the direction of the phrase for the duration of the phrase; switch directions when a new phrase begins.
3. *Exercise ball or other larger ball*: Students keep a real or imaginary ball in both hands and move it in ways that reflect the articulation of the music (performed or recorded).
4. *Full-body paintbrush*: Students move the full body in ways that reflect the articulation of the music (performed or recorded). This is especially enjoyable when a painting can be projected on a wall or screen that is in the same stylistic/historical period as the music the students are listening to.
5. *Balloons*: Have the students pretend to keep a balloon afloat by using their palms turned upward and patting gently the underside of the balloon.
6. *Chicken pecking*: Have the students hold one hand palm up in front of self, then with other hand, use the finger tips to "peck the feed" out of the other hand (used to reinforce light sound, staccato).
7. *Morse code*: Students hold one hand palm up in front of their bodies, then pointer finger of other hand tap the melodic rhythm of the piece.
8. *Rainbows/arches*: Have the students trace the phrase length from right to left in front of body, or have them draw the melodic contour in the air with a pointer finger in front of body. Change direction of the rainbow/arch movement for each new phrase.
9. *Conducting*: Ask the students to feel the primary pulses by using conducting patterns.
10. *Push forward*: Students stand or sit with both hands pushing forward on those pitches or text syllables needing emphasis within a phrase.
11. *Spreading peanut butter on bread*: Students pretend to hold a table knife in hand and spread a large and thick gob of peanut butter on a piece of bread (*legato*, energy through notes).
12. *Spiral hands*: Students show the sound moving from their mouths into a forward space. Use this motion while students sing a song in choir or play an instrumental part.
13. *Bow and arrow*: Students send their sound forth as a direct line into the back of the auditorium or other concert space. Students release arrow from the bow and follow the arrow forward with their pointer finger as they sing a song or play their instrumental part.
14. *Hand shakes*: At the conclusion of a phrase, students shake their hands in front of their bodies. This releases any tension and gives a sense of sound vibrancy that can wilt at the ends of long choral and instrumental phrases.

⊙ Observe singers of the Amherst Junior High School Choir using their arms to move the phrase forward and to energize the phrase during rehearsal. Go to the book's Companion Website and click on Video 6.4.

15. *Rubber band*: Students pretend to have their hands inside a rubber band, stretching it with the backs of hands as they feel a phrase and the energy needed to sustain longer and shorter phrases.

Visual Metaphors

When students listen to music with focus and intent, their minds and bodies might conjure up visual images of objects, people, scenes, and life events, as well as the images and sensations of movement (Kerchner 1996). Even visual metaphors provided as verbal connections between concrete objects and musical events seem to be rooted in the physical body. Implicit in many visual metaphors are movement references.

During rehearsals, teacher/conductors frequently use visual metaphors in their descriptions of musical technique, timbre, and interpretation as means for making familiar something that is abstract in musical sound or its production. Music teachers who use vivid descriptions and feedback inclusive of visual metaphors provide students with a vocabulary of descriptors that they may begin to use in communicating what they are thinking, feeling, and hearing in the music they or others perform. This might be especially true for students who struggle with verbal descriptions in general or those who seek examples for describing music in musical and nontraditional vocabulary terms.

To work on developing and using visual metaphors as descriptors of musical sound, prompt students to describe what they hear with phrases such as:

The music reminds me of a _____ when it _____ .
What color does the music remind you of? Why?
What object or story does this music remind you of? Why?

Here are examples of visual metaphors that teachers might use to describe sound production, the music students perform, and the music students listen to on recordings. It might be enjoyable to ask the students whether or not these metaphors fit the music they are listening to and/or performing, or if they could offer alternative metaphors to describe the musical feature or nuance.

1. Pretend you are a large, old oak tree with deep and firm roots. [stability, balance of body, body alignment]

2. Pretend the back of your chair is made of thumbtacks, and the spikes are sticking out toward your back. If you lean back, ouch! [alignment]
3. Squeeze the mustard or ketchup bottle so that it comes out evenly onto the hot dog. Try not to have the mustard or ketchup "splat" unevenly. [flow of air stream, moving bow over string, legato line]
4. The sound "melts" like the chocolate fudge over a sundae. [continuous flow of breath, legato line]
5. The sound is a train on the railroad tracks, without derailing. [focus of sound]
6. The sound is warm enough to melt a glacier. [quality of sound]
7. Each note is a dot. The musician is playing "connect-the-dots". [*legato* line]
8. Oatmeal vs. potato chip consonants. [hard or soft consonants to end words]
9. The sound is as rich as a deep, plush, velvet fabric. [tone color, expression, musical style]
10. The sound is warm red, orange, or purple. [tone color, expression, musical style]
11. The sound is as vibrant as the sunshine making the water on a lake sparkle. [tone color, expression, musical style]

In chapter 4, we defined music listening maps as teacher- or student-generated visual metaphors (i.e., drawings) that contain nonstandard, alternative music symbols to represent features of a music listening example. They consist of pictures, graphs, shapes, words, and lines that are created and "performed" as one listens to music repeatedly. Music listening maps are effective tools for drawing students' attention to features that occur in the musical texture, especially in parts other than their own. Alternatively, students can be asked to add symbols onto a teacher's music listening map or create their music listening maps that are representative of the students' personal music listening experience. In other words, teachers can momentarily peer into students' listening minds and bodies by observing and analyzing the drawings and words that illustrate what those students are thinking, feeling, and hearing while they listen to music. Furthermore, teachers can observe students' musicianship as they perform the musical maps kinesthetically.

▶ Observe these mapping demonstrations of the following pieces of music that can be used with ensembles and general music classes. You can use the videos to learn how to perform the maps for your class or to project the videos on a wall or screen in your classroom for your ensemble (or general music) students:

Video 4.13. Gliere: "Russian Sailors Dance" (*The Red Poppy*)
Video 4.8. Handel: "Hornpipe" (*Water Music*)
Video 4.11. Strauss: "Sunrise" (*Also Sprach Zarathustra*)

The process teachers use to engage ensemble members in music-listening mapping experiences resembles that employed with students in general-music classes.

There are three primary components to the procedure: creation, implementation, and reflection/assessment.

Presuming teachers/conductors select musical repertoire that "teaches something" in addition to performance skills, the first step in creating a map for use with an ensemble is to take an inventory of what musical concepts, features, intervals, rhythms, harmonies, textures, formal structures, dynamics, timbres, and special "effects" each piece of repertoire offers in terms of student learning. Not all music listening maps need to highlight pitch and melodic contour of a particular vocal or instrumental part, although these representations might be the easiest symbols for the teacher to create and for the students to grasp initially. For example, my map of the opening portion of "Sanctus" from Duruflé's *Requiem* contains symbols, in part, that represent "background music," or instrumental accompaniment for the vocal parts. This type of map focuses minds and ears to other important musical events that are not vocal but that still contribute to the ethereal, yet increasingly dynamic sounds that build to a climactic musical moment in this movement of the piece.

▶ Observe the mapping demonstration of "Sanctus" from Duruflé's *Requiem*. Go to the book's Companion Website and click on Video 4.14.

I encourage teachers to consider which music listening example clearly highlights features similar to the ones found in a particular piece of repertoire the students are rehearsing. If there is a professional recording of music from the students' repertoire, what is it about this performance that you wish to highlight?

Once you identify the goals and objectives for rehearsing and performing the music, creating a map becomes easy. Simply determine how much of the music to highlight (i.e., a phrase, a movement) and identify one or a few musical concepts, features, or characteristics from the music listening example to highlight and then create symbols to represent them. Of course, creating the map requires that you listen to the excerpt repeatedly to ensure the symbols depict the sounds you intend to feature.

In anticipation of hearing the musical excerpt and observing you perform the map, ask the students to describe what they expect to hear in the music, based on the types of symbols that appear on the music listening map. Be certain to list the students' responses on a chalkboard or white board; you will return to their responses during the debriefing phase of the mapping experience. Review the list of musical descriptors the students have provided, and then have them speculate which piece from their repertoire the map represents. Remember to prompt the students for rationales for their responses.

Next in the sequence of events, ask the students a focus question such as "What about the music do you think was captured on the music listening map?" Then perform the music listening map in an expressive manner while the students listen to the music and observe the performance. Subsequent to the initial listening, you and the students return to the original list of musical features that the students created prior to listening to the music. Ask the students some debriefing questions that are closely related or are the same as the original focus question, such as:

> "What about the music was captured on the listening map?"
> "Why did this map fit this particular piece of music and not the other ones you had mentioned?"
> "How could this map have fit another piece from your repertoire? What does this music have in common with that other piece of music?"

At this point in the discussion, have the students point to specific symbols on the map that reference their descriptions of the musical excerpt. The students might not correctly identify a feature of the musical excerpt. List it on the white board and have them listen again to the excerpt in order to find an accurate and alternate descriptor for the musical event. Similarly, the students might not have identified the correlation between a symbol on your map and the musical sound. This, too, is an opportunity for repeated listening and for you to guide the students to discover your symbolic representation of a musical event that you intended to highlight.

In another rehearsal, return to the music listening map just prior to rehearsing the music it visually describes. This time, have the students perform the map (students stand or sit) along with you. Invite the students to move expressively in order to feel the movement of the finger and arm in time and space. You might need to tell the students to exaggerate a bit as they trace the mapping symbols in the air. This experience could be followed by asking the students a debriefing question or directive such as:

> "Describe the weight of your arm as you followed the curvy line of the melody"
> "What did you need to do or think about in terms of pacing as you followed this section of the map?"

After the students have performed and discussed their performance of the music listening map, turn immediately to rehearsing the piece of repertoire for which the map was designed. Ask the students to identify verbally three or four things they will remember about their performance of the piece, based on the music listening map experiences. Record these performance reminders on the chalkboard. Ask the students to locate where the musical features of the map (and the performance reminders based on the map) are located in the score. Ask them, "Which vocal part or instrumental section plays this feature that is found on the map?" [list the feature such as melody, articulation, etc.].

Finally, perform the section or phrase of music that was highlighted on the music listening map, being certain to include the students' performance reminders in your conducting gestures. This might be an opportunity to record the students' rehearsal so they can review and reflect on their musical sound. Continue by asking the students to reflect on the following questions:

"Did you remember the performance reminders? Were there any reminders that you forgot?"

"Where in the score did you forget them/it? What will you do next time to remember them/it?"

"Were you able to hear the entire group performing the reminders consistently?"

Ultimately, you will recognize the effect of using a music listening map if information, knowledge, and use of metaphors translate into musically expressive performances in rehearsals and performances. However, if students forget or simply do not incorporate the musical mapping concepts into their performances, return to the music listening maps. Have them once again perform the map and add or change the map so that they will remember the inherent musical meaning of the invented symbols. Using a music listening map will not solve all technical or expressive issues; however, it does facilitate students' internalization of musical sounds, features, and concepts via multisensory rehearsal techniques. Teachers can refer back to the maps to jog students' memory of what a particular section of music "calls for" in performing it.

▶ Observe ensemble members from the Oberlin Youth Chorale experiencing and contributing to the mapping process as they listen to and follow the teacher-conductor's music listening map of "Lacrymosa" from Mozart's *Requiem*. Go to the book's Companion Website and click on Video 6.6.

▶ Observe ensemble members from the Amherst Junior High School choir as they move during their choral rehearsal of "C'est L'Amour" by J. Estes. Go to the book's Companion Website and click on Video 6.4.

▶ Observe the Northern Ohio Youth Orchestra experiencing and contributing to the mapping process as they listen to music they are rehearsing, the overture from Bizet's *Carmen*. Go to the book's Companion Website and click on Video 6.7.

▶ Observe the Norwalk High School Choir experiencing and contributing to the mapping process as they listen to music they are rehearsing, "Sing with Joy" from Handel's *Judas Maccabeus*. Go to the book's Companion Website and click on Video 6.8.

▶ Observe members of the Northern Ohio Youth Orchestra working in small groups to create their maps of the "Trout Quintet" (Schubert). Go to the book's Companion Website and click on Video 6.9.

A variation of the ensemble music-listening mapping process is to introduce world music or popular music that highlights a musical feature also found in the students' rehearsal repertoire. For example, a former student teacher used a portion of Led Zeppelin's "Kashmir" to highlight modal sounds; students had been studying tonality and modalities as they rehearsed their performance literature. The teacher created a music listening map in which she tracked instrumental and vocal sounds of the song, especially Arabic-sounding ornamentations and the modality. As a part of the final mapping symbols, the teacher placed a question mark (?) on the map, inviting the students to speculate what part of the music she had represented. While this song did not directly relate to the students' repertoire, it did reinforce the notion of tonality and modality that they had learned in prior rehearsals. Additionally, students had fun hearing how those musical concepts were used in other musical contexts.

Observe Amherst Junior High School Band members experience a music listening lesson that was a part of their rehearsal. The song is Led Zeppelin's "Kashmir." You will observe the teacher and a student performing the music listening map and the students' verbal responses to the mapping process. Go to the book's Companion Website and click on Video 6.10 & 6.11.

YOUR TURN

Think about creating (and/or maintaining) a comprehensive performance curriculum at your school. Select literature to perform that challenges the students' current music knowledge bases and technical skills. After all, it is the literature that is the foundation of the ensemble curriculum. In many respects, the repertoire dictates the types of music listening and other comprehensive musicianship lessons that you formulate. Some questions to consider as you plan for the semester or grading quarter include:

1. Why are you giving this piece to the students?
2. What is its inherent value as a piece of music?
3. What learning opportunities will the students encounter as they rehearse the music?
4. What challenges will the students face as they learn the music?
5. What technical aspects of singing or playing do you want the students to learn?

Then determine when you might use mapping and movement as organically infused experiences that permeate your rehearsals. Some additional questions to consider during your curriculum (lesson) planning include:

1. When might it make sense to include movement experiences in rehearsal?
2. When might it make sense to include mapping experiences in rehearsal?

3. When in the rehearsal schedule will I have a bit more time to include mapping and movement experiences, and when will we need to focus on preparing for the concert (i.e., polishing music, perform memorized music)?
4. Which pieces from the students' repertoire lend themselves to mapping and/or movement?
5. What musical concepts of this piece of music do you wish to highlight?
6. Which part(s) do you want to highlight in this section of the piece of music?
7. How much of the piece do I wish to focus on during a music listening mapping, movement, or verbal description experience?

REFERENCES

Broomhead, P. (2001). "Individual Expressive Performance: Its Relationship to Ensemble Achievement, Technical Achievement, and Musical Background." *Journal for Research in Music Education* 49(1): 71–84.

Consortium of National Arts Education. (1994). *National Standards for Arts Education: What Every Young American Should Know and Be Able to Do in the Arts.* Reston, VA: Music Educators National Conference.

Davidson, J., and J. Correia (2002). "Body Movement." In *The Science and Psychology of Music Performance,* edited by R. Parncutt and G. McPherson, chaps. 15, 237–50. New York: Oxford University Press.

Godøy, R., and M. Leman, eds. (2010). *Musical Gestures: Sound, Movement, and Meaning.* New York: Routledge.

Hendricks, K. (2010). "Investing Time: Teacher Research Observing the Influence of Music History and Theory Lessons upon Student Engagement and Expressive Performance of an Advanced High School String Quartet." *Bulletin of the Council for Research in Music Education* 184: 65–78.

Keller, J. (2004). "Let's Play the Music (and Dance)." *New York Times,* July 11, 2004.

Kerchner, J. L. (1996). "Perceptual and Affective Components of Music Listening Experience as Manifested in Children's Verbal, Visual, and Kinesthetic Representations." Unpublished doctoral dissertation, Northwestern University.

Pierce, A. (2007). *Deepening Musical Performance Through Movement: The Theory and Practice of Embodied Interpretation.* Bloomington: Indiana University Press.

Reimer, B. (2000). "What Is 'Performing with Understanding?'" In *Performing with Understanding,* edited by B. Reimer, chapter. 2, 11–29. Reston, VA: Music Educators National Conference.

CHAPTER 7

Teachers and Students Assessing

This book began with an exploration of why music-listening skill development is worthy of inclusion in general music and ensemble curricula, what types of teacher presentational skills and learning environments are conducive for engaging students in musical experiences, and how teachers and students might experience multisensory teaching and learning strategies to bolster students' music-listening skill development. It makes sense to conclude with the following questions: "My students have now experienced multisensory music-listening skill development strategies. They provided verbal and nonverbal responses that I have compiled. So what? What do I, as the teacher, do with the students' responses? What do I do to analyze these data?" How do I track student development over the course of the school year? How do the students' verbal and nonverbal responses inform how I plan for and teach future music classes?"

However, these same questions that involve issues of assessment and reflection must occur not only as ending points of teaching and learning but also as part of a continuous teaching–learning cycle. That is, instruction and learning (curricular) experiences drive assessment, and assessment drives teaching and learning (curricular) experiences (Brissenden and Slater, n.d.). Effective music teachers begin their instructional planning after they have formally or informally observed, assessed, and/or evaluated their students' current levels of knowledge and skills. Only then can they design music lessons that build upon the students' concrete prior experiences, current knowledge bases, and skills. Subsequently, teachers assess students based on what they have experienced in class and what they are expected to learn in order for the assessment (or evaluation) to be valid. The results of the assessment, then, cycle back to and inform the teacher's planning for future music teaching strategies and student learning experiences; this cycle is the teacher's "plan-for-action" in the classroom or rehearsal.

ASSESSMENT AND EVALUATION

The purpose of an *evaluation* is to compare the quality of student performance (i.e., a "product") based on a judgment (i.e., a score or grade). Learning goals, based on evaluation, are provided by an external source, usually an authority figure such as a teacher, a set of national standards, or a testing agency. The criteria for evaluation and the method of scoring are fixed, standard, and inflexible. All students' final performances of a skill, for example, are evaluated based on the same criteria, regardless of the student's base-line competency. Music teachers set the course goals, and the students are expected to meet specific performance standards. Furthermore, these standards include achievement levels with indicators that describe "excellent" achievement versus "average" achievement. Because of its inherent comparative function, evaluation can become quite competitive in terms of status and rewards among those who have an investment in the evaluation outcomes (i.e., stakeholders such as students, parents, teachers, school district, states, and countries).

Assessment is based on learning goals that students and teachers set together, rather than goals established by an external agency, institution, or teacher. Farrell (1997, 1) states that "in order to be fair, useful, and valid, the assessment goals must match the knowledge, skills, and attitudes that teachers are teaching as well as those which students are expected [and want] to learn." In that sense, assessment is also deemed reflective, since it is a collaborative effort between the teacher and individual students, which reflects those musical skills the students have and/or need to develop. For example, the teacher and a student might determine as a learning goal that "the student will develop instrumental and vocal timbral discrimination skills during music listening lessons."

Because students are not expert assessors, the music teacher must mentor students in diagnosing the skills that they need to improve and collaboratively defining learning goals; both are a result of the teacher's and students' observations and descriptions (and perhaps testing) of skills that students demonstrate. The key is that the teacher *guides* the students to discover what needs improvement and how to achieve those improvements, based on models of "excellence" in creating maps, movements, or verbal descriptions. In other words, teachers assist their students in recognizing what possible levels of achievement "look like," so that those students know what an achievement target might be.

Theoretically, assessment is an ongoing process that is nonjudgmental (e.g., not good or bad, not passing or failing) and noncomparative (i.e., the teacher does not compare Joey's music listening map to Suzy's). Instead, the teacher and individual students set goals that are described and compared to a student's own starting achievement levels of particular skills.

While it seems common for our profession to use the terms *assessment* and *evaluation* interchangeably, that is nonetheless erroneous. A holistic view of student progress in music includes qualitative and quantitative information solicited from a variety of assessment and evaluation sources.

Realistically, individual and group assessments and evaluations impart logistical challenges for music educators because they involve large numbers of students throughout the academic year. Furthermore, music educators have the obligation to assess and evaluate individual and groups of students in classes or ensembles. As was mentioned in chapter 6, individual student progress can become obscured when many students are taught in groups and teachers interact with students for only short periods at a time. Therefore, assessment and evaluation can be cumbersome, and the types of data required and strategies for collecting them are time-consuming.

Yet, because assessment and evaluation are components of our society's educational fabric, it behooves music educators to design solid, sequential curricula that include observable, if not measurable, learning goals and outcomes. Given the qualitative nature of the verbal and nonverbal student data (maps and movement) described in this book, it seems plausible to consider them in terms of potential assessment rather than as evaluation tools. This is particularly true because the data often rely on a teacher's subjective inference of students' multisensory, metaphorical representations of musical events. For purposes of this chapter, we will concentrate on how to manage systems of assessment relative to music-listening skill development, in both general-music and ensemble classrooms.

GOAL-SETTING

Experience has shown me that music students become invested in the teacher-student learning partnership when they are involved in determining their own music educational goals and assessment plans. Considering the teaching–learning cycle (assess-teach-assess-teach), setting goals is a viable way to begin tracking the development of student music-listening skill. Regardless of the grade level, collaborative goal-setting between teacher and students can be an overwhelming task unless the teacher first takes the time to guide the students through the *process* of creating goals. One template for guiding student goal-setting is as follows:

1. The music teacher relays the "content" of upcoming musical experiences that will occur in class: for example, "For the next couple of classes, we will explore [melodic contour, rhythm, texture, form] in the musics we listen to, sing, play, and compose."
2. The students individually address exploratory questions posed by the teacher: "What about [program music] would you like to explore?" "What about this topic interests you?' and "What types/styles of musics would you be interested in exploring during this listening unit?"
3. The student and teacher collaboratively determine the student's current level of music listening skill.

4. The teacher assists the student in designing personal goals for the music listening unit.
5. The teacher assists the student in planning her or his path toward goal achievement (i.e., physical evidence that the student is working toward achieving her or his music listening goal).
6. The student, teacher, and peer assessors reflect on and assess the student's progress toward or fulfillment of the music listening goals by reviewing concrete goal evidence (e.g., listening maps, movements, vocabulary lists, recital attendance, journals, reflections, critiques, performance recordings, blogs, listening center tasks, etc.).
7. The student and teacher create "next step" plans for continued work on and development of music listening skills.

The music teacher must be transparent by stating what her or his learning and participation expectations are for the music class or ensemble. The students also need an overview of the types of experiences and bodies of knowledge they might experience in a particular lesson unit. Based on this information, the students take inventory of their music listening interests and a musical concept or element they want to explore. For example, a student might choose to focus on how composers use dynamics or instrumental timbres in program music. Perhaps the student and teacher create the following goal: "During music listening lessons, Sarah will focus on identifying musical timbres that are used to create an object or event in program music."

The next step is for the teacher and students to determine the plan for achieving their individual music listening goals. Returning to our example, Sarah and the teacher might determine that she will focus her attention on instrumental timbres in select program music excerpts by mapping them, creating a vocabulary list, creating a movement sequence for timbral interactions, maintaining a reflective journal, and/or critiquing three listening excerpts during which she will describe how the instruments did or did not depict an image or event. Frequent teacher, peer, and self-reflective feedback is vital during the goal-setting process; this feedback serves to guide, refocus, review, question, suggest, and informally assess a student's efforts as he or she works toward goal achievement. Feedback must be provided throughout the *process* of working toward fulfilling a goal, and not only presented at the time of a student's final *product* completion.

The final step is for the teacher, student, and student's peers to review and assess the goal evidence for signs of progress, and then reflect on the "next steps" in teaching and learning. This involves maintaining, accessing, and assessing the evidence with student- and teacher-generated rubrics, and then using this information to plan for continued work on and progress toward refining the student's music listening skills.

MUSIC LISTENING PORTFOLIOS

How might the students' learning-goal evidence be preserved and presented? A portfolio is a tool for collecting, organizing, analyzing, and reflecting on student work. Items collected in a student portfolio can serve multiple purposes. For example, the portfolio can be used to document a student's class work; evaluate, assess, and show progress over time; highlight "the best of" a student's work; or serve as a repository for all student assignments. The portfolio is a collection of evidence with which students present themselves to the instructor or another audience member and declare: "Here is my work. This is how I approached it. This is why I value it. This is how I [assess] it. This is how you [assess] it. This is how I have changed. This is what I can tell I should work on next" (Winner, Davidson, and Scripp 1992, 77).

Music teachers will need to determine who, in the teacher-learner partnership, "owns" the portfolio (teacher, student, or co-ownership between teacher and student) and for whom the portfolio is being maintained (teacher, student, parent, and/or administrator), and who will be the portfolio reviewers. Thus the teacher helps insure that the content of the portfolio reflects only its intended purpose and audience. Otherwise, portfolio evidence can be cumbersome to maintain and analyze. "More" evidence collected in a portfolio does not necessarily provide "the best" indicators of student progress; therefore, choosing and pruning portfolio content are recommended.

Questions to consider regarding portfolio maintenance include: Will the portfolio "follow" the student from year to year in music class? Will the portfolio transfer from elementary school to middle school or from middle school choir to high school choir? What are students' options for how the portfolio content should be handled when it is no longer needed (i.e., take home, erase, teacher keeps evidence to pass along to another music teacher for another academic year, etc.)? Will there be a music portfolio portion of parent conference evenings or back-to-school nights, in which the students describe their experiences and learning that occurred in general music class or an ensemble?

How does the teacher store the students' portfolio contents so that all "audience members" can access and assess it? Before today's many technological opportunities existed, teachers were tied to storing paper copies, bulky audiocassettes, and video recordings of work samples, placed in folders and bins in the music classroom. While this storage method certainly remains an option, there are more economical ways to deal with the learning evidence.

For instance, teachers can give the students responsibility for maintaining their own music portfolios—filing the documents, selecting and organizing the content, and submitting the work for audience review. There are both expensive (e.g., NVivo 10, HyperResearch) and inexpensive portfolio-building software packages for teachers wanting their students to maintain online or electronic portfolios. Technologically savvy music educators and students can also create e-portfolio websites. Finally, students and teachers tend to have access to the following software from which they can build electronic portfolios for text, audio, and video data storage and access: PowerPoint,

Keynote, HyperStudio, Google Apps for Education (including free and premium packages for the programs "digi[cation]" and "R Campus ePortfolios". Quite often, electronic portfolios can be created with password protection. This more or less guarantees security; only intended "audience members" (i.e., teachers, students, parents, etc.) are able to access, view, provide feedback, and assess the student samples.

Students can easily upload digitized video, audio, and documents using technology that is readily available and that they probably already use for such purposes when dealing with social media. They can upload video recordings of mapping and movement tasks using a video camera, pocket camera (since most have a video function), and video recorders found on students' computers or smartphones. Furthermore, students can use voice recorder applications on their smartphones or computer devices to record their talk-alouds while listening to a piece of music. Students can capture their maps and upload them into electronic portfolios by taking a photo of the map using a pocket camera, video camera, smartphone, or computer device, or simply use a scanner to turn the document into a picture file (i.e., jpeg, etc.). Finally, students can create and upload Vodcasts, the video version of a podcast, with which they can talk about their thinking and listening processes as they view a video of themselves moving or mapping while listening to music.

Once logistical details surrounding portfolio assessment are resolved, the music teacher's next task is to determine the categories of evidence the students will enter into the portfolio. Portfolio "purists" might take issue with teachers making this decision if the students are truly to "own" their music portfolios; however, my experience has been that students need parameters, at least initially, within which they utilize their flexibility and co-ownership of the portfolio contents.

Music portfolios might consist of evidence for a variety of musical skills, or they can be devoted to one specific skill such as music listening. Music listening portfolios might include: students' music listening maps, movement sequence descriptions, vocabulary lists, recital/concert attendance and reviews, journals, reflections, listening critiques (concerts and/or recordings), recordings and critiques of student performances or practice sessions, blogs, listening center tasks, and compositions in the style of a particular listening lesson focus (e.g., a composition in the style of the blues, Italian Renaissance, John Cage, etc.). Giving the students the choice of providing evidence of music-listening skill development and goal achievement in perhaps only three of five categories you have suggested is also a way of empowering your students as they select the types of portfolio evidence they will include, according to their own interests and preferences.

ASSESSING MUSIC PORTFOLIO CONTENT

You might be thinking, "Portfolios can be implemented only in music classes geared for older students." However, even elementary school students can provide descriptive observational comments about the quality of their work. The language they use will be different from that used by older students, but nonetheless they can reflect on and critique the material contained in their music portfolios. Of course, all of this is dependent on the music teacher's having provided ample opportunities for students to witness teacher reflection-for-action, explore models of quality work, and practice providing feedback on their own and on their peers' work.

Whether students become involved in assessing portfolios or individual items in the portfolios, it is important for the teacher to provide assessment practice sessions. Imagine, for example, that a teacher creates two maps of "The Swan" from Saint-Saens's *Carnival of the Animals.* One map includes drawings of the instruments, melodic contour, phrase structure, pictures, and words to describe the musical style and feel of the music. The other map consists of a word and a drawing of a few quarter-notes and eighth-notes. The music teacher shows the maps to the students, performs both maps, and asks the students which map best captures the music and why. In the students' analysis, they begin to understand what constitutes robust, replete music listening maps and why.

Students must work with models of the maps, movements, and verbal descriptors in order to build the scaffolding for plausible possibilities. When music teachers share their thought processes during actual or trial assessments, they provide students with models for their own reflection and assessments, perhaps even mimicking (at least initially) the verbal phrases and descriptions that the teacher had used while presenting maps in prior classes.

As students provide feedback on their own or other students' work, music teachers play the role of coach. That is, they coach the students in providing feedback that is observational, specific, and respectful. For example, Jennifer comments on her peer's music listening map:

"It's good. I like it."

The teacher might respond by asking, "Jennifer, what about the music listening map was 'good'? What did you notice about the map?"

Jennifer continues, "I noticed that Will's map had a lot of instruments on it. And, it showed dynamics and the way the tune moved up and down."

The teacher concludes, "Jennifer, when you are specific about what you see on Will's map—instruments, dynamics, and melodic contour— he understands much more of what you observed than when you say that the map is 'good.' Keep working on giving that kind of specific feedback! Do you have any specific suggestions for Will? How might he make his map even more complete?"

Teachers can facilitate student discussions by providing "question prompts," such as:

> "Why do you think so?"
> "What did you notice?"
> "How did you know that this symbol was...."

Teachers' asking these questions model for students how to question, analyze, and reflect on their own work, so that their critical thinking processes move to deeper levels than might otherwise be possible.

It is probable that, no matter how analytically descriptive you and your students are as you assess the portfolios or pieces of evidence in the portfolios, you will need to assign an evaluative marker—a grade—to it. This is the antithesis of the philosophy and pedagogy behind using student music portfolios as an assessment tool. However, grades that employ a comparative standard are also a reality in our educational system. How do you handle this?

One way is for students and the teacher to co-construct sets of rubrics that guide you and the students through the assessment process. (We will discuss rubric design and use later in this chapter.) Another way is to have students, in conversation with you and possibly the student's peers, assign their own grades to the portfolio portion of the music class. The "grade conversation" might consist of three parts: (1) The student guides the teacher through the music (listening) portfolio by stating what the documents demonstrate in terms of the student's learning; (2) the student assigns a grade to the music (listening) portfolio or piece of evidence and provides a rationale for the grade; and (3) the teacher assigns a grade to the music (listening) portfolio or piece of evidence and provides a rationale for the grade. When discrepancy exists between the grades assigned by the teacher and those by the student, negotiation begins. The teacher asks the student to tell him or her why the grade should be higher (or lower) than what the teacher determined. This portion of the conversation returns to the discussion of the student's goal, the student's "starting point" (prior music-listening skill level), and the quality of evidence showing goal completion or progress toward reaching the goal. From my experience, students are more difficult graders than the teacher. In fact, the teacher often provides a rationale for a higher grade than that assigned by the student! Finally, both the student and the teacher sketch a plan for continued progress at this temporary point along the music-learning journey.

MAKING SENSE OF MULTISENSORY MUSIC LISTENING EVIDENCE

Collecting multisensory data—evidence—of music-listening skill development can be quite challenging, since it can include audio, visual, and text data. Furthermore, these multiple data sets exist for each student that the music educator teaches, in the many music classes and/or ensembles throughout the academic year. Perhaps even more daunting, then, is the task of organizing, analyzing, and making sense of the information.

In chapter 5, verbal protocol analysis was discussed. The basic principles include repeatedly reviewing verbal data (i.e., talk-alouds), selecting a unit of analysis (i.e., word, sentence, paragraph), and assigning a label (i.e., code) to each unit. These labels categorize data units that are of similar topic, thereby enabling teachers and researchers to recognize major themes that emerge from students' verbal descriptions. These same analysis procedures can also be applied to nonverbal data.

In my own research, for example, the findings were the result of labeling (i.e., coding) movements, drawings on maps, and sentences of transcribed verbal data from talk-alouds. Because the students' multisensory responses cannot be regarded as complete representations and descriptions of any musical event, feature, characteristic, or inherent affective import, music teachers must often infer what the verbal, visual, and kinesthetic metaphors "mean" in relation to the musical events. This information is gathered when teachers observe students create and/or perform the multisensory tasks relative to the musical events that occur at the time the students offer their musical representations.

What would it look like to code multisensory—verbal, visual, and kinesthetic data—for an entire class or ensemble, or for individual students? It is my recommendation to use one coding system to analyze and assess individual student work and another, more simplified system, for informally assessing a class's mapping experience.

Assuming the students are creating their own maps and movements, the music teacher can assess the class by using a checklist of potential topics (see figure 7.1) or just jot down topics in order to document general topics or themes captured in most student responses. These informal assessment strategies are relatively simple ways to survey the topics and themes that occur in students' multisensory responses. However, these strategies also lose the specificity of information provided by individual students.

To assess individual students, a music teacher will want to review a video and/or audio recording of the student responding to the music by mapping, moving, or talking aloud. Granted, this process is time-consuming. However, imagine a music teacher who does a comprehensive analysis of students' multisensory responses perhaps twice per academic year. The time spent can lead the teacher to an understanding, albeit partial, of the students' focus of attention, style of responding, vocabulary, and level of detailed description during the music listening experiences. These are levels of understanding that the music teacher might not otherwise glean from informally assessing a class full of students.

The teacher must be consistent in assigning codes to a set of data during the analysis phase, especially if the codes are used for assessment or evaluative purposes (i.e., student comparison). First, determine what the *unit* for coding will be. In my research, I coded individual sentences as the basic unit of analysis. Therefore, every time a student mentioned a perceptual or affective topic related to the music listening excerpt, I assigned at least one code. If the student told a story inspired by the excerpt, I inferred how the story elements related to the musical elements, structure, style, or mood. Quite often, I posed follow-up questions in order to clarify, solicit additional information, and uncover relationships between the story and music. Teacher prompts and questions are vital to analyzing verbal and nonverbal response data.

Coding the information that students captured on their music listening maps would be impossible without verbal descriptions of the representations from the students and having them point to them while simultaneously listening to the musical excerpt. Therefore, there are several layers to analyzing a listening map: (1) coding

Figure 7.1. TEACHER INFORMAL CLASS ASSESSMENT CHECKLIST

Directions: As you walk among the students, place a " √ " in the frequency boxes each time you notice a student representing a topic in her/his verbal, visual, or kinesthetic responses

THEME	FREQUENCY
Instrument/Voice	
Pattern	
Sections of music	
Texture	
Melody	
Beat	
Notational duration	
Tempo	
Dynamics	
Musical style	
Mood of music	
Effect of music on listener (including affective response)	
Student preference	
Programmatic association	
Kinesthetic association	
Music performance experience	
Prior music experience (not of self as performer)	

each different marking or drawing relative to the music; (2) coding students' verbal descriptions of the map; and (3) observing students as they point to their maps and then inferring the relationship between the symbols and the musical sounds. Similar to the verbal protocol analysis, the teacher codes each item on the music listening map, such as a drawing of an instrument, person/conductor/performer, object and words, word phrases, and standard musical notation.

Students who draw a scene of a story typically include its details in their kinesthetic and verbal descriptions of the music. However, there are "topics" that are embedded in the story scene—details that can become apparent when the student points to the map while simultaneously listening to the musical example. In some cases, especially with young children, they tend to point to all of the markings simultaneously during the pointing and listening task; therefore, the whole story is labeled as a "story" or "graph."

Students find it particularly difficult to re-create and follow line graphs during repeated listenings, since the students' hands and colored pens move in a particular way during one listening and in a different way during subsequent listenings. The lines may or may not coordinate with specific musical elements or structures, during either the initial listening or repeated listenings. When the students are able to follow the lines on their maps, however, the teacher infers the information about the relationship between the movement of the line and the music being heard.

Much like analyzing visual representations of musical sound, the teacher must rely on his or her own inference skills and on students' verbal descriptions when attempting to unearth the meaning of kinesthetic representations. The coding procedure is two-pronged: (1) coding students' movements relative to musical events, and (2) coding students' verbal descriptions of their movements. Students might also represent various musical features in different parts of their bodies, so multiple coding might be necessary. For example, a student might keep the beat in a foot, show the melodic contour in one hand, and show musical articulation such as *staccato* with the other hand. Key to understanding student movements is to recognize a change of movement when it occurs. Similar to talk-alouds or maps, students' movements might also depict a story. A crucial follow-up question for the student is, "What about the music made you create this story?" and/or "I noticed the action in the story changed. You began doing [name the motion or story action], and then you changed to [name the motion or story action]. What about the music made your movement change?"

Once the teacher has gathered and coded all forms of student data, he or she creates the coding clusters. That is, the teacher groups all codes that are similar and places them into clusters. For instance, a cluster might consist of the following codes: solo/*tutti* sections, different "parts" of music, chunks of music, foreground/background music. Once the codes are clustered, the teacher tries to find a general "theme" that arises from the codes. In this example, the larger theme or topic might be considered "formal musical structures." The next question to be considered is, How *prominently* does this theme appear in the students' responses?

My research (Kerchner, 1996; 2001, 2005, 2009) showed that students' multisensory responses fell into three general categories—perceptual, affective, and association. Note that the perceptual and affective categories are also the primary components of "cognition," as defined in this book. Regardless of age, grade, or extracurricular musical instruction, the K–12 research participants primarily depicted perceptual information related to the music.

Perhaps more interesting than those categories, however, are the themes or "topics" that appeared in each of them. It is important to remember that the themes emerged from data collected from students during individual interviews and as the students listened to an excerpt from Bach's Brandenburg Concerto #2 in F movement 1 (BWV 1047). How might the coding and thematic structures shift if students had listened to a different style and genre of music? This is definitely an area in need of additional research. From informal assessments of student responses, however, I can anecdotally report that the broad categories and most themes are represented as students listen to a variety of Western and non-Western musics.

Perceptual topics included:

1. Instruments (specific instrument, instrumental families, ensembles, timbral comparisons, tone quality)
2. Pattern (same and different, repetition, change)
3. Sections of music (chunks, solo/*tutti* sections, same/different sections)
4. Texture (individual musical parts, foreground/background music, harmony/melody)
5. Melody (melodic rhythm, pitch, contour, register, continuous motion, embellishment, articulation)
6. Beat (pulse, subdivision, downbeat)
7. Notational duration
8. Tempo (speed, fast, slow)
9. Dynamics (volume, loud, soft)
10. Musical style (genre, composer, historical period)

Affective topics included:

1. Mood of music
2. Musical effect on listener ("the music makes me feel happy....")
3. Musical preference ("I like the way the trumpet moves....")

Association topics included:

1. Programmatic association (music associated with stories, images, events)
2. Kinesthetic association (music related to movement, action, physical activity)
3. Music performance experience (comparison of music heard to student's music performance experience, awareness of performance process, awareness of performance skill, mention of performer and/or conductor)
4. Prior musical experience (comparison of music heard with music experienced at a different time and place; student is audience member or listener)

In addition to coding the talk-alouds, maps, and movements for specific perceptual, affective and association topics, teachers should consider labeling the data with additional descriptors that indicate students' personal, perhaps cognitive, style of creating their responses while listening to a musical example. These descriptors are: (1) degree of repleteness, (2) global or differentiated presentation of musical events, and (3) linear or nonlinear depiction of musical events.

The term *repleteness* was used by Nelson Goodman (1976) as a criterion with which to evaluate the aesthetic quality of a visual artwork. He stated that replete art forms exhibit many facets to which one can focus one's attention because the artist had used the visual artistic medium to its fullest potential. While I borrowed the term for use here, I do not consider students' talk-alouds, maps, and movements to be works of art. In fact, students create their multisensory responses not with the intent to be artistic but, rather, to communicate the essence of their music listening experiences in ways that words alone do not permit.

In my data analyses, I described the repleteness of students' verbal, visual, and kinesthetic responses in terms of the robustness of their responses. That is, if a student represented many and varied musical, perceptual, affective, and/or association topics during a particular music listening task, I considered it to be "replete." However, if all of a student's markings on a map depicted only one or two themes/ topics, then the map would not be considered replete with information in that particular response mode. Expect students' repleteness to vary per response mode as they describe a music listening excerpt.

Other descriptors, such as *global* or *differentiated*, can be applied to the level of specificity (detail) that students' provide in their multisensory responses. *Global* representations refer to those words, pictures, drawings, or movements that describe general, broad features of the music. Perhaps a student draws a picture of a ballerina and says that the music reminded her of the ballerina. This would be an example of a global depiction of something musical, perhaps the mood of the music. Contrarily, a *differentiated* response might be a student's representation of specific, detailed musical events or related associations. For instance, a student's map that includes an orchestra and then a picture of each featured solo instrument might be considered differentiated, since the student discerned the timbres as solos while also recognizing that an orchestral ensemble is playing the music.

Finally, responses that students present in linear or nonlinear fashion refer to the cognitive ways of organizing and representing musical sound. Students who demonstrate *linear* thinking and responding speak, draw, or move in response to musical events as they actually occur, in the order in which they occur in the music. *Nonlinear* thinking and responding are demonstrated when students describe musical events *not* in the order in which they occur. Nonlinear thinking can also be demonstrated when students return to an earlier portion of music to depict something they did not initially depict, or they create a story and depict its detail not as one-to-one music-symbol connections but, rather, as a holistic representation of the musical sound entity.

Figure 7.2. TEACHER INFORMAL INDIVIDUAL ASSESSMENT CHECKLIST

Circle all that describe the student's verbal, visual, or kinesthetic responses to music listening

PERCEPTUAL TOPICS	AFFECTIVE TOPICS	ASSOCIATION TOPICS	*RESPONSE DEVELOPMENT	*TASK APPROACH
Instrument/Voice	Mood of music	Programmatic association	Repeated information from one listening to another.	Linear thinking
Pattern	Effect of music on listener	Kinesthetic association	New information presented during repeated listening.	Nonlinear thinking
Sections of music	Student preference	Music performance experience	Elaboration of information presented during prior listening	Global events
Texture		Prior music experience (not of self as performer)		Differentiated events
Melody				Replete responses
Beat				Non-replete responses
Notational duration				
Tempo				
Dynamics				
Musical style				

*Dependent on opportunities for repeated listening

A checklist for recording music listening topics or themes in student responses is provided in figure 7.2. As the teacher reviews a student's responses in a particular mode, the following questions are asked and the information is recorded on the form.

1. Does the student focus on and depict a particular theme/topic? (repleteness)
2. How many times does the student depict the theme/topic? (frequency of topics)
3. How might you describe the manner in which the themes/topics are depicted? (linear/nonlinear, global/differentiated, replete/not replete)
4. How do the themes/topics depicted in this listening task compare with those depicted in prior music listening tasks?
5. How do the multisensory representations compare with those created during earlier music listening tasks?

CREATING RUBRICS

Once the teacher has collected, organized, coded, and analyzed the students' multi-sensory responses to music listening excerpts, there is the challenge of conveying to students, parents, and other stakeholders the degree of music-listening skill development and learning that has occurred, from one point to another in the music curriculum. Teachers might use rubrics to assess or evaluate individual music listening tasks (i.e., student-generated movement sequence) or the entire music listening portfolio. Before creating a rubric, ask the following questions:

1. Is the purpose of the rubric one that is generic—that provides information in a holistic manner about the overall task or portfolio impression? (assessment rubric)
2. Is the purpose of the rubric one that is task analysis-oriented—that focuses on a specific criterion, such as how the student kinesthetically depicts perceptual information gleaned from music listening examples? (assessment rubric)
3. Is the purpose of the rubric one that is evaluative and task analysis-oriented? (evaluation rubric)
4. Who is using the rubric—teacher, student, peer, or some combination of the three?

Rubrics are designed in order to ensure teacher reliability in assessing or evaluating student work. Rubrics include a numerical scale with accompanying descriptors for each scale degree, indicating the degree to which a student has met a particular learning goal and the skills that still need improvement (except for the highest rating on the rubric). Teachers need not be the only people to create rubrics. If teachers and students are co-creating the learning goals, then both parties should also be involved in the assessment or evaluation processes. Furthermore, student peer assessments can be powerful tools for communicating student progress, noting areas of learning that remain challenging, and determining the "next steps" in the learning trajectory. Figure 7.3 is an example of a student self-assessment of his or her verbal, visual, and/or kinesthetic responses during music listening. What information might the data found on the form provide the teacher that he or she might not otherwise have during assessment or evaluation? How might the student's self-assessment inform the teacher's understanding of the student's music listening task responses?

Taking cues from my students' perceptual, affective, and association codes and topics, I created a rubric (see figure 7.4) that might serve teachers who are evaluating individual students' multisensory responses to music listening. Notice that the rubric follows a logical gradation of criteria, indicating the highest and lowest possible scores. Furthermore, the rubric enlists the teacher to quantify what are primarily qualitative data in verbal and nonverbal forms. What this rubric does not indicate, however, is what performance level the teacher deems acceptable—what students are expected to achieve in a particular music class.

Figure 7.3. TEACHER RUBRICS FOR EVALUATING STUDENTS' TALK-ALOUDS, MAPS, AND MOVEMENTS

Score	Perception/ Repleteness	Affect/Repleteness	Music Vocabulary	Global/ Differentiated Descriptions
5	Student represents at least 5 different perceptual topics in a multisensory mode	Student represents at least 3 different affective topics in her/his verbal, visual, and/or kinesthetic responses.	Student uses at least 90% standard musical vocabulary, terms, and names to describe her/ his multisensory responses.	Student relates specific, detailed, differentiated multisensory responses to specific musical events, elements, structure, or mood.
4	Student represents 3 or 4 different perceptual topics in a multisensory mode.	Student represents 2 different affective topics in her/his verbal, visual, and/or kinesthetic responses.	Student uses at least 80% standard musical vocabulary, terms, and names to describe her/ his multisensory responses.	Student relates 80% of her/ his multisensory responses to specific, detailed, differentiated musical events, elements, structure, or mood.
3	Student repeatedly represents a single perceptual topic in a multisensory mode.	Student repeatedly represents 1 affective topic in her/his verbal, visual, and/or kinesthetic responses.	Student uses an equal combination of standard and non-standard musical vocabulary, terms, and names to describe her/ his multisensory responses.	Student and teacher relate 50% of global and/or detailed, differentiated multisensory responses to broad/ general musical events or features.
2	Student presents a story, scene, object, event that the teacher infers (through observation) to be related to musical information, events, elements, and mood.	Student represents only 1 topic in her/ his verbal, visual, and/or kinesthetic responses.	Student provides 20% verbal information using non-standard music terminology or alternative means of description (movement, singing, tapping, vocal sounds) to describe her/ his multisensory responses.	Student and teacher relate 20% global multisensory responses and descriptions to broad/general musical events or features.

(Continued)

Score	Perception/ Repleteness	Affect/Repleteness	Music Vocabulary	Global/ Differentiated Descriptions
1	Student provides words, drawings, or movements that the teacher cannot determine their relationship to musical information, events, elements, and mood.	The student seems to provide no specific reference to an affective topic in his/her verbal, visual, and/or kinesthetic responses.	Student provides sparse verbal information using non-standard music terminology to describe her/ his multisensory responses.	Neither student nor teacher can relate the multisensory responses to musical events, elements, structures, or mood.

Figure 7.4. STUDENT SELF-ASSESSMENT FORM

Student's Name:_____ Date:_____
Name of Musical Excerpt:_____ Composer:_____

Type of Music Listening Task: (circle one) Talk-aloud/Written Mapping Movement
Other

1. List all of the topics you included in your responses (see topics chart in classroom). Aside of each topic, list how you described the topic.

Topic	Where it is found in your map, or movement...What does it look like? (SKIP THIS PART IF TALK-ALOUD or WRITTEN TASK)
Example: Melodic shape	Example: Curvy blue lines at top of page

2. List three things about the music that stood out the most to you.

3. Did you enjoy listening to the music?:
   (lowest enjoyment) 1 2 3 4 5 (highest enjoyment)

4. How focused were you as you listened to the music today?
   (lowest focus) 1 2 3 4 5 (highest focus)

5. Did you enjoy performing the listening task?
   (lowest enjoyment) 1 2 3 4 5 (highest enjoyment)

6. How detailed are your descriptions of the music?
   (not detailed) 1 2 3 4 5 (very detailed, specific)

6a. Explain your rating.

7. As a result of this music listening experience, what about music would you like to explore?

8. As a result of this music listening experience, what music listening "topic" would you like investigate? (see topics chart in class)

To assist in determining age-appropriate student achievement levels in music listening, we return to the *National Standards for Arts Education* (Consortium of National Arts Education, 1994) Music Content Standards and the *Performance Standards for Music, Grades PreK–12* (Music Educators National Conference, 1996). Music listening as a content standard is described as "listening to, analyzing, and describing music" (1994, 181). Indicators of progress for each achievement standard (1996) provide teachers with assessment benchmarks that signify desired student performance demonstrated at the basic level, proficient level, or advanced level of achievement. The presumption is that teachers present the music aurally to the students and that the students have several opportunities to listen to the music as they engage their critical and analytical thinking skills.

Of course, the achievement indicators and levels are goals that teachers and students hold as they reach for target performance levels. But, depending on the students' prior musical experiences and understandings, the grade-level achievement indicators and goals must be adjusted to reflect students' baseline "formal" music listening, analytical skills, and descriptive skills. "Informally," students come to music class having had vast music listening experiences, but they have probably not been asked to listen to, analyze, and describe music in ways that they will in formal music education settings. As you read the following achievement standards, imagine how these benchmarks might be made manifest in students' verbal, visual, and kinesthetic responses while listening to music and how the music teacher might use these standards for creating rubrics and assessing student progress.

The music-listening achievement standards (Music Educators National Conference 1996) prescribe that preschool learners are expected to identify musical and nonmusical sound sources and describe them using their own, as well as traditional, music vocabulary. Children in grades K–4 should to be able to listen to and identify simple musical forms (i.e., ABA, AABA, *rondo*), express their perceptions of musical sounds kinesthetically and orally, and use musical vocabulary more extensively than in earlier grades. Notice that the students are encouraged to enlist multisensory modalities (verbal and kinesthetic) to express that which they hear.

By the time students reach middle school (grades five through eight), they should to be able to describe specific musical events, such as melody, harmony, accompaniment, and variation, as they occur in diverse musical styles, genres, and world musics. These students are also to analyze music aurally, in terms of harmony, rhythm, tonality, intervals, and chord progressions. Finally, students in senior high school are expected to define musical technical terms and symbols, including those that refer to *tempi*, chord names and functions, cadences, meter and key signatures, formal structures, and stylistic descriptors. The students should then be able to apply these musical terms to diverse musics they listen to in class. High school students should also be able to discuss music compositional techniques and list repertoire that demonstrate them.

NOW WHAT?

Now that we have explored possibilities for analyzing and assessing students' multisensory responses to music listening tasks, you might be asking, What are the next steps in the teaching–learning partnership, now that I have a pretty good idea of what my students are focusing on during music listening and their ways of verbally and nonverbally describing music they hear? Now what?

This question calls teachers into action by reflecting on their practice. Music teachers engage in assessment (and evaluation) at multiple levels—curricular, lesson plans or unit plans, student learning, and teacher efficacy and effectiveness of lesson presentation and facilitation. Teachers reflect on their observations of students' multisensory responses that were presented during music listening, their conversations with students, analyses of students' multisensory responses, and class or rehearsal lessons and teaching strategies. In doing so, music teachers are able to plan subsequent lesson experiences that take students, as individuals, as a class, or as an ensemble, to the next levels of music listening development. The curricular cycle—assessment, teaching/learning, assessment—continues.

Other reflective questions the teacher might wish to pose in order to facilitate future music listening lesson-planning include:

1. To what extent are your students achieving the desired music-listening skill development goals (think national, state, and school district achievement standards)?
2. How much time might you allocate in class to nurture this development?
3. Will you need to reintroduce, rework, review, or revise something in order for the students to access the particular music concept, element, or feature highlighted on the map or movement sequence? Will you need to select a different musical excerpt?
4. How might you teach for music-listening skill development in a more efficient or effective way?
5. How will you change this music listening task/ multisensory tool the next time you use it?

YOUR TURN

Now it is time for you to record and assess the evidence of your students' music-listening skill development. Jot down what you think the student is conveying about her or his music listening experience. What perceptual, affective, and association topics do you notice? What information will you need to infer? Write down questions you would want pose to the students after the mapping or movement task is completed. Then, prescribe a plan with which the student could develop her or his music listening skills. What perceptual, affective, and association topics need development? What about the student's musical vocabulary needs development? How will the student get to the point of providing differentiated multisensory responses during music listening? Finally, what will you, the music teacher, do to nurture this student and other students in the next music classes or ensemble rehearsals so that they can begin setting their own learning goals and assessing their own work?

A final reflective question might be posed to music educators about their students' music listening skill development: How have you maximized the opportunities for all learners to: Experience a variety of musics?; Discern musical elements and expressive musical qualities that make music artistic?; Express perceptual, affective, and associative features of their music listening experiences?; Make informed decisions about their musical attitudes and preferences with my guidance and encouragement? (adapted from Webster 2012). The essence of these questions served as the backbone for this book about multisensory music-listening skill development. The idea is to facilitate music listening experiences that propel students into learning about music through active music listening with their body-mind-feeling-spirit selves as individuals and as collections of individuals who gather to partake in the mystery of music experience. As facilitators of learning, we have explored how we can listen to, observe, and learn from our students about how they organically listen to music, so that we might align these processes with our primary pedagogical tools for the classroom and in ensembles.

I call upon you and your students to be collaborators in the teaching and learning partnership. You have been summoned to plan-for-action, teach for lifelong musical engagement, and reflect-for-action. The students have been called to listen-for-meaning and listen-for-understanding through active multisensory music listening experiences. Plot a course unique to your own teaching environment, and creatively listen to music and collaboratively learn from each other.

RESOURCES

Brissenden, G., and T. Slater (n.d.). *Field-tested Learning Assessment Guide.* Retrieved from http://www.flaguide.org/start/assess_in_context.php.

Consortium of National Arts Education. (1994). *National Standards for Arts Education: What Every Young American Should Know and Be Able to Do in the Arts*. Reston, VA: Music Educators National Conference.

Farrell, S. (1997). *Tools for Powerful Student Evaluation: A Practical Source of Authentic Assessment Strategies for Music Teachers*. Fort Lauderdale, FL: Meredith Music Publications.

Goodman, N. (1976). *Languages of Art*. Indianapolis, IN: Hackett.

Kerchner, J. L. (1996). "Perceptual and Affective Components of the Music Listening Experience as Manifested in Children's Verbal, Visual, and Kinesthetic Representations." Unpublished doctoral dissertation, Northwestern University.

Kerchner, J. L. (2001). "Children's Verbal, Visual, and Kinesthetic Responses: Insight into Their Music Listening Experience." *Bulletin of the Council for Research in Music Education* 146: 35–51.

Kerchner, J. L. (2005). "A World of Sound to Know and Feel: Exploring Children's Verbal, Visual, and Kinesthetic Responses to Music." In *Music in Schools for All Children: From Research to Effective Practice*, edited by M. Mans and B. W. Leung, 21–33. Granada, Spain: University of Granada.

Kerchner, J. L. (2009). "Drawing Middle-schoolers' Attention to Music." In *Musical Experience in Our Lives: Things We Learn and Meanings We Make*, edited by J. Kerchner and C. Abril, chap. 11. Lanham, MD: Rowman & Littlefield.

Music Educators National Conference. (1996). *Performance Standards for Music: Strategies and Benchmarks for Assessing Progress Toward the National Standards, Grades PreK-12*. Reston, VA: Music Educators National Conference.

Webster, P. (2012, October 14). "Creative College Music Teaching: Issues of Definition and Assessment." [Lecture handout]. Case Western Reserve University, Cleveland, OH.

Winner, E., L. Davidson, and L. Scripp (1992). *Arts PROPEL: A Handbook for Music*. Cambridge, MA: Project Zero, Harvard Graduate School of Education.

INDEX